Martin Edward "Marty" Crowe (1914–1999)

*"A good man who is not great
is infinitely more precious
than a great man who is not good."*
–WILL DURANT
adapted by Martin Crowe, c. 1943

GOODER

The Writings of Marty Crowe

*Selected from Five Decades of His Thoughts
On Teaching, Coaching, Humanity,
God, and Life*

Edited by
MAUREEN SLAUSON

Published by Grand Ave. Press
Copyright © 2024 Maureen Slauson

Printed in the United States of America.

ISBN: 979-8-218-49325-7

All rights reserved.

Photo credits are provided in captions for individual photographs. Used with permission of the copyright holders.

This is a work of nonfiction. All of the events in this book are true to the best of the author's memory. Some names and identifying features have been changed to protect the identity of certain parties. The author in no way represents any company, corporation, or brand, mentioned herein. The views expressed in this memoir are solely those of the author.

*To my husband, Tom,
my steadfast supporter in this project.*

*And to my siblings,
Terry, Mary Aileen, Kathy, Mickey, and Mara.*

CONTENTS

Preface	xi
Introduction	1

THE EARLY YEARS

His Father	7
The WPA	16

TEACHER

From Advertising to Teaching	33
Baptist Minister Becomes Assistant Coach	37
Teach Them to Be Human	41
The Literature Teacher	48
Commitment to Teaching Literature	52
School Days	58
The Impact of a Teacher	61
Beyond Classes	66
Guidance Is Misguided	68

THE STUDENTS

All Kids Count	75
That Was Our Job	79
The Power of Goodness	85
Slow Learners Have Merit, Too	88
Influence	93

EDUCATION

What's Wrong with U.S. Education?	97
The Inanity of Social Studies	101
The Censors	106
Robin Hood	109
Wrecking Ball	113
Competency Tests	117
School Does Not Have to Be a Grind	120
Much More to Learning	123
The Awards System	126

COACH

The Case for Being a Coach	133
Why I Am a High School Coach	137
Gratitude	148

WHY NOT?

Why Not?	155
The Fighting Irish Basketball Team of 1947	160
Billy Haugen	165
Austin Pacelli 1958, State Champions	171
Austin Pacelli 1959, Washington, D.C.	173
Orrie	174
We're from Central	176
State Tournament 1964	179

THE PLAYERS

Tribute to a Sub	191
The Night Billy Regan Made the Team	195
A Memoir from Vietnam	199
The Eddie Decker Story	203
Good luck Keno Larkin – you'll be a good coach	206
Mickey's First Road Trip	211

PARENTS

It's the Kids	217
Dads	221
Joe Donovan	224
Mothers of Athletes	230

SPORTS AND SOCIETY

Jackie Robinson	235
Black Ballplayers	239
Summer 1950	244
Gale Sayers and Brian Piccolo	250
Athletes as Role Models	255

ADVOCATE FOR GOODNESS

Lynching	265
What Color Is Democracy?	268
Cost of War	275
Body Counts	279
Geraldine Ferraro	281
Slaughter of Innocents	283
A Prayer for My Darlin'	285
Hubert Humphrey	288
Christmas 1950	293

BELIEVER

Rules	305
Pope John XXIII	309
The Eucharist	313
Mary Chaput	317
Youth and Religion	321
Think of This Homily	326
Someone Must Give In First	329
Is There a God?	333
Uncle Bob	336

NO MAN IS AN ISLAND

Dan McAuley	345
Loneliness	349
The Lost Son	353
Moments that Matter	357

FAMILY

What Is Important?	363
The Growing Up Years	367
Cars and the Family	371
Good-Bye to a Car	376
Eating Out	379
Henes Park 1970	382

THE ROAD LESS TRAVELED BY

Good Men	389
Father Winfred Herbst	392
The Brothers	394
JFK Prep	397
Remembering Aristotle	401

TIME AND WASTE OF TIME

Time	407
Waste of Time	412
Joyride	417
Epilogue	421
Last Column	422
Biographical Sketch	427

Iron, Trim, Tape

PREFACE

The cardboard boxes had sat for decades in the back of a little storage room at the end of a long closet in our old Victorian house. Built in 1881, the three-story, 4000 square foot duplex has been in our family for 75 years.

My parents bought it when they first got married, July 23, 1948. My dad was drawn to the big old homes with their large rooms, heavy woodwork, and unique character. He also saw the place as a source of needed income as he began his career teaching in Catholic high schools, a profession that would span nearly 50 years.

His first job was at St. Patrick's High School, only three blocks down the street. That job ended in the spring of 1950, but the house remained our family home. No matter where his job took us, we always came back to Eau Claire for the summer, mainly to get set up for renters for another school year, but also because it was our home. Tom, my husband, and I bought the house from my parents in the mid-1980s and still live here.

On the first floor was a large bedroom with the walk-in closet off to one side. At the far end, a small oak door led to a hidden room, a place a child would seek out for imaginative play on a winter's day. But the children were grown, and the room was now full of the remnants from a family's life. In the back were the boxes, piled on top of each other, waiting patiently. One finally gave way spilling papers across the floor. The time had come to sort through the archives.

The contents filled nine large totes and surrounded a pool table in the front room for months. As I carefully sorted through family memorabilia, pictures of ancestors, letters—and my father's writings, the jumbled history of a lifetime unfolded. I even found the letter my father wrote to my mother only days before their wedding telling her about the great house he found for them, "A 14 room duplex-seven up and seven down" he wrote, and "only about 25 years old."

He loved this house.

After the sorting, I was left with three crates of my dad's work spanning five decades:

- From his first teaching job, an "Anthology of Creative Writing, Class 1938-39, W.P.A. Adult Education."
- Playbills from 1940s theater productions he acted in or wrote.
- Scripts from his radio show that broadcast from 1947-51.
- Pieces he wrote that were published in various newspapers and journals, from the late 1930s through the end of the 1980s.

- Copies of his weekly column which ran from November 1962 to December 1976 in the Green Bay Diocesan paper, *The Register,* later *The Spirit.*
- Yellowed pages of handwritten copy, sometimes in pencil.

The pieces had been collected by my mother in envelopes that were torn and deteriorating, with faded script identifying the contents, multiple copies of articles held together with straight pins.

My early work focused on organizing—ironing, trimming, and taping the tattered papers so they could be read. Some were nearly lost causes-but worth the effort.

I set a regular reading time at ECDC, a local coffee shop, every Monday, Wednesday, and Friday. I became friends with the young people who worked the counter, and sometimes shared my project with them. It was time I held dear. As I read, I heard my father's voice. Though more than 20 years since his death, his writing spoke of earlier more vibrant times, the young man starting his career in teaching, the struggles and triumphs of his life. I became immersed in the project. I laughed. I cried. I was inspired.

To get a broad view of this writing compendium I began entering data into a spreadsheet, Title, Source, Date, Category, Rating (my response to the piece), and Other (special things that I wanted to note). His work fell into five main categories, Education (he was a teacher), Sports (he was a coach), Politics/World Events (his involvement in politics began as a child campaigning for his father in 1921 running for the Minnesota Legislature on the Farmer Labor ticket), Religion (he was a devoted and practicing Catholic all his life, but he also challenged the Church), and Human Interest (stories about people he encountered in his lifetime). The spreadsheet grew to over 50 pages.

I came to believe that there was much in his writing that can speak to us today. I hope his words speak to you.

—Maureen Slauson
April 2024

INTRODUCTION

In his January 1941 State of the Union Address, President Roosevelt spoke to the Four Freedoms that all citizens of the world deserve, Freedom of Speech, Freedom from Want, Freedom from Fear, and Freedom to Worship. Two years later, historian and philosopher Will Durant was commissioned by The Saturday Evening Post *to write a piece to accompany a painting by Norman Rockwell that represented "Freedom to Worship," (*The Saturday Evening Post, *Feb. 27, 1943).* The quote featured on the title page comes from a line in that essay. Durant wrote, "A good man who is not great is a hundred times more precious than a great man who is not good." My dad adapted the line to:

> "A good man who is not great is infinitely more precious than a great man who is not good."

The idea was one he often spoke to and was a core belief that directed his work as a teacher, coach, advocate, practicing Catholic, and human being. In one of his columns, "People Were Gooder in the Depression," he calls for the word "gooder" to be added to our lexicon.

* * *

"People Were Gooder in the Depression"
Green Bay Press Gazette
March 6, 1977

I grew up during the Depression years and I heard then, and still do, what a terrible time that was for the country and the people in it.

Well—it was bad all right. I remember the long lines of those waiting for a chance to apply for jobs that they knew were not likely ever to be there.

I even remember the bread lines, though I was never in one. I did help out at the Hospitality House of the Catholic Worker in Minneapolis while I was still in college, and I remember all those people with their dead dreams and wasted lives.

Most of all I remember, I guess, the morning when I heard my dad crying in the bathroom. My old man was a tough guy, and nothing really got to him most of the time. But that day when I was maybe a sophomore in high school, the desperation he felt must all of a sudden have been too much.

I heard him crying but I never let him know. I never forgot that morning, though. It shook me up more than things usually did. When you are young you don't get shook too easily.

I guess that is why I never really was touched too much by the depression nor destroyed by it. I never even understood it. Not then.

But one thing I do remember pretty clearly. People were gooder to one another than they are now.

I know there is no such word as gooder but that's not my fault. There ought to be. I could say better but better is not what I mean.

I mean gooder.

Maybe because each guy was as scared as the guy next to him. Or as desperate. Anyhow people sort of came to depend on one another—maybe even lean on one another just a bit, which the psychologists will tell you is not good, but it is not all bad either. Not all the time.

I remember I hopped a lot of freight trains right after I got out of high school because I wanted to taste a little of the world and there was no other way.

I was in the Green Bay switchyards one night and I had my dog with me. He was pretty old by then and pretty scared because sometimes the passing of the years can take your confidence or your courage whether you are a dog or a man.

Anyhow, we had left him with friends in Minnesota when my folks moved to Manitowoc because my dad, all at once, got a job there—and the dog had started to bite people like the garbage man and the paper kid, and I had orders to come get him. So I did, and I headed back with him on the freights.

There was no other way.

And I remember the yard man in Green Bay that night who told me: "Take your dog and sit on the platform of that passenger coach over there. It's dangerous in the yard at night. You'll be out of the way there. I'll let you know when your train is made up and ready to go."

He meant my freight. You don't forget a guy like that.

Or like the time I went out to the hospital in Saint Paul with my mother to pick up some medicine for my dad.

Freebie stuff. The only kind my folks could afford. (My dad was a vet but that's another story and has no point here).

Anyhow there was this one guy waiting with all the others.

The man was in pain and that was obvious to all of us.

My mother (who never got beyond the eighth grade but who had learned about justice and right and wrong and like that) suddenly grabbed the coat of a young but slightly pompous intern going by—embarrassed the hell out of me, she did—and she said: "That man is in pain. Take him next."

The intern looked down that proud thin nose of his and he said: "It is not his turn. He will have to wait his turn."

And my mother held onto his coat, and she said: "The man's in pain. His turn is now."

And that young doctor looked around and he saw all those quiet people watching him. The terrible meek. And so help me, he cracked.

"Okay! Okay! He can be next."

Hey, sure she was embarrassing to be with at times. And she didn't know from nothing about an awful lot of subjects. But when it really counted my mother was never afraid.

And she cared.

And that was something to remember from the Depression days and something to learn from them. A lot of people cared. We have all been running so fast for so long maybe we have forgotten how to do that.

Maybe we ought to slow down.

THE EARLY YEARS

HIS FATHER

My father's father was a descendent of Irish immigrants. He was a simple man but heroic in my father's eyes and had a profound influence on him. My grandfather was a political activist, an advocate for the working man and unions. He was one of the early founders of the Farmer Labor Party in Minnesota. My father campaigned for his father when he ran for the Minnesota Legislature in 1920. He was six years old. Those early days set in motion my dad's commitment to speak up and speak out for his country. He wrote about his father and those early years.

* * *

"It Was Funny About My Dad"

Typewritten manuscript
Date unknown

It was funny about my dad. Kinda sad, too. He always wanted to get a new roof on the house and get the place fixed up real good. I wish I could have told him it wasn't necessary.

All I needed was the old man inside. And mom. And how it was. But it was always hard to explain that to my dad.

He ran for public office twice when my brother and I were pretty young. State legislature and register of deeds. He never had a chance in either one.

It was funny, now that I look back, about that Bolshevik and Commie stuff. My dad never knew who Karl Marx was. I mean he was real smart and all that, but he never did get much schoolin' in. Most people were like that then.

So my dad maybe heard of Marx or Lenin or some of those guys, but I doubt it. I know for sure he didn't know what a Commie was.

That didn't stop the French priest in our town.

I mean Father Hubbard wasn't French, of course, or anything like that, but he was the pastor at St. Anthony's and since that was the French church (although most of the parish were Italians) he was the French priest. Well—anyhow, he put some printed notes in the pews one Sunday which said that no Catholic could vote the Farmer Labor Party and stay a member of the church. Father Hubbard said that the Farmer Labor Party was just another name for a bunch of Communists.

My dad was awful mad about that. He quit the church, and he never went back again, either, until a couple of years before he died, and that was more than twenty years after that.

I realize that quittin' the church because some priest is a well-intentioned jackass is no reason at all. But I mentioned that my dad was no real educated man and so maybe you couldn't really expect him to figure things out all clear and straight.

My dad was a deep thinker, though. Maybe when he quit the church he wasn't thinkin' very deep, but that's because he was so mad.

I woulda been mad, too.

My dad got wiped out in the election, of course. But that didn't stop him either. He kept pluggin' away.

I remember that, in 1924, he had my brother, Bob, and me out passin' out literature and pins boosting Bob LaFollette for president. Old Fighting Bob.

He was my dad's number one hero of all time, I guess.

He didn't have a chance—LaFollette, I mean. He was matched against Coolidge who was the Republican president since Harding had died a couple of years before—and against a man named Davis, whom the Democrats had nominated when they decided that Al Smith wasn't ready because he was a Catholic.

It was pretty much in the bag for Coolidge, but my brother and I would rap at doors, anyhow, and when somebody came, we'd hand out a leaflet and say, "Vote for Bob LaFollette."

Sometimes they would slam the door in our face and sometimes they would snarl, "Communist!" or "Bolshevik!" or something. Once in a while, though, some old lady would invite us in for an apple or cookies. We got to kind of like campaigning.

I guess we didn't convince too many voters because LaFollette didn't do too well in our area—or in the state of Minnesota for that matter. He did carry Wisconsin, though. That was his home state, of course, but it was very unusual for a third-party man to win even in his own state. Besides that, LaFollette got more than four million votes in the country and that was a lot in those days, and a big surprise for a third-party candidate.

My dad felt pretty good about that.

Besides, the Farmer Labor Party elected a dentist named Shipstead to the United States Senate from Minnesota. And, later on, they elected Magnus Johnson, a big Swede farmer who was honest and innocent, to the senate, too. And then they elected Floyd Olson to be governor.

Olson was a great public speaker and a very sharp man and a shrewd politician. He also had a lot of guts which is what it took to be a member of the Farmer Labor Party in those days. He was, I think, one of the best governors that Minnesota has ever had.

Floyd Olson would probably have been a third-party candidate for president himself, sooner or later, but he died as he came near his peak as governor. I remember I went to his funeral at the Minneapolis Auditorium (I was in college, by then) and Phil LaFollette, who was the son of old Bob, and Governor of Wisconsin, gave the eulogy. He quoted from Edwin Markham's, "Lincoln, Man of the People,"

> ....*he went down*
> *As when a lordly cedar, green with boughs,*
> *Goes down with a great shout upon the hills,*
> *And leaves a lonesome place against the sky.*

It was very sad.

I sensed that when Floyd Olson died an era was over. The glorious, exciting fight that the Farmer Labor Party had made was won. The pioneers were gone but the victory was there.

Since then, men like Hubert Humphrey and Eugene McCarthy and Walter Mondale, as well as many others, have come along to capitalize on what the handful of trailblazers had done way back, when it was clean and dangerous—and a fine and splendid joy.

My dad, like a lot of others, never got anything out of it all. Personally. I suppose it hurt a little. It always hurts to get passed by.

But my dad was essentially a dreamer. You never hurt a dreamer where he really is.

I remember, too, that my old man was one of the founders of the book-binders union in our part of the state. Unions weren't very popular in the early 1920s. It was always rough going.

Once the printers in our town went out on strike. It was just a small place with a bindery and a print shop which put out the little daily paper in our town. My dad didn't have to go out. He wasn't a printer.

But he did.

I didn't understand it then—but I do now. I understand my dad much better than when I was a kid and only knew that his not having a job made things pretty tough around the house.

The main trouble was, of course, that the printers did not win whatever they were striking for, so they gave up and went back to work. But my dad never went back.

I don't know, of course, what the strike was all about nor who was in the right nor any of that. I only know that my dad never went back, and I am glad that a man like that was my father.

IT WAS HARD ON THE FAMILY, of course. I know, now, it was harder on my dad. After a long time, he got a job in St. Paul and for years he traveled back and forth every day to work. Twenty miles each way. Either on the streetcar or—some years later—with some other men who worked in St. Paul, too—and drove a car.

It couldn't have been very easy because my dad was getting old by then. But I never thought much about it.

I can remember one night when he came home, though, because that was just before the end of my senior year in high school and that afternoon we had beaten Cretin High of St. Paul in baseball, and it was their first loss in three years, and they were rated the best team in the state.

I had pitched the game and had set Cretin down with three hits and had fanned a flock of batters—fourteen, I think. I was feeling mighty good and mighty proud.

I waited for my dad to come home that night so I could tell him about it, and I could see he felt good, too. You could tell by the way he had of waiting, sometimes.

"You musta had a good day," he said.

"The fast one had a hop on it today. The deuce was breakin' sharp."

He didn't say anything more then, but I knew how he felt about maybe I might make the big time some day and I knew that was a very good day for my dad.

When I knew that, it was the best part of the day for me, too....

My dad used to try to win prizes in contests. Like Liberty Magazine, for instance. They used to put in pictures of the heads of presidents, only it wouldn't be all of one man.

Like it might be Jefferson's chin and mouth and Van-Buren's nose and Jackson's eyes. And like that. You were supposed to divide up the pictures and match them with the other parts from other issues of the magazine. This sounds easy but I remember it got awful hard late in the contest. Much harder toward the end.

My dad would carefully cut out those fool pictures—he was very neat and meticulous with a pair of scissors—or with anything for that matter. (Which is the exact opposite of the way I was then—and am now). I would get pretty furious at the darn things, but my dad had almost infinite patience.

Well, after all the weeks had gone by and all the pictures were in, my dad would take his over to the shop in St. Paul and put a binding on the whole thing. The result would be a very fine-looking book. Then he would mail it in—and wait.

He never won a dime.

Not once in all the contests through the years did that patient, kind, persevering man that was my dad win one little round dime.

I remembered that years later when Liberty Magazine folded—and I was glad they were out of business. By then, of course, my dad had been dead for quite a few years….

And one Christmas my mother was pretty sick.

She used to get "spells" and that Christmas she got a bad attack. She was out—cold.

I was twelve that year and Bob was ten.

I didn't expect anything much for Christmas because I knew my dad hadn't been able to go out shopping. And I was right. That Christmas morning I came down the stairs and there was almost nothing there—except a note on a chair. The note said that Santa had a policy not to leave anything at a house where somebody was ill—but that he would make a special trip back in a couple of weeks.

The note was signed. Santa Claus.

I was twelve years old and besides, I recognized my dad's handwriting and besides, did the old man think a twelve-year-old believed in things like....

I guess that was the day I began to believe....

I threw out my pitching arm my freshman year at St. Thomas College. By that time, I had come along well enough as a baseball pitcher that it looked like my dad's great dream (and mine) of my making the big leagues just might come true. A few scouts had shown a bit of interest.

I pitched on a Monday; warmed up a whole game on Tuesday because the starter was in trouble all the way; went in in relief on Wednesday down at St. Olaf. My first pitch, the ball sailed over the back stop.

I could never throw fast again.

After that I got by in college with a combination of slow curves, blooper balls, and good control. I managed to stay on the college team and, in fact, made a letter each year.

But the dream was over.

I knew it. No big team is going to be interested in a young pitcher with a lame arm. It was over.

My dad would not give up.

Even after I was through college and reduced to pitching, on a Sunday afternoon, for some small-town team near our own town in Minnesota—somebody who didn't know I had a bum arm or couldn't afford a pitcher with a strong one—my dad stayed with it.

Like always, he wouldn't quit.

I'd come home from a late Mass and my dad would have put my uniform and my spikes and bat and glove in the car and he would be ready to go out—to wherever it was that week—and watch me pitch another game. It was a quiet time, but it was good driving out to the game.

We didn't say much but I think we were both glad that we were there.

One Sunday, standing out there on that mound, all at once I realized a pretty wonderful thing. All of a sudden, that day, it came to me that as long as my old man was in the stands there was exactly one person who cared. And, later on, when he was dead, the number was none.

And that's the most important lesson in mathematics that I have ever learned in all of my life.

THE WPA

My father graduated from the College of St. Thomas in St. Paul in 1938. The country was amid The Great Depression. President Franklin Roosevelt created the Works Progress Administration (WPA) in 1935 to get people back to work. My dad was hired for his first teaching job in 1938 with the WPA working in a school in St. Paul with Hubert Humphrey serving as the school administrator.

* * *

"Depression to War to Prosperity: What Got Lost?"

Handwritten manuscript
c. late 1960s

Hubert Humphrey wasn't always vice president of the United States. Or a senator from Minnesota. Or mayor of Minneapolis. Or a political science teacher at Macalester College.

Once upon a time, he was a supervisor for the WPA adult education program in Minneapolis and St. Paul and I was a teacher on the staff.

I was very young and very brash, and Humphrey wasn't much older and a bit brash too, and the Humphrey-Crowe debates at a couple of our teachers' institutes were the big happenings in our program.

Back then.

Many people have the idea that because Humphrey talks a lot and talks fast he really doesn't say very much. That's wrong. He marshals his facts and his arguments as well as any man I ever knew. Some people think because Hubert talks fast he is trying to put over some kind of a fast deal—that he lacks sincerity.

Wrong again. HH was strictly on the level. (Some say he has changed since the old days when he had to fight for a place in the sun. Could be. I doubt it though.)

My debates with Hubert Humphrey were typical of the adult education program in 1939. Most of the teachers in the program were fired up with excitement about it.

It was new and different, and it had no established guidelines to go by and that was the thing of course. Unlike much of education it had no chance to get tired or stuffy.

It is too bad the whole thing died when the WPA went out. It was one of the better programs among all the wonderful hodgepodge of those glorious days.

I suppose part of it for me was that I was young. When you're young nothing scares you very much. I was often hungry in my youth and so what about it? I was usually broke but who needs capital when you're young?

The Depression was all around us. And the challenge of it was tart to the tongue each day.

You remember WPA. If you were a truck driver you raked leaves. A schoolteacher—you drove a truck.

One field I had had no experience in at all was the theater. I had never been in a play in my life. (Except in Noah Bibeau's barn when we were ten). So, part of my assignment was to direct plays.

One of the great jobs of my life.

I taught speech classes, too—and there my college experience qualified me a little. My major was English, but I had been on the school debate team. I had been the orator for a while, too.

Into that marvelous class in that marvelous program came the humble and the proud. The quiet ones—the loud ones. Angry people. Defeated people. Cynics. Dreamers. A few who were on fire. A lot of ones whose name nobody else knew—and they barely remembered themselves. A few whose names I knew well and whose presence, therefore, surprised me.

Men who wanted to get a better job. Many who wanted any job. Quite a few neurotics. Some psychotics.

(Somebody said once the difference is this: "A psychotic doesn't agree that two and two is four. A neurotic agrees but he's unhappy about it.)"

Unhappy people. Happy ones. Some lonely. Some who just wanted to be with others for a little while. Some who came in from the night—or the cold.

Wolfram Hill, whom many found obnoxious because he so often dominated the discussion, but who had the real nature of Nazism labeled long before the rest of us did. Wolfram, who wrote angry letters to the editor, and got angrier answers in return.

Johnny Adams, who had been a top-ranking professional boxer, but who was over the hill and down on his luck. His wife, from the glory days, was gone. His little girl stayed with somebody up North, Johnny said, and he would stand in class with the flattened nose and flattened ears, and he would read little poems that he had written.

"Calendar baby on the wall...."

Tough Johnny Adams, one of the gentlest men I ever knew. Yet, if you pushed him too far....

Like that welfare case worker one time.

I got the call at my home, and it was Johnny, and he was in jail.

Apparently, what had happened is that he had gone to see a welfare man at an office somewhere because a friend of his had tuberculosis and they wanted him to go out with a work crew.

Otherwise, they were going to cut off his help.

Johnny went up there with the sick man and what happened was so typical of that good little guy.

He tried to explain that his friend was too ill to work. But the caseworker would not listen. I can see Johnny doing it. I knew him. Gentle. Patient.

I can see him explain it over again. Johnny never did learn, I guess, that with a certain kind of very small man, especially a man in a bureau with new and sudden authority, it is no use to explain.

He wouldn't listen. But Johnny tried it a third time. When that time he failed too—when the caseworker said, coldly and finally, he either works or he doesn't eat—that's when Johnny quietly opened the little gate in the divider, which in those offices in those days always separated the people who counted from those who didn't, and he walked through it, and he tagged the caseworker. Hard. Final. Right on the button.

I was told he was out for 15 minutes.

So, Johnny called me from jail, but before I got down there, Tommy Gibbons, who had fought Jack Dempsey, and who was sheriff then, had heard the story, too. Johnny was gone when I got down there.

So far as I know, the case never came to trial.

You used to say, Johnny Adams, how much you owed me—how much you had learned. Never so much as you taught me, Johnny. I was the wise guy fresh from college. My answers were too fresh and too ready.

You taught me true.

Agnes Ouradou. From some tiny town somewhere. Walnut Grove. Or something. No talent in public speaking. Nor dramatics. Nor creative writing (I taught a class in that, too.)

Yet with a rare gift. You could count on her.

She was the only woman I ever knew who was, as far as I could ever see, totally incapable of guile. We all came to depend on her. Only when we looked back did we know how much. The theater would have collapsed without her.

Never walked on a stage in her life. Yet when she was needed, she was there.

She wrote a piece in class once. No flair. No style. But the greatest writer in the land could not have written something like that. Maybe wouldn't have wanted to.

Couldn't. Either.

She wrote that she was working in a restaurant, and somebody came in and left some free tickets for a dance. Agnes wasn't going to go, but since the tickets were free....

She got another girl, and they went to the dance.

The address turned out to be a dark street in the flats on the far side of the river. Took a little nerve to walk down there after they got off the streetcar. But since the tickets were free….

The street number was a building that was pretty boarded up. Looked abandoned. But they heard music from upstairs somewhere. So, since the tickets….

Once in the place, they discovered that almost everyone there was a Negro. Agnes had no feelings, either way, about Negroes. (Bigotry never occurred to her.) But it was a surprise. Still, the tickets….

They stayed.

Apparently, they had a good time, too. It was late when they came out on the dark street and headed up a few blocks for the place where the streetcar stopped.

A big, black car—a limousine—pulled up and somebody in the car asked the girls if they wanted a ride. Agnes wrote that she could see in the light in the car that there were two men in it, and one had a scar on his face and the other had one shrunken arm.

The girls were dubious about accepting a ride from a stranger on a dark street late at night. Still, since the ride was free….

They got in and the two men drove them home.

Agnes identified the two men in her paper. She found out who they were as they drove the girls home. The one with the scar was a member of the City Council in St. Paul—and I forget his name, now. The one with the one bad arm, said Agnes, was John McDonough, at that time mayor of Saint Paul!

I suspect that both had been at the dance as part of good political procedure. That never occurred to Agnes. It wouldn't.

The men drove the girls home as an act of kindness—which I am certain it was. There was no attempt at any hanky-panky, of course.

And the ride was free....

One year, my boss in WPA (not Hubert) put me in charge of a class in "Personality Adjustment."

That was a dandy.

Every person in the place had a problem. One woman, I recall, told us that she had been followed on her way to class, by a man. She named one of St. Paul's most prominent business figures.

After a real look at the woman, I could only conclude that if the man really was following her, he needed the class even more than she did.

One lad, about twenty, came up to speak to me on at least five occasions and was never able to get past the first few words.

"Mr. Crowe—I—I—I want to—I—I...."

After a few weeks I was pretty humbled by it all. I think, when I started, I figured I would know how to cope with anything that came up. I was a very cocky young man. You can be when you're young.

I grew a little older in that class....

I got to know a lot of Commies in those days. Some came to my classes.

I think you've got to decide what you mean when you say Communist. If you mean someone who, in case of trouble, would side with the Soviet Union, then I only knew a few.

But angry young men who wanted to overthrow the status quo—plenty.

I never blamed them too much. For being mad, I mean. They saw a lot of dirty dealing going on. Many saw good people going hungry while ones who were far less good ate well.

Often the hungry ones were their own.

The trouble was—I just couldn't see Communism as an answer. Marx, in many ways, was a bore. And many Commies are bores. They have smug answers to everything, and what's wrong with our own system is too many smug people.

Besides communism lacks kindness. I know capitalism often does too. But that's what's wrong with it. Why change systems if you're going to hang onto the main evil in the old one.

Some of the guys who considered themselves Commies, weren't so bad in those days. As guys I mean.

I walked out of play practice one night—an outfit called The Group Theater with much talent and a lot of political fervor—down in the warehouse district in St. Paul. We'd practiced in a loft and the guy who came out with me was a young man named Jack. Something.

A panhandler hit us for help. Jack reached in his pocket and gave him half a rock. Four bits. I knew Jack wasn't working and I knew he didn't have much.

He was a good guy, Jack. He didn't see Marxism for the phony pitch that it is—but he was a good guy. I remember him that way....

One night a bunch of Trotskyites were at play practice and some Stalinists walked in. I thought there was going to be murder for a moment. But the Trotskyites simply got up and walked out.

All Marxists. All Commies. But no one hated the Stalin lads like the Trotsky boys did. Like in 1934, I think it was, when they had the truck drivers' strike in Minneapolis. Much of that union, 544, was Trotskyite. So, the Stalin crowd was on the side of the strike breakers.

Some of the most violent street fights in Twin City history were during that strike. Many of them matched Commie against Commie.

I once saw a Trotsky newspaper which pictured the "four great enemies of the human race" across the top of the front page, Harry Truman, Winston Churchill, Pope Pius XII, and Joe Stalin.

What a backfield that would have made!

In 1940, the teachers' union from WPA sent me as a delegate to something called Peace Mobilization in Chicago. The idea was to protest the draft which hadn't come in yet but was well on the way. (A lot of young people these days, in my classes, for instance, don't realize that the United States didn't used to have a peace time selective service. It's all they've ever known. Before 1940, there was none. Since, there's been nothing else.)

An attempt was made at the Chicago rally to nominate John L. Lewis of the Mine Workers as a protest candidate for president. You should have heard the Commies on that one! One distinction Lewis had, he was hated by the Communists and the titans of American capital with equal fervor or even frenzy.

I don't know if that says anything about John L. Lewis or not, but it occurs to me, in retrospect, that it might very well do just that.

Congress passed the draft law while we were in session. Or immediately thereafter.

Once again, I was learning....

I ran into some of the anti-red hysteria which always grips some people in this land, and, under stress, grips a lot of them.

One night I was going to appear in a play at a Catholic Center in St. Paul and I was forbidden to go on because somebody had decided the script was "pink" (I had written it myself.) and that some of the other cast members were "questionable."

God knows I was seething with fury that night. But how do you combat a nut when he's got the wheel?

Later I tried to figure out just how in hell anyone could get a "commie" slant out of that one act play. It was actually a plea for peace.

I guess I nailed it down after a while. Peace was a commie idea in 1939 because Russia was allied with Hitler and if we fought the Nazis we'd be in there against Stalin's lads too.

So down with peace.

I suspect the same fanatics would have okayed the plan for peace a couple of years later—because by then war meant fighting side by side with the Soviets.

Peace, as some people see it, is wonderful only when the set-up is right.

Remember the pickets in front of the White House. You can tell the difference between the Commies and the pacifists if you really want to.

One day both had signs saying, "The Yanks are not coming." "I didn't raise my boy to be a soldier." And all of that.

Then Hitler invaded Russia.

The next day the commie sign said, "Let's open a second front."

The pacifists still carried the signs from the day before. You can tell the difference—if you want to.

One Sunday afternoon—early in 1940—I was going to lead a forum in a Catholic school auditorium in St. Paul. I had had scores of them.

This day I was told I would not be allowed to take over. The crowd was sent home. Somebody had told the proctor—and, apparently, the Bishop—that I might be a Red.

I knew Archbishop Murray a little and I knew that he knew such an accusation was a not very funny farce. I told him so and I forget his advice. Probably suggested I calm down and learn to live with the crackpots.

Good advice, I guess. But hard to take when you're young.

Still, my dad had gone up against the same stuff years before. And, even now, some screwballs see Commie plots in fluoridation of water, mental health clinics, pornography.

One lady wanted *Robin Hood* banned because she said it recommended taking from the rich and giving to the poor—and was therefore Marxist!

Some argue that attempts to help the Negro or the poor are obviously Communist plots—as if the Commies really gave a damn about the Negro or the poor. Or as if nobody but Commies would care.

Some of these idiots just don't know any better. They're hysterical. Others are so damn choked with bigotry or venom or hate, that they use these tactics fully conscious that they are vicious and contemptible.

Some politicians—a good many—play this game. They milk this thing for every bit of political mileage they can get out of it—fully conscious, all the way, that it is a fraud. I could name a number of such right now. So can you.

These are really despicable men. They actually are willing, if necessary, to gamble with the survival of the race in order to gain some two-bit political advantage.

Many of these are, I think, worse than Joe McCarthy ever was.

I only met McCarthy once. But I am convinced that he never forgot that the whole thing was a frame. Some, today, as they get deeper in it, forget that fact entirely.

McCarthy wanted to go to the top politically. Who can blame him for that? And he kept a certain kind of personal sense of humor about it all. The cheap connivers of our time don't have that.)

From the vantage point of more than a quarter of a century since those days, I can look back with little malice. I suppose some of the people who gave me—and many others—all the trouble were really just scared little men. Sincere of course. Hitler was probably sincere. Hysterics usually are.

Anyhow, a lot of Commies of all types—Stalinists, Trotskyites, and breeds that hated both—went out and died in World War II. And later on, in Korea.

Perhaps they were never forgiven by the fanatics. But time, at least, has forgotten them.

Anyhow, the war came along, and jobs were there. The depression never ended. It was replaced by war.

WPA, that crazy, wild, unpredictable product of the grim lean years was gone—and with it the adult education program and the attempts at a culture conscience and all the rest of it. Done.

The Japanese attacked Pearl Harbor and the arguments were over. I got a job at the airport. Making changes on B-24s.

I couldn't handle a monkey wrench or a screwdriver. I told them so. They hired me as an expediter. I asked them, "What is it?" and they said, "You'll learn."

I never did learn, really. Except that when I got out of the way, things were expedited more than otherwise. I learned to get out of the way.

Contracts were cost plans, and nobody cared. Suddenly, people were making money, and nobody cared. Somewhere men were dying, and you cared if someone was close.

But it seemed like nobody cared enough.

The days of being poor were over. Those terrible days that somehow had never seemed so terrible to me. Not as terrible as the days of men killing other men seemed. Somehow.

Finally, one day I was checking in a crew. I had, at least, found something to do—for about 20 minutes of an eight-hour shift.

The men came in with a monkey wrench in their overall pocket. Behind them, for the first time, came the women.

Straight from blueprint class—straight from vocational school. The new look on the American scene. The female mechanic.

My best friend was there with me one day—and he met his mother checking in. She'd been to school. She was ready for work.

One gal argued one day that the fact that she was insisting on putting a wire through the gas tank of a plane might seem odd, but the blueprint said that's where it belonged. She was hard to convince.

At last, a gal came in one morning carrying a toolbox as big as a small suitcase. All the girls had the big ones. "What's your name," I said, checking against my list.

"Watson," she snarled—and I looked at her. Hard, confident, ready. I would swear she was chewing tobacco.

That night I quit my job.

It was over.

The Depression. The glory of the battle. The easygoing days. The crazy days. The special kind of laughter. The pace we had once.

The days of our youth were done. The world had turned a corner.

It was over.

TEACHER

FROM ADVERTISING TO TEACHING

In 1941 my father was hired for his first teaching job in a school. He left mid-year and picked up another teaching job that he left in the spring of that year. He wasn't sure teaching was a profession for him. That summer he decided to explore other possibilities more directly tied to his interest in writing and ended up at an advertising agency. It was a clarifying experience.

* * *

"From Advertising to Teaching"
Published in "Something to Crowe About"
Green Bay Register
May 19, 1972

One afternoon, a long time ago in Minneapolis, I was looking for a summer job. I had just finished my first year of teaching. I wasn't sure then, that teaching was my bag.

I'd done a little writing in high school, and I'd written a column in the college paper (St. Thomas) my senior year. So I decided to check at an advertising agency.

I knew about advertising what I knew about most everything else. Nothing. I suppose it was natural I got the job. After all, I'd been a director of dramatics for WPA, and I'd never been in a play.

My boss turned out to be a little guy with a mustache, an arrogant manner, and the most expensive, low slung, foreign made car I'd ever seen up to that time. He really wasn't a bad guy to work for, but the job was a bad one for me.

"Remember—people are idiots. Never underestimate their capacity for stupidity."

"Write your copy as if everybody reads with his finger on the lines."

Oh, the gems of advice I received that summer! True, maybe. The men I was working for had got rich following such concepts. Only, even then, I knew there was something better to be than rich.

So, I plugged on—turning out those miserable slogans about "bread that makes tasty toast" and cakes that "stay moist."

"Can I say wet? Just once? Can I write that our cakes stay soggy?"

He froze me in that way he had.

When I quit, he was honestly amazed.

"You going back to teaching school?"

"I reckon."

"What they pay you?"

"Not enough."

"As much as you make here?"

"Half."

"Listen. There's no limit here. You got a lot to learn yet. But you write pretty well. In five years, you'll be making twenty thou." (That would be more than fifty now. Thou, that is. Gees. Grand.)

"That would pay for a nice funeral."

"Huh?"

"I'm half dead already......"

And so it was, I left the advertising business. Nothing wrong with it. Same as most businesses, I guess. The other guy loses, that means you win. The other guy's hard luck is good luck for you. Something like sports, maybe. Only in sports it's a game. Or supposed to be.

That agency was a way of life. And it was bending me to fit. You either fit in, in the end, or you get out. I wasn't waiting for the end.

It took me three more years to get to like teaching and coaching. To be honest, it was probably those great football teams we had at Hudson public high that swung it.

It's more fun winning. (The ad agency had that part right.) Anyhow, all at once I knew this was for me. The good bells were ringing, man.

I've never been sorry.

Some years when my teams got clobbered, I wondered for a day or two. When fans—and especially parents (who meant well but still hurt)—were on my back, I wondered for a lot longer than a couple of days.

But what the heck, baby—there was that theme that little girl name of Margaret Cary—straight C student—you know—one of the forgotten ones that are all over the place in every high school—the lost ones—you never know they're there—only all the meaning in life is in them.

Only you gotta take a look.

"I always felt like in your class I counted for something."

That's what that nobody wren wrote on that long ago paper. And all the little, lost ones since then in a thousand corridors. Sure, man—I'll never make a check in all my life like they would've handed me in that agency after a while.

But I could explain to you what you could do with that agency and it's checks, only this is a family type newspaper. (They may even cut this).

Thanks Margaret Cary and Eddie Decker and Billy Egan and Jimmy Nowak and all those wonderful shadows down the years of a man's life. To use the jargon of the young—you're where it's at.

And that's my message to all those college seniors who are, right now, waiting to grab those neat little diplomas in their hot little hands. You don't really need a Jaguar in the streets of Minneapolis. What you need is the good, good word. And this you'll discover late or soon.

Only better soon.

BAPTIST MINISTER BECOMES ASSISTANT COACH

The decision to try teaching again led my father to several brief jobs, until he was hired at the high school in Hudson, Wisconsin, to replace a teacher who had been called up for military duty. The job would last two years, until the former teacher returned to reclaim his position. My dad enjoyed his work in Hudson. I remember hearing the stories. This was one.

* * *

"Baptist Minister Becomes Assistant Coach"
Published in "Something to Crowe About"
Green Bay Register
October 13, 1972

A Baptist minister for my assistant coach! It was too much.

But Ben Chalmers was the principal and he had not been kidding.

"We have no one else and he's a good man. You'll like him."

Oh, sure. Watch your language coach because you're an Irish Catholic with a salty tongue. And Baptist ministers don't like that. You've known a few. Maybe we can have little sermonettes before practice.

You meet the guy and he's not bad.

A week later you grudgingly admit he's a good man right enough. And a good football player.

The alumni want to scrimmage your team. Most are guys just back from the war. A little out of shape—but they have a few tricks they've picked up. You hesitate about it—but then you say okay.

The scrimmage is a tough one for a while. Then the alumni start to tire, and your kids begin to whomp them. So that's when they start to get dirty.

You figure to lose a boy or two in this kind of mess and you're not sure it's worth it.

"That's it for tonight. Thanks, guys. We'll try it again some other time."

"Chickening out, coach?"

"You guys are getting tired. Besides, it's almost dark now."

"Gotta protect your little boys from the big, bad alumni—huh, coach?"

My kids are mad. One word you don't throw at high school kids and walk away.

Chicken.

"Come on coach. Let's stay with it. These slobs can't hurt us. They're big in the mouth."

It's an ugly situation and you've got a tough game coming up next week. You can't afford to lose your head.

An idea strikes.

You walk over to your assistant coach. The Reverend Dan Woods. He's 27—not much older than a lot of the alumni players. And he's in shape.

"Dan—would you take defensive end for a couple of plays?"

He grins. "Sure, coach."

And he gets in there—no equipment except football shoes. And a baseball cap. He always wore the thing. Not much protection for a defensive end.

"Ya think it'll be okay, Dan?"

"Don't worry, coach."

The alumni have the ball, and they see me put Dan in at left end and that's a challenge. They will teach the holy man a lesson. They set up their play. Single wing. Power. They're coming at Dan. Four blockers in front of the ball carrier. They will show him. And me.

A slight miscalculation.

The ball is snapped, and the blockers try to form but they haven't met the likes of the Reverend before. At the snap he's coming—fast and low and hard. He knows the game and he's not afraid. He knows a challenge when he sees one.

He goes through the blockers like they were never there, and he hits the ball carrier like a guided missile—one step after the guy gets the ball from center. The ball carrier's legs go high, and his chin goes low. It hits the ground, and the ball goes flying. Four-yard loss and loss of ball.

Dan jumps up and after a while the alumni halfback picks himself up too. The main mouth of the alumni team comes up to me. "I guess you're right, coach. It's gettin' a little dark. Hard to see the ball."

"Right."

On the way in, you throw a look at the parson. "You did good."

He grins. "Thanks, Coach."

And thanks to you—good friend……

1945 Hudson Raiders Football Team
Middle of Back Row, Rev. G.D. "Dan Wood" and Marty Crowe

When my dad left Hudson in 1946, the staff of the yearbook dedicated that issue to him. They wrote:

> With respect and admiration, we, the staff of 1946, dedicate this *True Blue Annual* to Mr. Martin Crowe, whose magnetic personality and understanding manner have won the friendship of the entire student body. He has not only served as an inspiration to all, but has left in the hearts of his students an idealism, a way of life, that shall never be forgotten.

TEACH THEM TO BE HUMAN

Those early years were the beginning of my father's formation as a teacher. At the center of that formation was a commitment that he held throughout his career, to help his students become good people. It was a core value with him. Sometimes he got in trouble for his commitment, but he never wavered from it.

* * *

"Teach Them to Be Human"
Catholic Digest
June 1945

In my history class we discussed the case, factual or fictional, of an American lieutenant said to have machine-gunned some surrendering Italian prisoners as they approached him upon one of the European beachheads. I chose to regard this officer as probably mentally irresponsible for a grossly immoral action of which he would not be capable in normal circumstances. Mine was a minority report.

"He did right," said one student. "You can't trust the enemy. The Japs have proved that. Safety first is the only rule to remember."

This boy plays tackle on the football team (which I coach). He is a nice boy. He has a pleasant smile. He is a better than average student.

"There are some things which are wrong," I said, taken rather off guard, "by their very nature. Nothing, not even reasons of security or personal safety, can make them right."

"The enemy doesn't recognize rules of right and wrong. If we attempt to, we'll be at a disadvantage." This from a short, blonde girl, an A student and co-editor of the school paper.

"Are we going to let the enemy set our behavior? Isn't it just because he has shown so few moral concepts that we are fighting him? Isn't that what this war is all about: decency, justice, morality, and belief in God?" Vaguely I felt that, somehow, I was combating the radio and the movies and comic strips and, probably, the youngsters' fathers and mothers. I kept on realizing that what I was saying was true.

And yet I now began to sense that it was mostly strange doctrine to the students; that some had never bothered to think, beyond the fact that if you shoot a man before he shoots you, his arguments or principles will never bother you.

"Look, Doris," I was becoming a little angry, I knew it, and wanted to hold it in check, "If you are in competition with someone and he breaks the Ten Commandments to defeat you, does that justify you in doing the same?"

I thought that would stop her. She was a fun-loving but good girl, her uncle a minister.

"You've got to get along in this world. You've got to take care of yourself," said Doris.

And with that I could almost hear the silent chorus of approval that went up from the high school class. Suddenly the anger inside me was boiling over, something no teacher is ever supposed to let happen.

"Listen," I said, "You've got to take care of yourself. Sure. But not when you hurt someone else who doesn't deserve it. We're studying history, and what is history except the record of a lot of scientific and technical advances man has made without an adequate advance socially? What is history but the story of countless men and nations who were never interested in doing anything except what helped themselves? And the misery they brought to the world because of that view?"

"That's how Alexander looked at it. And Caesar, Attila, Genghis Khan, Napoleon. And Bismarck and the Kaiser and Hitler. Is that all we've got to offer, the same bill of fare they had? Might makes right? Is that our answer?"

"I hope not. I hope our answer is Christ's answer when he told us that all men are our brothers, and we are our brother's keeper. I hope we believe Lincoln when he said that just as he would not be a slave, so he would not be a master."

The bell rang then, and the students grabbed their books and fled. I suspect there was a welter of dazed vaguely amused discussion in the halls.

"What in the world was he talking about?"

"Old boy sure was wound up, wasn't he!"

I sat there a long time that afternoon. A few students came in to pick up their books, glance curiously at me and depart. The early winter evening began to close in.

Still I sat there. A lot of things paraded before my mind. How many students had asked me, one time or another, "What good will history ever do me? I'll never use it after I'm through school." In other words, what is the value of your product in dollars and cents potential?

"I'm going to be a stenographer, Mr. Crowe. What do I need history for?" I could see her still, the bright girl in Minnesota with the notebook, willing to listen to an answer, confident there was none.

But suddenly I knew there was an answer. School boards didn't know it; history was taught because it had always been taught, as far as school boards were concerned. Superintendents didn't know it, except a rebel now and then. America didn't know it. But suddenly I knew it. I should have said:

"You're not going to be a stenographer, Julia. That may be what you will work at. But what you are going to be is a human being, which is what you are right now. And as a human being you need history for the same reason you need God. Because history is the story of man's struggle for and his failure to comprehend God in this universe. It is through his story, man's story, that you can learn of his errors and try to avoid them in writing your story. History is a record of man's struggle toward the light. And the Light, Julia, is God.

Julia, I'm sure, would have gripped her notebook a little tighter, smiled nervously, thanked me and departed.

And later she would assure her friends, "He's so funny. I can't make him out. Not at all like Miss Seymour was last year. I could always understand what she meant."

But if I would have confused Julia, consider how I would confuse most of the superintendents I've met or known.

"You will please deal in facts, Mr. Crowe. Dates, places, people, things. We will leave the theory to others."

"What theory, Mr. Jenkins? And what others?"

"You will be wise to heed my advice, Mr. Crowe."

So back to your books, teacher. Let's turn out some Quiz Kids, eh? Or some cute Information Pleasers. "How many heads had the royal duck of King Henry III? And how many wars did Charlemagne fight? How old was Alexander when he died?"

That's the language the students can understand. Ask us the questions and we'll try to answer no lies. But don't ask us to discuss. Please, teacher, don't ask us to discuss it!

I remember the impatience that always greeted me when we considered "ideas."

"What did Will Durant mean when he wrote that a good man who is not great is infinitely more precious than a great man who is not good?"

"Aw, teacher!"

"Who is Will Durant, then?"

"Will Durant is an American philosopher."

"What is a philosopher?"

"Aw, teacher!"

I remembered the eager boy in Detroit, so anxious to help me out when I was upholding the character of Jews against the assault of many students.

"Barney Ross is a Jew," I had told them, "Franz Werfel is a Jew. Hank Greenberg is a Jew. Einstein is a Jew."

I figured Ross and Greenberg would help anyhow. Then up pops Danny with his face shining, "And how about Roosevelt? And he's a Jew!"

But then as the darkness crept over the room, I remembered the shining eyes of the girl in the front seat in a

Wisconsin school when I finished telling the story of how Socrates had died.

"I'll always remember that," she said.

And I was glad because I believed she would.

And there was a boy in another Wisconsin school who had thrilled to "The Story of Victor" in Maxwell Anderson's *Key Largo* and how he had believed in something greater than himself. And how he had died.

But most of all there was that boy in the small Minnesota school, a sophomore, a student, substitute on the football team, who'd written, "If I go to war, I'll fight clean and think clean. At least I hope I will. That way I may die sooner or be killed easier, but if I do, I'll die clean. And I'd rather do that than live dirty."

Remembering that, I know that I, in this year 1945, by grace of God in a position to help form the minds of those who will soon be men, have a solemn duty to teach what is right rather than what is expedient.

I shall try to show them, if I can and when I can, that a man must live with himself always. And that, rich or poor, big or a little, he will appraise himself and know himself for what he is. And that, for him, he must create his own peace by his own life and thoughts and deeds. That is what a teacher is for.

And as for "winning the peace" in the world, I shall try to show, and I shall pray that I succeed, that world peace will be won, if it is won, not by force of arms or by coalitions or blueprints or obliteration of peoples, but by the existence in the world of men of a disposition that deserves peace. For peace will come to us only if we are deserving; and if we are not, nothing then can guarantee it. And right now, as anyone who looks about with a fair and open mind must admit, we are not really deserving of very much that is good.

I am not teaching my students to be secretaries or scientists but to be human beings, not so much to be great as to be good, not so much to fear to "die clean" as to fear to "live dirty."

THE LITERATURE TEACHER

My father taught high school English. He loved literature and shared that love with students in his classroom, with readers through his published work and in scores of banquet speeches over nearly fifty years.

He wrote fondly about his early days growing up in Stillwater. That passion for literature, however, was nearly snuffed out, in his own high school years. Rather than introducing students to the wonder of the written word, teachers often resorted to mind numbing tasks like passage memorization assignments and the intricacies of correct grammar and punctuation.

That all changed when he met Father James Moynihan in his junior year at the College of St. Thomas in St. Paul, MN.

* * *

"Father Moynihan"
Typewritten essay found in files
Date Unknown

I was in his office one day—he was president of the college as well as a literature teacher—and the office girl said, "Father—don't you think you'd better get to class now?"

"Oh, yes. That's right. What time is that class, Miss Brombach?"

"Eight-thirty, Father."

"Oh. What time is it now?"

"Nine o'clock, Father."

"Oh. Oh my. Yes—I better get over there immediately. Immediately."

And that's how it was with Fr. James Moynihan. Even in these days of the informal look, few would call him Jim. He was absent-minded. He came late. We used to try to time it so we would get there just before he showed. But he was the greatest literature teacher I ever saw. By a long country mile.

Five minutes in his class was worth five hours in most.

I'd come out of high school hating literature because no one had ever shown me how it was, and I didn't know how—nor care—to show it to myself.

And then, all at once, there was this man.

He'd stand in front of us and quote Coleridge on prayer: *"He prayeth best who loveth best … all things both great and small."*

Or Keats on truth: *"Beauty is truth, truth beauty,—that is all you will ever know in this world.… It is all you need to know."*

Or Donne on the communion among men: *"No man is an island… When the bell tolls, therefore…… it tolls for thee."*

Or Shakespeare on life: *"… And each man in his time plays many parts."*

I'd majored in English because I wanted to learn about writing at St. Thomas and they had nothing else to offer in this field. But now—suddenly—I was filled with the glory and the exaltation of words themselves—in language and ideas and dreams.

I was alive in a way I'd never known before, and I knew I wanted to go out and carry the message to all the kids everywhere trapped in classrooms taught by pretenders like Sandra Buckley or by well-intentioned but ineffectual instructors like Agatha Simmons who simply didn't know that it was there.

Suddenly, teaching no longer seemed like a chore performed by uninspired individuals who put in so many hours a day keeping a semblance of order among kids who only waited for the school day to end.

Sure—I was angry because the tender time of being seventeen would not come my way again and it would have been so much better if these wondrous things to which James Moynihan had brought me had been there for me to see and know and taste and believe in and be lifted up by when I was young in the special way that is only there for a little while.

Still—here it was—and there was no going back. I had it now and my job, it seemed to me, was clear. Take it out from here to those who are still as young as you were then.

It all began for me in Father Moynihan's class. I do not feel I would've become a teacher without my having known him for that little while. Certainly, I would not have taught English.

Maybe the quotation that sealed it all in for me was that one he gave us from *Hamlet*:

> *This above all: to thine own self be true,*
> *And it must follow, as the night the day,*
> *Thou canst not then be false to any man.*

That, I guess, laid it on the line. I would start from here. God willing, I would never turn back.

Marty in the Classroom
c. 1948

COMMITMENT TO TEACHING LITERATURE

My dad did not turn back. He ran into conflict, sometimes from administrators who wanted him to pursue a restricted curriculum, sometimes from fellow teachers who had a more traditional approach, and sometimes from parents who worried about their children missing out on "the basics" or "not having proper college preparation."

But then there were the students. My dad knew the power of the written word and inspired his students in literature classes for nearly fifty years.

There was the girl who said, "I never liked poetry till I was in Mr. Crowe's class. Now I want to be an English teacher." And she is.

Or the man who stopped me in church one day, one of my dad's students and a football player from over 50 years ago. He reminisced about those days and said, "I never read a whole book until I was in Marty's class and read The Grapes of Wrath. I would never have gone on to college if it hadn't been for him."

And there was the girl, who on a trip east, took a detour to visit Walden Pond. There she collected a small container of water and some leaves to bring home to her boyfriend who had *been drawn to his coach's story of Thoreau and his two-year retreat in that very place.*

What is inspiration worth? A lot. My dad knew that from the time he was a young man and he never wavered. He knew who he was.

* * *

"Commitment to Teaching Literature"
Handwritten copy found in files
ca. 1957–58

"There are two things we ask of our teachers," the superintendent said. (This was long ago when I was very young and so I waited for the pearls of wisdom to drop). "We ask that they keep roll accurately and that when they leave their rooms after school all the shades are at the same height." (I must have been staring). "That way the passerby sees a neat looking school."

That was more than fifteen years ago and there have been a good many school officials since then, but things haven't changed very much.

Keeping roll and keeping records. Keeping things neat. Orderly. Calm. Fitting the pattern. Remembering that what seems to be is probably more important than what is.

That was Mr. Morgan's credo on that night in North Dakota long ago—and it holds for most of them, everywhere, today.

I've fought it—but they win the fights.

I've told them I will not spend most of my time teaching usage and grammar to seniors because if seniors haven't mastered usage by the time they reach the twelfth grade, my efforts are not going to change matters very much.

I have told them that I am not too much impressed by the oft-repeated cry of that businessman: "Give me someone who can write a decent sentence!"

I've told them that if I believed said businessman was really interested in the decency angle, I might be more concerned. I happen to know that what he is asking for is someone who can punctuate correctly and spell correctly and put the words down in the correct order and that decency has nothing whatsoever to do with it.

I've told them, too, that from every ten seniors in my English class I can provide at least two who can write a sentence correctly—who know a phrase when they see one—who would never mistake a preposition for a conjunction or an indirect object for one that is more head-on.

My trouble is, as it has always been, to find one of these masters of the correct form who has anything to say.

So, I've argued for ideas.

I've argued that there is as much point to Shelley as to the subjunctive—and probably a good deal more. I've told them that if they could understand how it was with Keats when the medics let him know he had had it—that he was running out of days and hours—he sat down—and wrote:

When I have fears that I may cease to be,
Before my pen has gleaned my teeming brain–

I have told them that a student who can understand—even kind of—how it was with that young man that day—and how a man gets to be that way—that they would understand far more of what is worthy to be understood then if I could suddenly bring them the kind of light which would clear up the matter of the dangling participle.

And so, what has the answer been?

It has always been the same. Some administrator behind some over rated desk has told me that I am being shifted to English II next year where we will, "use the grammar workbooks, you know. Very valuable, really." Or else that I am to teach a class in current affairs or social science instead of my English IV group.

(It hasn't been so bad, sometimes, because I like to teach about current affairs and social science—and Shakespeare had as much to say for the students in those fields—and these times—as he did for anyone else. Trouble is when I quote from the Bard too often, I'm accused of leaving my domain and invading the territory reserved for the teacher who has replaced me in the literature class).

A teacher can fight the administration, of course, but he can hardly expect to win the decision. Still—the fight itself is a lot of fun.

I remember that, as a student in high school, I thoroughly despised poetry. It seemed to me to be mostly about daisies in the breeze or pansies on the hill—and we were constantly under orders to scan it and to memorize it.

(I once was ordered to memorize Portia's "Quality of Mercy" speech from *The Merchant of Venice*. So, I did memorize it and recited it and got an "A" for doing so. Ten years later I found out what it meant and that it contains some of the finest concepts the mind of man has ever written down. It seems to me that was too long to wait).

It was shortly after I was graduated from high school (I was a good memory man in the history class, too, so I finished as a member of the "honor roll") that I came across a poem in the public library in Saint Paul which changed my whole point of view relative to poetry.

It wasn't much of a poem, I guess, and it was by a little-known Irishman named Shaemas O'Sheel. But the lines which rocked me went something like this:

Bravely they fought, but they fought not well
And on the field of battle, they always fell—
They heard strange music that no foeman heard
Who on the field of battle always fell—
Yet they will scatter the red hordes of hell
Who on the field of battle always fell.

It is a sardonic note I think that I, who hated poetry because it was presented to me dead, should have found in a poem the kind of answer that I needed years later to wage the kind of fight that I feel I must wage in my chosen profession.

(I hope O'Sheel realized that it is no fun to be one of those who "always fell"—but I do believe we shall yet scatter those hordes—which though not, I am sure, "of Hell,"—yet, I am convinced, keep so many a mind from the upward looking, the light shining, and the dream.

Mr. Schaefer, wherever you are, I want you to know that I have not forgotten the day when you said, "What these kids need to know is how to spell and how to puncturate (sic)" (in my scorn perhaps I create your pronunciation, sir, but I think not)—I have not forgotten but I agree even less now than I did that day so long gone. You could hurt me then, Mr. Schaefer, but not now. Your successors have hurt me since and will again. But never enough, sir, and never in a way that really counts.

And so, I still give them Thomas Wolfe instead of the semicolon—or at least I spotlight him more. Because, Mr. Schaefer, Thomas Wolfe once asked the question, "Do only the dead know Brooklyn?"

And I ask you Mr. Schaefer. Do they? I asked my kids that too, sir. And I think it's a question worth asking. Because I think it's important for them to realize that the question that Tom Wolfe raised is much greater than the knowing of Brooklyn—or the Bronx—or Jersey—will ever be. Much greater than the knowing of the semicolon will ever be either, Mr. Schaefer

Because you see, sir, there are a lot of answers we can't come up with—but we shouldn't forget them because they're out of reach. Wolfe said that sir. And that's important if anything is. You see, sir, it's even important to know some questions. Some questions are worth knowing more than the answers. That's deep, Mr. Schaefer, maybe—but not too deep. Not for some of my seniors. After I left your school, I tried them out. Yours wasn't the only school I left.

SCHOOL DAYS

My father taught for nearly fifty years and each of those years, as summer ended, he looked forward to coming back to the classroom.

* * *

"School Days"
St. Paul Pioneer Press
August 1983

Well, here it is near the end of summer and another school year is about to begin. For me, this will be the 45th. How does a guy's mind run at a time like this? What seems to be the important thing? What is No. 1?

It won't be the salary, that's for sure. I've spent most of my life teaching in private schools in medium-sized towns and there has never been much money available. And there isn't now.

Many of the schools I've been in have had to fight to stay alive. So what? That's been part of the excitement and the fun. And teaching in high school is nothing much if joy isn't there. With it, there are fewer jobs any better.

So, I won't get a new car this year and I have never had one. Again—so what?

To walk into my classroom and try to teach what is right and what is worth it—this is better.

The emphasis at the moment is on mathematics and science and computers. The emphasis is on making money and creating the easy life.

There is no fun in teaching that kind of stuff. I don't want a kid to walk out of my class who has only learned to be smart, or clever or how to manipulate. How to win the close ones. How to use the other guy. How to be top dog.

What a bore.

I want to turn out a dreamer. I want to find the guy or girl who is not interested in wiping out the other side (or beating them to the pots of gold), but who, instead, feels the hurt when others are hurting and feels good when their tears are dry.

I want my kids to believe in love.

Not sex. There's nothing wrong with sex and they know about it already. The merchants of sex are not kids. And they are not interested in love but in profits. If they ever believed in love, and I suspect they did—once, they have long since forgotten what it was.

They want to tell the kids that sex and love are the same. And that is a shattering lie. My kids want to believe in love.

I teach literature and I can give my students Keats and Shelley and Wordsworth and Frost and Christina Rossetti. Some cynics sneer that *Romeo and Juliet* is all sex and a mile wide. But there is love there—and the cynics will always miss it.

And I want them to have God.

Not prayer in the classroom. That's for the kind of adult who wants to look better than somebody else. But let me have God. If I wanted to block him out, I couldn't do it anyhow. He comes through the locked doors.

So here we go again, kids. With love and faith—and unafraid.

Hey, school isn't as bad as some folks crack it up to be.

Marty discussing written assignments with
American Literature students, c. 1972.

THE IMPACT OF A TEACHER

My father wrote this column in response to a full-page ad taken out by a teacher who was quitting the Lakeview Heights Schools. In the ad the teacher spoke about his frustrations and reasons for leaving. I have changed the name of the teacher and the community, as I do not want to focus on the man or the city. It was, after all, nearly 60 years ago. I include this piece because right now, in 2024, we have a problem with teacher shortages. Many teachers have left the classroom; we have declining numbers in our teacher preparation programs.

My father's commitment to teaching comes through in this piece. He saw the potential of the teacher to impact lives, to support students who were struggling, to challenge those who could achieve more if they dared to reach. He could think of no better way to spend his life. He looked forward to each new school year, even his last one.

I am hoping his words spark an interest in some young person considering future options or reignite a passion in a teacher already out there working every day with the many different young people who are the students in our schools.

* * *

"Response to Public Letter from Lakeview Heights Teacher Who Quit His Job"

Published in "From the Bench"
Green Bay Register
April 23, 1965

A young man quit teaching in Lakeview Heights the other day. He did it to the sound of bugles.

This lad's name is Douglas Merrick, and he has been teaching at Lakeview Heights for five years. Lakeview Heights is a suburb and, apparently, like some suburbs, is populated by the kind of people who believe that status is everything and class symbols the only kind worth having.

So young Douglas is mad because the kids in his classroom are "self-centered; frivolous, frozen with sophistication."

Life has become, to them, "a shrill, handwaving, convertible riding round of trivialities," and they are "bored with themselves, with others, and with life."

So, Doug wants out.

Well, now, the symptoms of whatever the trouble are there—and they are as you describe them, lad. The kids are shrill and self-centered. And, for sure their thoughts and their actions are trivial indeed.

The trouble with you, teacher, is not your observations. Your solution is what's wrong.

You, simply, quit.

Don't you know, Doug, that's what these kids do best? If they have a weakness that flies above all the rest, this is it. When things don't go their way, they quit.

They take their ball and go home.

And so you offer nothing, Douglas. You point the finger—and we have all pointed our own for a long time, though few of us have ever bought advertising space to spotlight the whole thing.

Maybe we should have. Maybe we should say bravo because you had the style, the verve, the willingness, and the cash to do so.

I almost said courage. But not quite.

Because I am not sure how much guts you have, Douglas Merrick.

You say, "all my senses reel" from the sight of "the petrification of a once—vital young person." You say you "have seen enough of living death."

So, you stick out your tongue at the whole works. And then you run.

You're going to write a book.

Well, bully for you, sir. But soft pedal my bravo, please.

Sure, a lot of kids are slobs.

Soft. Whining. Cowardly conformist. Dull. Greedy. Blasé. Gutless. Decadent. Amoral. Selfish.

And a lot are self-pitying, whimpering quitters, too, Doug.

The question "why" pokes up its head.

In a world where the thing to be is rich, and what you are is determined by what you own, is all this surprising?

In a world of split levels and tri-levels and country clubs and cocktail parties and the absolute necessity of the private swimming pool and the barbecue pit, is this surprising?

Tune in their elders, Douglas.

Tune in the fortyish fry around Lakeview Heights or anywhere else.

You'll hear trivia, Doug. You'll hear talks of angles and promotions and what's in it for me. Amid the clinking of the ice in a thousand glasses, you'll hear dreary, dull, uninspired conversation about a score of trivial things, and, sometimes, you may tune in a bit more zest in the language about such things, maybe, as how to keep Negroes and Jews out of the area, or how to get a new minister at the neighborhood good fellowship church who will have less controversial ideas.

You may even, if a teacher is man enough and teacher enough to earn it, hear such a teacher called a few things which might at first seem to violate the basic niceness of the atmosphere.

This is the world the kids never made, Douglas.

Sure, I grant they haven't done much to improve it. They never will if the men who see what the trouble is, turn and run.

I'm not really sure you do see the trouble though, Doug.

I understand that you are an atheist. And that's your right.

And I read that you are an admirer of the cynic of the intellectual elite, Ayn Rand. Your privilege again.

But I have a suspicion now, Douglas. I suspect you are a bit of a poseur, maybe. Self-announced atheists often are. Ayn Rand devotees often are.

I think, maybe, you have a contempt for people, Douglas.

You like good music and good literature. So do I.

You teach English and so do I. And so you like poetry. And so do I.

How do you like the line from Coleridge: "He prayeth best who loveth best"?

Or the one from Burns: "A man's a man for all of that"?

What about the poor benighted kid with the low IQ, Doug? What about the bewildered guy with no special social grace, whatever?

How do you feel about the nameless guys, Doug? The beaten down, bloody handed ones of a lot of colors and creeds who scrounge and fight to exist.

How about them, Doug?

Do you like the poetry of Sandburg? What about Steinbeck, Douglas?

Or is it the cool sophistication of Rand—or no count?

I've got kids in my class who want to try the Peace Corps, Doug.

Where did they come from?

A boy told me last week that the plea of an assembly speaker for young men, "who would burn themselves out" in dedicated lives—like teaching for instance—was "the best talk I ever heard."

Who let him in, Doug?

And a boy who wrote in a theme, the other day: "To kill a lot of people and not to care because they are people who don't count—like the Vietcong, for instance,—isn't right. And we can't make it right because of what we say and who we are."—what about that boy, Douglas?

Don't run. Don't hide. Don't quit.

Unless you're a fraud and a fake, Douglas. Unless you really despise all people except the chosen ones. The elite. If you feel that way, you should have quit long ago. You should have never begun to teach at all.

There are a million kids out there looking for a way and a light and a dream. A teacher's job is to show them.

It's a good job.

BEYOND CLASSES

My father knew a teacher's work was challenging and he welcomed the master teachers he encountered who taught him. One of them was Sister Paul Marie.

* * *

"Model Teacher Looks Beyond Classes"
"Letter to the Editor"
St. Paul Pioneer Press
November 19, 1984

Each year I read about somebody who has been chosen "teacher of the year." Lately it has been someone who is sharp and strong in the area of computers. (Computers are "in" right now.) Sometimes it is a teacher of the gifted ones and sometimes someone who works with the retarded. (I tend to admire such a teacher most.)

Sister Paul Marie will never be chosen as the top teacher of the year. She is, though. Name your year. Any year.

She is the last nun to teach at our school. We used to have a goodly number. We have one now. She has been here 30 years.

The other day she talked with me about one kid she works with who is a very slow reader, and thus often is in scholastic trouble.

"It's slow going," she said. "He probably will never be very much in the classroom. But he comes to see me every day. He never misses. And he tries. He really tries."

The boy is a fine football player and I know some learned folks maintain that if a boy can't pass his courses he shouldn't be allowed to play football—or anything else.

"Would you vote to bar him from football, Sister?"

"Never."

Then we began to talk about some other kids who are not sold short on brains but who are a constant pain in the whatever—big mouth, big show. I mentioned one of these, whom, I admit, I have never liked. Liked? I can barely abide the guy.

"If you knew what that boy goes through, at home every morning before he comes to school, you might understand him better."

Thanks, Sister. For the first time maybe I shall try. Sister Paul Marie knows more about the background of the kids in our school because she has bothered to find out. And because she cares.

I shall ask her about some other "problem kids," and I shall listen to what she says. The president's commission and a lot of school boards would do well to do the same.

Sister Paul Marie is not very tall, and she's not very young anymore. She knows more about computers than I will ever know, but there are a thousand experts who know more. And there are teachers of special education with more imposing degrees. But she is my nominee for teacher of this year… or any year.

GUIDANCE IS MISGUIDED

My father once wrote an article critical of guidance counselors. The message in his writing was that many young people in our schools needed someone to listen and care, a counselor. He saw the counselors instead occupied with testing, career planning and assisting with selecting and applying to post-secondary schools.

I became a counselor, though in my time we were called school counselors. Interestingly, my dad's argument was my argument throughout my career. I was aware of the students my dad was concerned about. I did not object to assisting students with academic planning both in high school and beyond. It was a great way to get to know them. However, counselors were often buried in clerical work. Students needed more from us.

Despite his critique, the Wisconsin School Counselors Association invited my dad to speak at one of their conventions. Perhaps they agreed with him. At the time of this convention, I was in my first year as a school counselor in Nevada. When I returned to Wisconsin, I was a regular at the annual convention. Sorry I missed this one.

* * *

"Guidance Is Misguided"
Green Bay Press Gazette
February 27, 1977

I am scheduled to be the banquet speaker next week at a state convention of junior high school guidance counselors to be held in Stevens Point.

I am not sure just why they selected me for this opportunity. I am not trained in the field (my daughter, Maureen is a counselor at a school in Nevada) and some years ago I wrote a piece for a metropolitan journal about guidance counselors which had more reaction—pro and con, but more con than pro—than any other article I have written in a long time.

That particular piece was interpreted as being very critical of counselors, and since it was reprinted by a number of papers here and there, the hot responses came from a lot of places. I remember one principal of a school in southern Minnesota who accused me of putting the question to the function of advisors and counselors everywhere.

To say that he was angry would be to radically soften his position.

I am, therefore, somewhat surprised to be going to Point to talk to a whole battalion of people in the guidance field. I am also, I think, just a little bit scared by this assignment. Maybe I stand in need of a bit of guidance, myself, this time. And maybe that is why I am writing this piece today.

Because the original article was not an attack on guidance counselors and could only have been interpreted that way by people who are extremely sensitive and possibly just a bit paranoiac. Heck—some of my best friends are guidance counselors and I would not mind at all if my daughter (one of the single ones) should marry one.

Wait a minute—no, that's right. I'm pretty sure I would not mind.

The trouble with guidance counselors is not the man (or woman) in the field. It's the field itself.

Too many dedicated and highly trained people have to spend too much of their time giving tests and trying to advise little Annabelle that she belongs in beauty culture school rather than in college but that if she does go to college, anyhow, she would be far better off at the University of Michigan than she would be at Dartmouth or Cornell. Her IQ tests show it and so do her aptitude tests (ACT and SAT and maybe there are some more by now) and so do all the graphs which deal with her personality profile.

Now I do not doubt the wisdom of the advice for Annabelle. (I might suggest additional advice to her parents which might enable them to see that the kid is not meant for college and that college is not the magic carpet—nor even the door to prestige—which so many parents for so long have dreamed it to be.

Then Annie might be better able to abide things at home when the horrible truth about her—not being "college material"—is known.)

Should the beleaguered gal say to heck with all my advisers and all those tests and records—I don't want to curl anybody's hair ever and I'll show them all. I'll go to college, and I'll make it. Well—we all know she probably won't. After all—there are all those tests, man. But somehow you kind of hope she upsets that old apple cart. Some way. Some day.

The impossible dream.

Impossible. Impractical. Unlikely. Unwise. They said it all about one of my football players in Marinette some years ago.

"He'll never make it."

"For sure?"

"For sure."

Last I heard he had his master's degree and was teaching art in some college somewhere.

"Why did you have to tackle Mount Everest?"

"Because it was there."

Don't read me wrong. I think the tests are usually pretty reliable and that the advice based on them is usually good advice. Folks read me wrong on that before. I don't need a repeat.

What I object to is not the tests nor the predictions nor the advice but simply that this sort of thing has come to seem to be the counselor's job and if he does it well, he is doing his job.

And to that I say like hell he is.

Gertie downed a handful of pills in the lav a few minutes ago because her boyfriend decided she was too fat and headed in a new direction. Clint got slugged by his old man this morning because the guy was drunk, and the kid went to the defense of his mother.

Charlie is sitting under a tree somewhere because some fool coach wanted to know how come he can't play basketball like his older brother did.

Or worse—like his father did.

Too many tests in the guidance man's office. Too many charts and graphs. Too many catalogs. Too many arrows pointing. Your job is not the talented kids, man. Not putting them on the right roads. Your job is the troubled ones. They cry in the night.

You used to hear them. Remember? When you had the time.

Given the chance, I think you still will. If not, you should test for another job.

Now get mad if you want to.

* * *

In 2000, I was named Wisconsin High School Counselor of the year. As I drove into town on that Friday afternoon following the convention, the award on the seat next to me, I considered stopping at school. I was only a block away, but I decided instead to go home.

A little further down the road was the cemetery where my dad was buried. I thought, "I'll go show dad." I pulled into the road closest to his gravesite, parked, picked up my plaque and looking over my shoulder to be sure no one was watching, I made my way to the stone that marked his grave. As I stood there holding my award, I heard his response as clearly as if he was there,

"Don't let it go to your head."

I laughed. I knew that was exactly what he would have said. I was grateful for my dad's bit of advice one year after his death and was happy for my visit. I headed home.

THE STUDENTS

ALL KIDS COUNT

My dad loved working with all students, but he was especially aware of those on the fringe, the lost ones, the troubled ones, those who lacked academic skill. I worked with many students who fit that description in my career as a School Counselor. I was the "At Risk Coordinator" in one school. "At Risk" meant credit deficient with graduation in jeopardy. The mission statement of the plan we wrote for that program was "Each One Reach One."

My dad didn't need a program or a mission statement. He just did it—for nearly 50 years. He felt it was a critical part of his job, though his advocacy was sometimes met with resistance.

* * *

"Why Shouldn't All Kids Count?"
Green Bay Press Gazette
September 4, 1977

A few thoughts as another school year begins…

The best thing ever said to me by a student was in a year-end evaluation of our class. A little gal name of

Margaret Carey wrote: "In your class I always felt like I counted for something."

Now that was more than 20 years ago at Pacelli High School in Austin Minnesota, but I have never forgotten it. It has always been a source of gladness for me that that little girl felt that way and a source of anger that she should feel she did not "count" in her other classes.

I suppose the way she wrote it was a little bit strong, but nevertheless, I think most of us know that a lot of kids feel just that way—and often with much justification. So many drift through the precious years of being young with the feeling they are nobody.

Maybe if girls' athletics had been around in 1955 Margaret would've been an athlete. She was small and slight and quiet, and I doubt it—but maybe. She was never in a play, or a musical or whatever. She was a very average student.

Like so many through the years—she was just there.

Many teachers say that is the way it is—you can't do anything about it. It's the kids' fault—not ours.

Maybe.

But a lot of teachers try, and I think we all ought to try. Margaret may have felt that she counted in my class, and I'm glad she did, but I'm sure I missed it with a hundred more. Maybe a thousand.

Missed it because I had too many things to do, or because I was too much in a hurry. Whatever. And this haunts me still—because once in a while I didn't really care.

We've got to care. If we don't care we should not be teaching, because we are not really teachers. Above all the rest—we've got to care.

Every teacher will say he cares. I will say I do. How is it then that so many kids get lost? Their fault? They were born to be lost? That answer lacks a lot.

I remember a kid named Lefty, and all the meetings we had to talk about kicking him out. (I don't want to say which school it was, but it was a long time ago). Lefty had a problem… drinking.

I voted against giving him the sack. Fought it all the way and, with the help of an old nun there, managed to win. Lefty stayed.

Some of the teachers were savage about it.

"It's because he's the quarterback," they said.

He was, too. And maybe that was part of it. No coach likes to lose a good QB. But in this case, it was more than that. He had a strange kind of lonerism. A pride. I thought it was too good a thing to see it waste.

I left that school at the end of Lefty's junior year. Three weeks into the next one they got rid of him, surprising exactly no one, I guess.

Anyhow, I went back there for a reunion years later. Somebody told me that the left-hander had had a pretty rough life. Never shook the habit, I guess. Kicking him out didn't change him. Or save him.

"We told you he was a lost cause," one teacher who had been there said to me. I did not slug him.

"You didn't only tell me, man. You guaranteed it."

I figure if you are going to kick out everybody but the saints, there's nowhere left for the sinners. Honest—there ought to be. Teachers should want there to be.

It's more important, I think, than what text you use or how much homework you assign. More important than records or tardy slips or lesson plans or hall passes. More important than any of them—or all of them together.

It makes teaching harder, I guess. But who said it was meant to be easy. Besides, in there somewhere is all the fun and all the glory the job has to offer. Dammit, man—it's worth your best shot—over and over if necessary. Mine too.

We may miss again. Many times. Like I have and you have. Many times. But we don't miss every time. Sometime—somewhere—we are there when the cry for help comes along.

That's why the job is the good job, man. The goodest job there is.

THAT WAS OUR JOB

For most of his career, my father taught in Catholic schools. He felt that his commitment to developing a sense of humanity in students was less challenged in that setting and important in the school's mission. However, as in all educational venues, the appearance of "excellence" was important, and some students got in the way.

* * *

"The Public School People Are Laughing at Us for Accepting Her"

Handwritten manuscript, c. 1960

*Note: Names in this piece have been changed to protect anonymity.

"The public school people are laughing at us for accepting her."

That statement, made by Sister Margaret Claire, was the worst thing I ever listened to as a teacher.

Sister Margaret Claire was, of course, the principal at one of the Catholic high schools in which I've taught. And she had no right to make a statement of that kind.

Because if Catholic school people are going to start being conditioned in their judgments and decisions by what the "public school people" think about them, then there is no reason for a Catholic school to exist.

I would like to make it clear that I believe the Catholic school system is the finest thing that has happened to American education. So there is a reason for it to exist. There is no legitimate reason why Sister Margaret Claire should be part of it.

Yet there must be thousands like the Sister, lost in the desire for human respect, in the system. I have met at least twenty. It is remarkable that the Catholic school system remains, for me, an admirable thing in spite of them. (There are those who will argue, of course, that it remains so because of them).

The girl about whom the above statement was made was not a very intelligent person. God knows why he created girls like that—and I don't know that he is under obligation to explain his actions to Sister Margaret Claire She is under obligation to accept them.

To deny the girl a chance to be part of the four fine years in high school because she doesn't quite measure up intellectually might make a lot of sense to the Russians. It doesn't sound like a Christian sense of conscience to me.

The girl, whom I will call Rose Marie, also had a rather questionable reputation. So, as I recall, had Mary Magdalene.

Criticized for consorting with sinners, Christ reminded his critics that it was the sinners he had come to save. I think it is necessary for all the Sister Margaret Claires to remember that. If too many forget, then the time has come to let the Catholic schools crumble and the weeds grow through. Because the weeds will be there anyhow.

It happens that Sister was wrong about Rose Marie. She became a daily communicant at mass—and, ultimately, even nourished, probably in vain, the hope of becoming a nun herself.

But even if Rose Marie had turned out badly, we still owed her a chance. And a second and a third.

The confessional stands in every Catholic Church as a constant reminder that Sister Margaret Claire and I, and every Catholic—yes, every man alive—is doomed indeed without a second chance. And that the second chance is there.

I read a short letter in a Wisconsin newspaper some months ago in which a public junior high school student had this to say: "They criticize the deportment of our students. They choose to forget that we accept all the students they kick out."

Out of the mouths of the young, I think, come, often, words for us to remember.

I have fought to keep boys from being expelled for as long as I have taught in Catholic schools—and that's thirteen years now.

My motives were seldom altruistic. The boys in question were usually athletes and I needed them on my teams.

But I kept remembering that the point still held. If Catholic schools had a reason for being, surely that reason existed most clearly for the not so saintly ones. And it was never the saints who were up for expulsion.

I remember, for instance, one boy who smoked. Now smoking in itself was not reason enough to be kicked out of school—it depended on where you were standing when you lit the weed.

In some schools, you had to light up inside the building to rate the gate. Some schools set the distance at one hundred feet. One thought two blocks would do it.

Well, Henry had smoked, I guess, since he was four. He didn't trap the dames in a corner. He didn't lap up the waters of joy. But he did weed it.

His main trouble was that he refused to lie about it.

Thus, when three boys were suspected of smoking in the lavatory and questioned about it, two would deny it—and Henry would own up.

They used to try to get Henry to put the finger on the other guys too. (Lots of school authorities, Catholic and public believe this to be a worthy procedure). But Henry would give them that cold smile and suggest that he hadn't been watching the other guys—he'd just been quietly inhaling for himself.

So, Henry was always on the verge of the sack.

Sister Leo used to pass me in the halls for months at a time without a greeting of any kind, because she was the best one on the faculty at getting the goods on Henry and I was the one who got him off the hook.

Henry would sit in most of his classes with apparent total lack of interest. In my class he did B work often—never lower than C. Some of the sisters accused me of favoring Henry because he was an athlete. They were probably right. But he earned his mark in my class.

"Well, of course," Sister Leo sneered once. "He likes you."

"Try that approach sometime, Sister," I said.

(There is a legend abroad in the land that only the teachers one dislikes ever teach him anything. I checked this once because I found myself buying the idea. It didn't test out).

In a Catholic school, it is traditionally accepted among the students that if a boy is in the "sisters' doghouse" as a sophomore he will never get out. There is much to this idea, I think. It is probably true in great degree in a public school as well.

If something is stolen—look for Louie. If something is broken—check on Chuck. I have known many a boy who with a wry grin confided to me that since he was going to take the rap anyhow, he figured he might as well be guilty of the act.

I once asked for a boy to be student manager of the basketball team. One of the sisters vetoed the suggestion because he'd been suspected of stealing a dime in the seventh grade.

I got him the job anyhow. So far as I know we never missed a shoelace. But much more important, he went on to college, where he became a straight A student and beamed much reflected glory back on all of us. The missing dime got lost again.

No one would recommend Red Francis for college. Not enough personal integrity nor responsibility. He'd never stick. He'd never make it. He'd hurt the standing of our school.

I got him in because he was a mighty mean man at left guard, especially on defense. He graduated this June from a college in Wisconsin. His recommendations are good. He'll be a teacher now—and a coach. He'll do both jobs well.

They did kick out Henry. It took a while, but they got it done. A year later Henry was in minor trouble with the law. Two years later a girl was in trouble and Henry had to get married. A few months after that he was dead in the crash of a "borrowed" car.

Sister Leo met me in the hall one day.

"Did you hear about Henry?" She asked me.

"I heard," I said.

"It's a terrible thing but I suppose it was bound to be."

I let it go then but I say it now.

"Bound to be, Sister? Maybe. How do we know? How will we ever know? Henry was like an unpleasant bug—and we brushed him off. And now the bug is dead."

But was it really a bug, Sister?

Ask yourself the question some night. In the quiet time, Sister.

I have.

Henry was a problem. Sure. Hard to solve—too hard. So, it came to the time when we didn't care. Then nobody cared.

Maybe that was our job, Sister. Maybe we should have cared.

THE POWER OF GOODNESS

My dad paid attention to goodness when he saw it. Goodness is easy to miss because so much focus is on pursuit of "excellence," achievement and recognition. Goodness usually gets lost, but my dad was attuned to it.

* * *

"The Power of Goodness"
Green Bay Press Gazette
August 29, 1976 (excerpt)

The hierarchy, the dignitaries and the bigwigs of the Catholic Church gathered in Philadelphia recently for the International Eucharistic Congress. The last time in this country was exactly 50 years ago, in Chicago.

Anyhow, the topic of the time was world hunger. And the one person who drew most of the attention—by no design of her own—was the little nun from the streets of Calcutta, Mother Teresa.

How can it be, that men with great intellect and great education—and reputations to match—do not catch the imagination of the multitude as does this little old lady who has spent most of the years of her life with the poorest of the poor?

The nameless and forgotten ones.

Maybe, that is because, in the midst of all our arrogance and cynicism and pretense and greed, we really are looking for a good person. And, in Mother Teresa, we find one who is, indeed, good.

I think I wrote here once that the philosopher and historian Will Durant, once said:

Goodness is more precious than greatness,
and a good man of more value than a great one.

Sometimes we sneer at such a statement as sentiment and idealism. But underneath we do believe it, I think. The light of it shines through.

For some reason that brings my mind to remember a lad named Norman. Or rather, what happened to him.

He had a big mouth and a big temper. He came from a "broken" home and somehow, he wound up at a school I taught at a long time ago. He antagonized just about everybody. I once had him by the front of the shirt (I was younger then) at football practice, I remember.

Well, anyhow, Norman was fair game for expulsion. Inevitable, as the poets say. And finally, when he cussed out a couple of the nuns one time too many, he got sacked.

"We don't want you around here anymore."

But he came back one day months later. I think maybe because there was nowhere else for him. And he had felt—maybe—that we did care a little once. And maybe we did, a little.

Anyhow, this one priest did not care—at least not anymore. He was not too bad a guy, I guess—but he was out of patience.

"You're not welcome here," he told Norman.

Somehow, though, Norm stayed around for the rest of that morning, and he was still there for the noon meal.

Hot lunch.

Mrs. Snyder, who was one of the cooks, spotted him.

"Well, Norman! It's good to see you again! You know something? I pray for you every night."

And that's when that tough kid cried.

SLOW LEARNERS HAVE MERIT, TOO

M*y father believed in recognizing and appreciating individual differences each student brings into the classroom. He looked for opportunities to celebrate talent whatever that may be. He also inspired students to pursue challenges they might not have considered. Each resulting accomplishment built confidence, a worthy objective for a classroom teacher.*

* * *

"Slow Learners Have Merit, Too"
Green Bay Press Gazette
May 22, 1977

Last week, we were talking about the idea that some educators insist is the right one now—namely that you pass a student only when he can do the work at the level he is at, no matter how many years go by and no matter how he outgrows his classmates physically.

I said, then, that there were weaknesses very evident in this approach, but I did note that I could not object too much if a teacher decided to fail the vandal or the bully or the deliberate lout. But I had to take the stand on behalf of the guy who tries but can't cut it anyhow.

Like a guy named Eddie I had in class in Minnesota a long time ago.

I was teaching at a Catholic high school, there, in those days, and Eddie flunked religion. I could not quite believe that.

"He gets to Mass every morning," I told the priest who taught the class. "There are only four kids in the whole school who do that. Eddie's one."

"He can't pass my tests."

Well, he passed mine, Father. I know that didn't make any difference because you were in charge. I wasn't.

But I just want it in the record. From where I was sitting. Eddie passed religion. And I have a hunch that if there is a God (If there isn't, religion class becomes a farce anyhow, doesn't it?), He passed Eddie, too.

I had the same guy in English class and there I was in charge.

Eddie couldn't spell. I'd give 20 words and he'd blow 15.

"That ain't so good, is it?"

"I've seen better, Eddie."

"Give me the list. I'll study it some more and take the test over again."

Next time he'd miss 12. Or eight. I guess maybe he never cut it down to fewer than eight out of 20. He was a lousy speller.

He wasn't any better on verbs and pronouns. You know—the sacred word. Usage. He'd work hard but he'd blow most of them there too.

I wonder if it takes any genius to see that Eddie was not meant to be much of a student. If so, then I must be a genius because I never flunked the guy.

I don't think it takes any genius. It takes a guy who gives a damn. And giving a damn is a teacher's job.

I had a guy named Gordy once.

I guess Gordy was just about the worst student I ever had and that was way back during the first year I ever taught. A little school with 13 kids in the senior class and Gordy was sitting solidly at the bottom.

I was teaching history that year and I'd call him in to see me half an hour before a quiz. I'd go through the ten response questions I was going to ask in class.

"Ya got it now, Gordy?"

"Yeh, I got it."

The class would meet, and Gordy would strike out on nine of the ten.

That year I was directing the senior class play and one of the key parts was that of a dumb Irish cop. Gordy seemed to fit it all right.

"He'll never be able to learn the lines."

"I guess you're right—but we'll give him a shot at it, anyhow."

Don't ask me how or why but Gordy knew his lines before anybody else in the cast. Came the night of the play and Gordy stole the show. Brought down the house as they say it in Minneapolis. I guess it was just about the greatest night the kid ever had.

They knew who he was. They said hello.

Twenty years later I met Gordy in a restaurant in Hudson.

"Hi, coach. Remember me?"

Twenty years is a lot of kids and maybe I hesitated.

"Casey," he said with that great toothy grin of his. (Casey was the cop in the play.)

"By damn," I said, "You're Gordy."

I ask you, teacher, should I have left him out of the play because on production night he might forget his lines? Blow it, as the poets say? Look, man—everybody deserves a chance at something in this life. You don't think so?

Your privilege.

That's why, for instance, I think to "declare a boy ineligible" for the football team because he can't make it in English or math is a travesty and probably a fraud. It would make as much sense to deny him a chance to take shop because he doesn't recognize a gerund when he sees one.

The same Eddie I was talking about could fix my car when nobody else in town could. There'd be twenty different size wrenches hanging on the board and he'd reach for the right one.

Every time.

One of the two greatest halfbacks I ever had played for me in Eau Claire. There was hardly a class he was any good in, but he was a good kid and he tried. The faculty there was unusual. They passed him.

He could run the ball and catch it and block and tackle, and he did it all with a fierce and wonderful kind of joy.

I said last week I don't think I'm good enough to second guess Whoever created you and me. And Jimmy. He couldn't handle an infinitive and I am witness to that. But he sure could run with the football. In one game, an official sent him to the sideline. Jim had a bit of a temper, and I thought maybe it had got in his way.

He showed me his hand, and somebody had stepped on it. Hard. Cleat marks—deep and brutal. We put some disinfectant on the wound and bandaged it up. Then he wanted to go back in, and we let him.

Maybe we shouldn't have. I've never been sure about what you should do in a case like that. You don't want to play an injured player—ever—but Jim was more hurt than injured. There is a difference, man.

Besides, if you're not careful you can sometimes hurt a boy in ways you can never tape up. We've done that. Often. As parents. As teachers and coaches. As people.

Anyhow, I've noticed "dumb" kids can often "take it" better than the rest of the guys. Maybe it's just that they've had more experience.

I thank God for guys like Eddie and Gordy and Jim, who, for a little while, walked through my life.

And taught me.

INFLUENCE

I close this section with excerpts from a letter to the editor sent to the Marinette newspaper from one of my father's former students. I came across the letter as I sorted through the boxes. I think her words are an apt tribute to my father, the teacher.

* * *

"Crowe's Influence Felt Many Years Later"

By Mare Lindsay Hare
Excerpts from a Letter to the Editor
Marinette Eagle Herald
March 24, 2007

I wish to speak to the relationship I had in high school with my teacher Mr. Crowe. We all hear stories about how a teacher can impact your life, change your direction. Such was Marty Crowe's influence on my high school years.

Mr. Crowe never followed the predictable lesson plans, yet I learned more in his classes about life and the world than in any college classroom. He wasn't a teacher who favored or played to the popular kids. No, Marty befriended the "fringe," the kids who needed him, who were searching for self-esteem and were lost.

Mr. Crowe made you believe that all things were possible—that it was up to you. Some honor students used to joke about the "losers" who took Crowe's classes like economic geography. In those classes, TIME magazine was our textbook. He showed us what the rest of the world was doing.

He portrayed true Catholic values in teaching about the sin of racial prejudice, segregation and hate crimes. He gave ideas to the faces of the politicians who were running and challenged us to become informed voters. More than anything else Marty Crowe taught humanity from the heart. He was often painfully honest about himself and his life experience. He had a humility that made you stop and think about being more compassionate.

I'd never have finished high school, gone on to college, or become one of those honor students without the support of this man who always wore black, looked a bit unkept but had the soul of an angel. I only hope that he continues his work in a higher place free of judgment. Thanks, Mr. Crowe, for making a positive difference in my life and many others.

EDUCATION

WHAT'S WRONG WITH U.S. EDUCATION?

When my father died, a Milwaukee Journal reporter called me. They were doing a story on him. The caller said, "I can't believe the file we have on your dad, letters, columns, years of submissions."

My father believed in speaking up. Sometimes his commentary was controversial. Often, he was calling on us to be better people, to be "gooder". His writings addressed educational philosophy, but also talked about the human beings who populate a school, teachers and students. He wrote about the impact of education on our society.

* * *

"What's Wrong with US Education? The Answer Involves Our Values"

Milwaukee Journal
January 29, 1973

I've been reading a lot of arguments lately about whether modular scheduling or the old traditional kind is better for high school students. I tend to prefer modular, especially since I've been at JFK, and it works so well here. But maybe that's because we're a small school and that kind of thing is best when the school is small.

Or maybe it's because our faculty is so involved and dedicated and because the people on it really do care and, therefore, when a kid has free time there's somewhere to turn to.

And someone.

Anyhow, what's wrong with education has nothing really to do with scheduling. Or very little at any rate.

It has a lot more to do with Watergate. Or, better yet, Cambodia.

The guys you watch on television who were so slick and sly and ambitious and arrogant and smooth—they are products of what American education is. They are the direct result of the directions they were given.

To beat the other guy. In the classroom, on the football field, wherever. To finish first. Colleges are not interested in losers.

Business wants men who can get the job done. Image is everything. Look good to those around you. Con those who must be conned. And if you have to do something wrong—don't get caught.

Only suckers get caught.

I'm certain many will say that's not the philosophy of American education and to that I reply that American education has no philosophy. Wisdom is for hermits—or for men in distant, lonely rooms. The thing to be is clever. And the place to get is ahead.

Ask any hep student, high school or college, and he will tell you that many guys he knew who finished on the honor roll—or maybe cum laude—got there because they knew how to play and please and manipulate and anticipate the teachers.

Is that cheating?

Well, no. I guess not. At least, you can't get caught. And no covering necessary. It's not cheating. It's clever.

It's smart.

And in there somewhere, is what is wrong with education. Marks are the thing. Rank. The colleges want to know where you stood in your class, not whether you respect or even care about learning.

Learning and wisdom are for the guy on the mountaintop. I want a pad in suburbia.

And so now all the bright young men come on TV with their new haircuts in their expensive business suits—not unkempt, dirty crusaders for some forlorn cause at all. Smooth. Neat. Nice smiles. Nice teeth.

Their crime? They got caught. They were not quite clever enough. Quite embarrassing, really. Bad for our image. Ours. The party's. The country's.

Inexcusable bungling. Only boobs get caught. Inexcusable...

In the meantime, our B-52s fly over Cambodia and unload their cargos and nobody knows just why. And old men in funny straw hats die on the ground and that's a bit of too bad isn't it? Just isn't right somehow...

You won't change that by a change in scheduling, man. The disease is deeper than that.

Here at JFK we know that—and we're trying. We haven't all the answers but we're looking. But even here you come up against a statement like this from a faculty member—a young and excellent teacher—Critical of the tendency to emphasize literature in our English classes.

"These kids need spelling and grammar and punctuation. They need to know how to write a decent sentence."

I'd like to say to him that what they need is a decent sentence to read and understand. And that decency has nothing to do with spelling but has a lot to do with Cambodia.

I'd like to give him a sentence by John Donne. For instance.

"Any man's death diminishes me, because I am involved in mankind."

And I would like to say that it is the idea, not the structure, that makes that sentence decent. But he would be impatient with that. He wants a performer, not a philosopher. He is a young man in a hurry.

Even here.

And in there, somewhere, is what is wrong with education.

THE INANITY OF SOCIAL STUDIES

In 1960 my father wrote an article advocating for the critical importance of social studies in our schools' curriculum. Reformers were advocating removing it, calling the issues considered in social studies "inane." The push was a return to the "basics" with a focus on civics and history. The argument is right out of today's educational discourse. I think his message is timely.

* * *

"The Inanity of Social Studies"
Madison Capital Times
April 27, 1960

One more group of educators met the other day. (An educator it seems, is a teacher who is afraid he isn't impressive enough unless he has a more significant title.)

This one came up with the idea of more emphasis on science, mathematics, and English. This proposal is getting to be the cliché of the profession. It's as new as an old joke. And just about as tired.

But this solemn panel added a touch. They would do away with the "inanity" of "social studies" and go back to "good old civics and history." Well, now, there's one.

The one great mark of most star students in high school this day is their ability to repeat and remember. Most of them lack something else—the ability to think and the urge to come up with a creative idea.

Quiz shows and "objective tests" and other forms of intellectual silage have led many a lad to believe that the one who can memorize the words on a list—the one who can fill in the blanks—is the learned one and wise.

Civics and history—and good and old both may be—are two courses which have traditionally paid dividends to the kids with the photographic mind.

"Social studies" deals with inane subjects such as race relations, family problems, hunger amidst plenty, crime. It takes a look at the lame and the halt and the blind—and the lonely and the desperate and the lost. The man without a cause or a hope or a dream or a name. It has a gander at communism and fascism, and it raises some questions about war and peace.

It tells no one how to make the big bomb but it reminds all the results of using one.

The subject may be an inanity, but I would remind you educators that it asks the questions that had better be answered—and fast.

It is easier to build a bomb than to know what to do with it when it's done. It's easier to learn how to fertilize the soil or even to irrigate the desert than it is to discover a way to get the food out of storage and into the mouths of the hungry.

The answers are on no list and there is no formula to be memorized for Friday.

A man must be thirty-five to be eligible to be president and the civics books will say so. Cornwallis called it a day at Yorktown and General Lee gave up his sword at Appomattox Courthouse. Your history book says it and I guess it must be so. Mine said it, too.

But they've been mowing old men down outside Johannesburg and councils of white men meet outside Atlanta to plan dark deeds. The French have their bomb and the Chinese want theirs. And there are many fresh graves in Budapest.

Social studies raise the questions why. And also, where to and what next.

These are good questions. I think.

Social studies might even bring a man to look at the stars. Might bring him to a kind of concept of the immensity of space and the puny futility of an attempt to "conquer" it. While science makes some men proud, social studies might bring some to be humble.

Civics won't. History should but it never has. Social studies might.

I better end this now.

Sure, I teach social studies. It's not my major, though, whatever that is. (Some educator can tell you). It's my minor. Whatever that is.

You know what my major is?

English.

That ought to set all right with the educators since next to science and math, English was recommended when the panel sat around the table.

One trouble though.

What the educators mean by English, I suspect, is how to spell and how to punctuate and all that jazz. Some educators might say the kids should write themes because they should learn to express themselves. A theme a week, some educators say. Maybe two a week would be twice as good.

One trouble, I think. One fly in the ointment, educators. That's a cliché, too. But that is ointment you have there isn't it?

The fly is this.

You teach a kid the words and the commas and the population of Pittsburgh and how tall was Lincoln and how many spuds will the cylinder hold and then you say you're ready. You say write me a theme.

Trouble is the kid hasn't looked in the eyes of a lonely man or a hungry child. Trouble is the kid has seen an Indian on television but not on a reservation. Kid hasn't seen what pride is like after it's dead. Kid has never seen six in a room at the county hospital—nor heard how it sounds. Kid knows what the general says about the bomb—what the physicist says. But he doesn't know what the mother in Nagasaki said that one day. Nor why.

You've taught the kid to write. Trouble is he has nothing to say.

Social studies might help him. I think. It might not give him answers—civics does that—but it would give him questions civics doesn't even know exist.

The questions are a beginning, I think.

When I taught English many of my kids could do a good job in spelling and punctuation and they could diagram a sentence with the best.

But I asked them once what Coleridge meant when he wrote: "He prayeth best who loveth best." And what

Shakespeare had in mind with: "The quality of mercy is not strained." And, most of all, what Christ was driving at when he said: "The meek shall inherit the earth."

You know something? Nobody had an answer. The best sentence diagrammer in the class couldn't tell me. And the next year it was the same. And the year after that.

So, I shifted to social studies. I think maybe that's where Shakespeare belongs too. And Coleridge. I know Christ does.

Because it's a subject that provides no pat answers. But it raises the hard questions.

And that, I think, is something.

THE CENSORS

Another timely article addressed the issue of censorship, a challenge that is front and center in our schools today. The books were different, but the motivations and the costs to learning were of concern then as they are now.

* * *

"The Censors"
Typewritten manuscript
c. 1968

A long time ago, I ran into trouble teaching Steinbeck. There are parts of *The Grapes of Wrath* and *Of Mice and Men* that I think are great. The writing is great, the ideas are worth the consideration of any man.

But some of the pious people in the town were convinced that Steinbeck's writing was obscene. Few, if any, had read any of his work. They just "knew" it was off-color.

I was young then and I was not afraid. So, I fought back—and I won. Others have not been so lucky.

One teacher in Wisconsin had Salinger's *Catcher in the Rye* on his reading list. The school board in the town wanted him to take it off. He refused. So, they got rid of him.

In another place it was Orwell's *1984*. Another time, it was *Brave New World* by Aldous Huxley. But the most absurd thing of this kind I've come across was brought to my attention a few years ago while I was going to summer school at Carleton College in Minnesota.

I was part of a big seminar involving teachers of English from all over the country, and one young man told me of his experience with the law in his hometown.

Seems that one lass spotted a copy of the play, *Mr. Roberts*, on his bookshelf one day after school and wanted to know if she could borrow it.

"Why not?"

So, he gave her the book to read and thought no more of it until the cops raided him! So help me God.

The sheriff told him the girl's parents had contacted him to insist he was leading their daughter astray.

"By reading *Mr. Roberts*?"

"Exactly."

"My God. That's ridiculous."

"I don't agree. It's a dirty book."

"Have you ever read it?"

"I wouldn't read a book like that."

"How do you know it's dirty then?"

"I just know, that's all."

And there it was. The young teacher had a mighty tough time of it for a while. *Mr. Roberts*! Good grief.

I suppose some of the vigilantes mean well. That doesn't excuse them, but it's better than nothing.

A lot of them don't mean well at all.

A good many are arrogant, self-righteous, smug types who really believe they are better than the rest of men. And thus, better able to decide what is best—and what is bad—for everybody else.

We have progressed. This breed seems a bit pathetic and more than a little ridiculous now in most places. But not everywhere. Not by a darn sight. Not yet.

One of my finest hours in this connection came when I read where some book, I think it was *Catcher in the Rye*, was banned from the public high school libraries—and lists—of a major American city. It may have been Cleveland.

Then the nun in charge of a large girls' academy in that city announced that the students in her school were welcome to read "Catcher" if they wanted to—and she was sure that some of them would lend their copies to any public school students who might be interested.

Sister, I love you. . . .

ROBIN HOOD

"Was Robin Hood a Communist?"
Green Bay Press Gazette
May 8, 1977

It seems that this time of year, almost every year, somebody somewhere gets all stirred up about the books being read by high school students and a big hassle ensues. This year, the one I know about took place at a little town in Iowa—name of Volga, I think.

I suspect there have been similar furors elsewhere. There have been a number in Wisconsin in recent years. One, as I recall, was at Neillsville a year or two ago.

Now I can see how a lot of good folks can get pretty disturbed by pornography. There are plenty of porno books and magazines around and they serve little purpose except for sexual titillation for those who need, or want, that kind of thing.

If all such stuff should somehow wind up missing, I don't think we'd be losing anything. I just am not convinced that censorship is the answer because censorship involves the judgment and taste of those who do the censoring. And most people don't care to have others tell them what they should—or should not—read.

Besides all that, self-appointed censors tend to get carried away.

I doubt whether there are many high schools which use—or teachers who recommend—porno books.

But over-enthusiastic censor types come up with titles like *Catcher in the Rye* and *Mr. Roberts*.

(I mention these two because I know both have been "on the list" in certain towns where rigid "moralists" have insisted that these books be banned). And this makes the whole crusade look ridiculous.

(It reminds me of the overzealous "communist hunters" some years ago who decided that *Robin Hood* should be banned because in it, Robin took from the rich and gave to the poor. Therefore, they argued, the book gave its blessing—however subtly—to communist doctrine.

Robin Hood!

I doubt if the commies ever got a better press than they did out of that one.)

I remember, almost 30 years ago, that I recommended to my classes at Eau Claire Saint Pat's (now Regis) High School that they read John Steinbeck's *Grapes of Wrath*, which I considered then—and still do—the best American novel that I had ever read. I was immediately besieged by the voices and demands of the outraged.

They insisted that Steinbeck's book was both "immoral" and "red."

Granted, there is some earthy language in *Grapes of Wrath*, but it is certainly not a sexually stimulating book—unless one is almost pathologically vulnerable to such stimulation.

I wanted the kids in my class to read it because I wanted them to be aware of what had happened to a sizable segment of the poor in rural America during the dust bowl years and the depression.

I wanted them to come to understanding and, perhaps, compassion. I don't think the reds are much interested in either.

In one town in Minnesota, a teacher told me how he had actually been arrested by the sheriff because one of the girls in his class had borrowed his copy of *Mr. Roberts* and read it.

"Her old man is really burned up."

"Has he read the book?"

"I don't think so. He doesn't read dirty books."

"Have you read it?"

"No. I don't read stuff like that either."

It happened that the teacher didn't have to spend much time in stir. But for letting somebody read *Mr. Roberts*!

(It must've been the binoculars and the showers in the nurses' quarters that did it. And if that scene would bring little Annabelle to perdition, I can simply say that I suspect she's going to get there, anyhow. And fast.)

One woman on television the other night—she was from the town in Iowa—quoted somebody in some book who said: "Good Lord, Cousin Amy!"

And that, said the good lady, is, of course, "taking the Lord's name in vain."

Well, I suppose it is.

But if you're going to become all worked up about a line like that, you are, frankly, going to make yourself ridiculous and you are going to lose a battle which might, conceivably, be worth waging before it even begins.

And you are going to have the young in hysterical laughter.

And if you don't care about the young, then what is all your crusading about? And whom is it for?

You can censor much of Shakespeare and even more of Chaucer. But should you? I don't. I don't believe I should.

You can censor many of the things written in scripture, too. (And a number of Bible students I know do just that.) The story of Susannah and the Elders, for instance, is pretty blunt and leaves little to the imagination.

I wonder, if you do that, if you do not wind up with those who were going to stone the woman "taken in adultery."

"Let him who is without sin cast the first stone."

And it is written that each man there put his stone down and went home.

Might the same thing under such a directive not happen in Volga? Or Neillsville? Or Edgerton? Or wherever?

Ethics and integrity and decency are virtues worth having and holding to. Fanaticism is not.

WRECKING BALL

My father never wavered from a commitment to his students he wrote about in the 1945 article, "Teach Them to Be Human." He saw that our humanity is often put on a shelf in favor of ambition with a blind eye to the cost, to others, to society and in the end to ourselves. The story as told here is still relevant today. The players are different but not the underlying dynamic.

* * *

"Wrecking Ball Made His Point"
Green Bay Press Gazette
August 28, 1977

The other day, in reading the *Minneapolis Tribune*, I came across an article which kind of stays in my mind. It was about the wrecking ball.

Not really, I suppose, since the huge steel ball which has obliterated so much of the past in most cities in the land was never actually mentioned. But I have watched it at work before.

In Saint Paul, for instance, almost 20 years ago, it utterly wiped out the house where my mother had lived the last years of her life and wiped out the whole neighborhood, besides. I am sure the place looks better now than it did, but I liked it better then. I guess that's because no architectural improvement can ever quite replace the memory of that old gal standing on the porch waving a sad goodbye after visiting.

I used to hate to come because I hated to leave. So I reckon my lack of enthusiasm for the wrecker has a pretty personal touch to it, and maybe that is why the story got to me.

Only it wasn't just that.

This piece I am talking about dealt with an area of old stone houses—apartments now—which are being knocked down to make room for high rent replacements. It seems the people who lived there did not want to leave. They had been picketing and protesting, but, as usual, the power of low rent people is not very great.

Especially in the thinking of the speculators who are going to build there.

"You say the new apartments will be in the $400-per-month range," one old lady said. "None of us here can afford that kind of rent—or even come close."

The reply of the manager of the new project stands as a classic in my mind. I have rarely read anything which matches it in coldness and logic.

"I am not here to rent property. I am not here because I see any of you as potential tenants here. I am here to clear this land to get on with our business."

Hey now—that says it pretty clearly. It happened that in another section of the paper educators and others were making the point that we must put more emphasis on reading and writing techniques—on spelling and grammatical usage and punctuation and communicative clarity in our schools or all may well be lost. Or certainly that the school system is, otherwise, in trouble and maybe in vain.

Well—they could hardly ask for more clarity in communication than that statement by the property manager. It is clear and it is to the point—and that is what the whole thing is about. Right?

Wrong.

That is not what life is about, and you would think educator types would realize that. Maybe they are, themselves, an indication of the futility of the education system. (After all, most of the Watergate lads—and others of their ilk—could spell well and communicate as they wanted to—in their case sometimes not so clearly to all, perhaps.

But then—it was intentional, and that, after all, makes all the difference. It is one thing to be misled by a charlatan who knows just what he is doing, and something entirely different to be confused because the poor slob you are dealing with is not too good with his adjectives or pronouns. There is no excuse for the latter.

Right?

My point is, as it has always been, that how you say a thing is important, but not as important as what you have to say. And what you have to say does not depend on your use of your gerunds and participles and infinitives, but rather on what you are and what it is that has made you what you are.

The point is that the lad who expressed himself so clearly and so coldly to the bewildered nobodies he was dealing with (nobodies in his scale of who is what, that is) is seven sorts of a skunk or a rat (with apologies to all real skunks and rats, everywhere) and that doesn't say what I want to say very precisely or very clearly, but I suspect most of you understand all right.

He is, in my opinion, a product of our educational system marked "approved" (just as I suspect, Haldeman—and a lot of similar types a good deal worse than he—also got good marks from the system. Most of these lads, as noted, can spell and communicate with the best.)

In the meantime, it might be well to remember that the greatest Teacher of all time once said something like this: "Listen, you klutz, you are really an ass if you think that how much profit you make on your property is what life is all about. Or if you think you can use or hurt or ignore other people simply because you have the temporary power to do so."

"What life is all about, man, is that someday it is over—and then we get to the final interview."

Is that really so hard to understand? Heck—way back in the fifth grade most of us knew what it meant. That Teacher made his point pretty clear.

Maybe as the years go by and things happen, we just forget.

Huh?

COMPETENCY TESTS

My father's last teaching job was at McDonnell High School in Chippewa Falls. While there he contributed columns to the student newspaper, Mac Matters. *I found this one written in his 40th year of teaching. His commitment to students who struggle was unwavering.*

* * *

"Challenge to Competency Tests for High School Graduation"

Published in "From the Crowe's Nest"
McDonnell High School, Mac Matters
Chippewa Falls, WI
April 1981

In what I am going to write about today, not all teachers will agree with me. Not all teachers at McDonell will agree and that's all right. So far, at least, it is possible to have a diversity of opinion in this land. God grant that it stays that way.

What's on my mind, right now, is these legislators in Bond Street suits who want to impose "Competency Tests" on seniors.

"If they don't pass, they don't graduate."

That strikes me as pretty smug. These tests will deal mainly or entirely with proficiency in reading and writing and 'rithmetic.' I guess these "basics" lads are well intentioned. At least I hope they are.

I think they are wrong.

I have one class this year in which most of the kids need a credit to graduate. They are earning the credit by doing acceptable work on the short stories of men like Conrad and Orwell, Galsworthy and Chekhov, and Victor Hugo. The course is called World Literature and if we include Dostoevsky and Ibsen most of these guys would be lost.

So, we won't include them.

They've done a pretty good job on reacting to something like "The Verger" by Somerset Maugham (that's the one where the old man is fired from his custodian job at the church because he's too dumb and then he goes out and makes a fortune) and the "Secret Sharer" by Joseph Conrad.

I suspect my students' reviews would never be accepted at Yale but none of these guys will ever go to Yale. They are accepted by me and praised by me—because the kids answered some rather simple questions with some surprising insight—and even wisdom.

But their spelling is lousy and grammatical structure isn't much. Better drill masters than I have tried to teach them all that and failed. I would fail, too.

There are some pretty good guys in the world who never did—or could—learn to spell or punctuate. You might say—understandably—what difference does it make if they're good, if they can't spell. What's goodness got to do with it?

It's got just this to do with it.

There are more good spellers in the world than there are good guys. We need some good guys, and we need 'em bad. And we need 'em fast. We need 'em in high places, but, of course, they won't be there because we put the guys who can spell and "cleverly articulate" in high places.

We've had our share of clever crooks running things. We have our share right now.

You want real basics, man? Try integrity, for one. Try decency and compassion and love and the ability to give a damn about the other guy.

Try peace.

Listen, men in high places, if your competency test keeps the good guy in my class from getting a diploma, then you have simply added one more kick to the kids who have been kicked too much already.

Their self-image is already very low. You want to lower it further.

Pardon me, sir, if I say, I think you are the dumb one. And pretentious and mean besides. What kind of a guy is dumber than a mean one?

You are honestly afraid that if we give a diploma to a kid who tried hard but could just never master his adverbs and prepositions, we might mislead the men doing the hiring in industry or the admissions in college?

Just get on the phone and call the high school office. Somebody there will tell you how the kid did in school and what his marks were like. I'm surprised a smart guy like you—with a necktie yet—never thought of that.

SCHOOL DOES NOT HAVE TO BE A GRIND

O*ne of the topics my father wrote about that garnered much feedback was homework. He knew that assigned written homework analyzing literature could make the whole experience burdensome. He sought, instead, to inspire his students, to bring them to thoughtfulness and compassion through the power of the written word. He encouraged them to take time to be alone, observe the world around them and experience its wonder.*

* * *

"School Does Not Have to Be a Grind"
Green Bay Press Gazette
ca. 1960s

We are finishing a three-day retreat here at Catholic Central. It seemed to be an effective and good retreat. The kids, for the most part, were with it. Most of them were quiet and a good many, I'm sure, took the chance to do some thinking.

Trouble is, it will be over tomorrow—and the bludgeoning grind will be on again.

The kids will be back in my class, with Beowulf and Chaucer. In the other classes, it will be parallel lines or the properties of nitrogen or the structure of the leaf, or the hooks and bars of shorthand, or the conjugation of the Latin verb.

Good stuff, I guess. (For instance, everybody has always assured me that Beowulf and Chaucer are good stuff.)

Homework will be back.

With the stars hanging in space a good many hundred million miles away and with the long, lean October night, with its thousand strange sounds and noises, waiting out there to tell a score of stories if anybody has the time to listen—and with the clear, crisp night wind ready to smack you in your teeth, and maybe in your soul—with all that, Eddie and Annabelle (separately, friend because this is no young love and romance story) will be slamming away at the answers to the questions on page 47.

Like, for instance, why did Beowulf slay the dragon's mother.

That is a good question and the answer to it has often troubled me. So has the elevation of Denver, Colorado, and the population of Istanbul.

Even more compelling, though, comes the question: Is there music out there in the night. Not "Beatle bop." Something else. Can you hear it? Is there a long calling down the night wind?

Where from? Where to? What next?

Are these questions unimportant because they are not in the book? Are they of no value because you can't look up the answers? Maybe there are no answers. Maybe some questions are meant to be questions forever.

Do you have to have answers all the time?

MORE TO LEARNING

"There's Much More to Learning Than Rote"
"In My Opinion" column
The Milwaukee Journal
August 1, 1976

Some time ago I wrote a piece for this section in which I suggested that the hue and the cry among "educators" about the lack of fundamentals in communication—for instance, spelling, punctuation, precise sentence structure—came pretty close to much ado about nothing.

The lack of proficiency in these areas is not really "nothing," of course. It simply does not, in my opinion, pose a problem equal to that to be found in the inability of the student to think—or, perchance, to dream.

A lot of parents are wondering which way their kids should go this fall. And a lot of kids are wondering, too.

So, I'm writing, again, on the subject of education and I will quote this time from a man who wrote better than I will ever be able to, and who wrote a long time before I got into the act.

His name—T. S. Eliot, the great English American poet. He is worthy of your attention and of mine.

> *Endless invention, endless experiment,*
> *Brings knowledge of motion, but not of stillness;*
> *Knowledge of speech, but not of silence;*
> *Knowledge of words, and ignorance of the Word.*
> *All our knowledge brings us nearer to ignorance,*
> *All our ignorance brings us nearer to death,*
> *But nearness to death no nearer to God.*
> *Where is the Life we have lost in living?*
> *Where is the wisdom we have lost in knowledge?*
> *Where is the knowledge we have lost in information?*

Man, that is great stuff!

For instance—"knowledge of speech but not of silence."

Silence has so much to tell us. To teach. I say to the kids in my class, "Take a walk. Take it alone. Let the cold wind of an old October smack hard against your teeth. Climb the high hill. Alone. Or walk the lonely shore. And then stand there and look up—and out. A million stars. Incredible space. Don't try to think this time. Let the message from the long silence come to you. Forget how big you are. Remember how big you ain't."

More than the comma or the gerund or the rule on "i" before "e." More than all the drills or all the words can ever give. Oh, so much more.

"Where is the Life we have lost in living?"

So many kids want to know, "What good is it gonna do me?"

They mean in making a living. They mean like in coin of the realm, man. The folding green. And in that framework, it is much easier to say to them why spelling is more important than poetry.

Only it really isn't. Is it? Or was Eliot wrong?

"…where is the Life…"

And "where is the wisdom we have lost in knowledge?"

I think that one hits most true. Like right on. Or whatever.

Because we have taught the kids so many things, they mistake their knowledge for wisdom. Or they never even know that wisdom exists. Or can exist. The teachers have forgotten, too—or maybe some of them never knew—that wisdom is far greater than knowledge.

And that knowledge can get in the way.

And so, "all our ignorance brings us nearer to death, but nearness to death no nearer to God."

And that is a tragedy beyond all dimensions.

Perhaps this sounds as though I am talking about religion but of course I am not. Eliot was a poet, not a theologian. When Coleridge wrote, "He prayeth best who loveth best…" he wrote as a poet. So did Keats "Beauty is truth…." So did Wordsworth: "Trailing clouds of glory do we come…."

So, for that matter, did Pete Seeger: "Where have all the flowers gone…" and Simon and Garfunkel: "The sounds of silence…."

There is much more to learning than rote and routine or the mastery of technique. To pretend that this is what it is, is to rob it of its greatness and its worth. And worse, it is to rob the learner of what Rachel Carson once called, "the sense of wonder."

No teacher, methinks, can do anything much worse than that.

THE AWARDS SYSTEM

My father often spoke at graduation ceremonies. He knew graduation was a momentous time in the lives of young people. They were leaving their youth and would not be back. He was also aware, amid all the recognition of accomplishments that highlight graduations, there sat those students who would not be recognized for special achievements, but for whom the occasion was also significant. He wanted to pay tribute to the graduates who were simply "good kids." He wanted them and their parents to know they counted.

* * *

"A Teacher Questions Award System"
Madison Capital Times
May 27, 1975 (excerpts)
Reprinted by UPI

It is the time for graduation once again in the high schools across the land. And so once again the various kinds of honor students will walk across a thousand platforms to receive their awards.

There will be special recognition for the lad (or lass) who got the highest marks for the whole four years. In some places he will be asked to give a short talk and he will tell all the parents and teachers and friends assembled there that he intends to go out from his hometown and conquer the world.

He will thank his teachers and his school—and he may even thank his dad and mother—for making him what he is this day. Usually, he will sound pretty earnest. Sometimes he may sound a little smug.

And then the salutatorian will be honored, too. He finished second in the battle for academic marks and while that isn't first it isn't bad.

(Was it Vince Lombardi who said winning was the only thing? Was it Leo Durocher who proclaimed that nice guys finish last? Well, second isn't winning maybe, but it is a long way from last.)

At some schools, an award will be given to the top student in physics or in math. And the informed people in the audience—and the teachers—will know that such a young man has the best chance of all to storm the portals to financial reward because nothing else on the academic charts pays off like science does. Or math.

This is the time of the computer, man. This is the time of fission and fusion. The time of electronics and nuclear stockpiles. Everyone knows that the world and the future belong to the man of science.

Of course, the school's top athlete comes in for special attention, too. And if he combined his skill on the field or floor with other things like "character and leadership and scholarship" he will take home a plaque or scroll that any man might well envy and desire.

There will be no award for the guy who was good to his mother.

Nothing at all for the kid who was never ashamed of his old man because he carried a lunch pail, and his use of the language was never impressive nor even very good. Nothing for the girl who spent so many hours helping a friend with their homework because that was the only way the less gifted one was ever going to make it in this ceremony tonight.

No award for the guy with social finesse and a touch of class, who used to ask the less attractive girls at the dances in the school gym to whirl a bit out on the floor because it seemed like the way to go and be.

Nothing for the halfback who never scored even one TD, but who did grab a teammate by the front of the shirt one night and demand that he cool it because said young man was going to stuff something into the john and cause a minor but messy flood.

"A janitor has some rights, too, man. Whether you think he does or not."

No award for the boy who said that.

Nor for the guy who sought out the lonely and neglected ones. Who shared his time and his laughter and himself with those others passed by. The quiet ones. The meek. The shy. The lost.

Damn it, man. There ought to be something for a kid like that.

Will Durant wrote once: "A good man who is not great is infinitely more precious than a great man who is not good."

Our educational system is not buying that idea, but I think it is true, even so. We are full up to here with great men. Powerful men. Men with medals. Men who can order planes into the air. Men who can drop a thousand bombs on farmers in funny hats. Such men are the product of an asinine system which teaches it is better to be successful than to be kind.

It isn't. It never was.

In the meantime, little old lady in the fourth row at the commencement exercise, you listen hard, but your son's name is never mentioned at all. But you know he is a good boy. You wish someone else knew, too. Or cared.

Someone does.

COACH

THE CASE FOR BEING A COACH

On a Friday afternoon in January, I was at the coffee shop reading. As I walked up to the counter to refill my tea, I noticed a young man and woman at a table. He was wearing a shirt with an emblem that read, "Regis Coaching Staff." (Regis is the Catholic school in town, formerly St. Pat's, where my dad had coached 75 years earlier and returned to in the late 1980s to assist with coaching until a broken hip forced him out in 1993). I struck up a conversation with the couple and found we knew several people in common. After an enjoyable talk we parted ways and I returned to my table and my reading.

The next column I came to was "The Case for Being a Coach". I had two copies. Should I offer one to the young coach I'd just met? I did. He was delighted. They both were. She said, "We'll frame it." I returned to my table wondering at the serendipity that had just played out.

Unexpected blessings, a good afternoon. I felt my dad's presence.

* * *

"The Case for Being a Coach"
Published in *"From the Bench"*
Green Bay Register
May 10, 1963

A lot of boys coming to the end of their senior year in high school are wondering now, as in all the years, what they should go about preparing for themselves as a way of life.

For one who might be giving a thought to becoming a high school coach, somewhere, I have a few notes.

First, you will never be rich—or even very far ahead of the bill collector on the first of every month. But what about it?

Whoever has enough money?

The guys I know and see and hear about who have clipped more than their share of coupons are reaching for more. So it gets down to it that the guy without enough money is reaching out for more to get along and the guy with plenty is also reaching for more because that's the way it is.

So, you won't get rich, lad.

And you'll take a lot of guff. You'll listen to a lot of parents and fans and second-guessing experts who don't know what they're talking about, and you'll have to like that because that's the way it is, too.

You'll have a few "Precious" ones on your teams—the prima donna, the ink hog, the superstar. These will make the season seem a little long once in a while.

You'll make your plans for the big game and see them wash down the drain because some kid tried too hard and fumbled the ball or another guy froze, or it rained that day, and you were going to throw the ball, or some other boy forgot, or another one didn't care.

But you won't find many of this latter breed.

And some night you will be sitting in your little room in the gym which passes for your office, and it will be late in October, and it will be dark outside because practice is over, and the guys have had their showers, and the dark comes all at once and quick in a Wisconsin October. And your window is open and there's a smell of burning leaves from somewhere and maybe just a taste of something which reminds you that the cold is waiting out there beyond the edge of the night.

It is a sad kind of a time. Bittersweet, but sad.

And then you start to listen to the voices of the kids as the door bangs behind them down below.

"See ya, Charlie."

"OK. See ya tomorra."

"So long, Al."

No high class dialogue. Nothing fancy. But the door slams—lots of times and then it's quiet and you know the last guy is gone and one more day of practice is over.

And one more precious day, you suddenly remember, of the swiftly flying days of being young for a lot of good boys.

And somehow the words still hang there in the air after they're all gone away.

"So long, Al."

And you remember then, too, that you're a very lucky guy and that there's something here you can't put a price tag on—or even say it in words. Something of wonder and maybe of mystery, too. Something little that's suddenly as big as there is.

You remember other doors that slammed once. And other voices hung in the air. In some old October long ago. You walk home quiet that night.

WHY I AM A HIGH SCHOOL COACH

In nearly 50 years of coaching there were plenty of tough times for my dad. His friends often asked why he continued. I came across this typewritten piece that tells the story.

* * *

"Why I Am a High School Coach"

Typewritten manuscript
c. 1950s

"You bonehead!"

The fan in the fourth row was expressing the most common evaluation of the average high school coach's intelligence. At that moment, the evidence was all in favor of his judgment. Yet it still hurt. Only it never hurts enough.

That fan can't make me quit.

Neither can all his screaming brethren. The ones who mean it and the ones who don't. They curse and screw their faces into horrendous masks of fury or heat. They sweat as they swear—and they may foam a bit at the mouth. Their eyes are wild, and their hair is wilder.

But I love 'em—bless 'em. I'd miss 'em if they weren't there.

They're part of the whole crazy business that makes the life of a high school coach. And in spite of them—and in spite of the comparatively low salary and the patronizing of the guys I knew in college who wonder why I never came to a better end—and in spite of the strain on the nerves involved—and in spite of the disappointments that are part of it too, I wouldn't trade this life for that of anyone I know.

Classmates of mine have turned out better. Some are doctors. Some are lawyers, editors, roofing contractors and interior decorators.

They can have it. This is for me.

Many people who wonder why might seem justified in their bewilderment. For instance, the chap who was analyzing the structural material of my cranium was motivated by a small matter indeed. I'd told my quarterback to pass instead of punt on a fourth down on our own six—and it hadn't worked out. We'd lost the ball in the danger zone.

And so he calls me "bonehead."

My best friends stare at me—listen to loud-mouth—and ask quite sincerely, "Is it worth it?"

And then my wonderful, incredible, superb, unbelievable, unpredictable gang of kids—my team—rise up on their hind legs and flatten the opposition on four straight cracks at the line and we take over again.

And I turn to the yak-bird in the fourth row, and I say, "I just wanted to see if they could do it."

And he snarls—or swallows a fly—and I turn back to my flabbergasted friends, and I say, "Now you see why?"

And they don't—and they never will. But I do. And it's my life.

You can't know how it is unless you've sat in the dressing room between the halves and heard a little Polish kid say, "We gave up a lot to get this far, and nobody stops us now."

You look around at that bunch of boys you've worked with hour after grueling hour through all the weeks and months pointing toward this one—pointing toward the golden dream. And now half the game is over, and everyone knows your team is done. You almost know it yourself. Only they don't know it—and a little guy named Krumlowski, whose old man wields a broom at the stockyards, won't let them believe it.

And suddenly there's something singing in the air, and you know your team is not licked. These are the comeback kids—no surrender guys. Remember them?

And you watch them storm out of there for the second half—muddy and wet and three touchdowns behind—and somehow you know their battle flags are still up—and there is going to be a ball game, brother.

And you watch them claw and fight their way to a fantastic victory. And you watch them hug one another in the wild and abandoned joy of the very young.

And maybe there are a few tears in your eyes. But you know it's worth it. All the way.

Or you're on the team bus on the way to another game in another season and another year. And there's a pug nose named Tully sits next to you after a while and says, "Coach, my dad's on a drunk again."

You've talked this all through with Tully before—given him the good word—the old advice. No dividends so far—but he's back. It's good to know he's there—that he wants to be there. You haven't got a son that age—with the terrible problems of adolescence. But Tully will do.

So, you talk it all through again. And just before he leaves to go back with the boys in the rear of the bus who are playing cards Tully faces you head on and says, simply, "Thanks, coach."

That makes up for a good many anonymous letters and sarcastic phone calls in the night.

It's a lot of years now since you've seen Tully—and since he's dead on a Pacific island somewhere, you won't see him again. But the memory comes easy.

And it's good.

Or the day the boys from Lesterville gave you the leather case for your clothes brush and the rest of it. Not much of a case or much of a gift. Not much of a team either. The worst basketball team you ever had—worst on offense—worst on defense. A pretty hopeless outfit.

And so, you'd landed another job in another state in the middle of January, and you were leaving.

"We want you to have this," Jimmy Peters says because he's the captain and the only guy on the team who can score. "Maybe it'll help you to remember us, sometime. We weren't much good—but we tried. And we know you tried, too. We're glad we had you for our coach."

And then you know you shouldn't be leaving these kids in the middle of their dismal season. You're walking out—and you feel like the heel you are. But you learn something as Jimmy hands you the case.

You know you'll never walk out on anyone again. And you never have.

There's Tommy Kennedy, too.

There is the night Tommy came into your office. It was a long-gone May, you remember, and it was raining.

"I got a letter from St. John's today. Mom gave it to me when I got home. So, I came back to tell ya. They're taking me on."

"I'm glad, Tommy."

"The letter said that my marks aren't good enough to get in—but they're taking me because of the recommendation you gave me."

Tommy Kennedy is no brain, but he's got a straight way of looking at a man.

"What I said in that letter is what I believe to be true, Tommy."

"Yeh. Well, I guess you're the only one coach. The principal said I should get a job and forget it."

"This time Mr. Adams is wrong, Tommy."

"Yeh. I just wanted you to know, coach—I'll never let ya down."

You sit there while the boy turns and punches back out into the night and the rain. A letter, you recall, isn't so hard to write. You're glad you weren't too tired—this time—like you were so often before.

A long time after that there's that other letter you still have somewhere, "Just to tell you coach—I'm graduating cum laude. How do you like that? Me!"

"I learned to work up here, I guess. I didn't deserve the chance I got. Maybe that's what did it."

"Anyhow coach—to make it brief—thanks."

Another long time after that you read somewhere that Captain Tommy Kennedy was shot down over Austria, Czechoslovakia, or somewhere. But you know that his life could never have hit a much higher point anyhow than it did the night they handed him that degree "with honor." You save his letter.

So that's the way it is with a high school coach. He's privileged to work with some pretty good boys before they are old enough or slick enough to be "smart." He gets 'em while the shield of honor still shines bright.

And what more is there than that?

It's enough to drown out the railings and the carpings of papa and mama when they feel their darling, who is an unskilled and very lazy halfback, is being "discriminated against."

It's enough to blot out the "demands" of papa—if he is "big" enough in the town—that you be fired.

It's even enough, believe it or not, to make up for the fact that you are fired.

And it's enough to compensate for the vocal trouncing you take from the Monday morning strategists.

"That pass which was intercepted should not have been thrown!" (You had rather felt, yourself, that it would, looking back, have been better to run the ball on that one. Or kicked it. Or given it to some kid in the stands).

"The defense was too weak!" (You'd had a hunch on that one, too, since the opposition did score 50 points).

"McGregor should be at left half instead of Ramsey!" (Possibly. Certainly, Ramsey hadn't done much in this one. Still two weeks ago he was the top ace on the team).

"There should be more power—less razzle-dazzle."

"There should be more razzle-dazzle—less old-fashioned power football!"

(You reflect that you're going to have a rather hard time making both lads happy).

There are the lover boys too, of course—and they are a real occupational hazard. If you tell them to skip sweet, little Daisy—and hit the sack earlier at night—your star, Teddy Morgan, is outraged. Nobody is going to tell him how to run his life. (You reflect that you'd hardly care for the trouble involved). You try to break up every "case," but you can't escape the fact that many of your "steady" lovers were the best ballplayers you had.

You try to assure many mothers—and some boys—that football is not a dangerous game. That very few are ever badly hurt playing it. You furnish statistics and quote from several famous men—but it's a hard tough fight.

You almost knock yourself out trying to keep the "school spirit" of the student body at a high pitch.

You have prima donnas on your team. And "ink hogs." They're hard to take but you take them.

You have a few kids like Brink who can really carry the mail, but who won't play at all unless they can have their choice of equipment—and practice their own way and at their own convenience.

At first you string along with such a lad, because he can do things lesser men can't approach, but when you get older in the game, and a little wiser, you send Brink back to his point of origin because you have to sacrifice Brink's brilliance or the team's good will.

The former is nice to have around. The latter is indispensable.

You have the sharp ones who try to make a quick buck—or a hundred—on the game, and who are ugly when they don't.

You have the pompous and unctuous one in the Kiwanis or Rotarians or the Elks or the Knights of Columbus who assures you that "who wins doesn't make any difference. It's how you play the game."

In a bad year, you test him. You lose four in a row—and suddenly he finds that he likes to win more than he thought he did. He doesn't take the time for a character check on your personnel. He goes after your scalp.

You have the administrator, sometimes, who thinks that "athletics is out of balance. Too much time spent on it. Too much emphasis."

You feel like reminding him that the six weeks of practice for the operetta takes time too. So does the Senior Class Play and the Prom. You've been excusing kids from study hall—and even from class—for years when the going got tight in regard to one of these "traditional" extracurricular activities. But you don't mention all that.

He feels that these projects have "educational value." He can't see any in sports. And you're not likely to change his point of view.

You find the good lady in the PTA—or the gal on the faculty—who deplores the "competitive angle" in sports.

"Victory means too much."

You don't say much to this lass either. You wonder how long sports would last if you took away the scoreboards. But you keep your mouth shut.

If it's a rainy day, you may mention the debate tournaments, the one act play contests, the declamation meets, the music festivals. You may mention the "loving cups" (a misnomer, indeed), the individual awards—ribbons, medals, scholarships. You may ask how many students would spend the hours they do in preparing their "card catalogs" or practicing on their flutes and clarinets—if there was no recognition at the end of the line—no chance to prove they were better than somebody else.

Or you might mention the competition in the classroom—spurred on by many an anti-athletic teacher. The fight for A's—or the dog-eat-dog struggle to be top dog—"valedictorian" is the title. Or if it's one of your philosophical days you might suggest that things were a bit competitive on Heartbreak Ridge. Or if Korea is in another world—make it Salerno or the Normandy hedges.

And then you are constantly meeting the man who deplores the fact that the colleges give the "breaks" to the kids who can lug the football or scorch the nets rather than do "something worthwhile."

You silently remember, (while you admit the countless and asinine abuses which are almost inherent in this college rat race to get the best material)—you recall Billy O'Brien, and you remember that he would never have been able to buy knowledge on the dough his dad made at the shoe factory. Football gave him his chance—and he took it—and now he's a social worker in a large city in the East—and he's a happy man—though he never will be a wealthy one.

You remember something Billy said to you once, "Ya know somethin,' coach—the way I see it, each of us was born to do what he can in the world for the other guys in it. None of us ever do much—but that's what we were meant for."

You know Billy was leveling with you—and you don't think he has lost the meaning along the way. And you're glad the way he could throw a football gave him his chance to be able to do his bit.

You almost feel like asking this objector to athletic scholarships how he feels about science scholarships.

You remember a few kids you knew who were scientifically sharp. They had their chance too. And took it. And some of them, no doubt, are today of value to mankind along the lines Billy O'Brien had in mind.

And a good many more have had their diplomas long since, and their houses on the hill, and their precision perfect automobiles, and maybe even a few citations for this and that.

But their value is strictly for themselves.

I should mention all this to this critic of sports—but I don't. "Something worthwhile" to him is something worth money—and he wouldn't understand Billy O'Brien anyhow. I'm not even sure I do myself.

But somehow, I know I should.

Anyhow that's it. That's why I can take the beefer boys and the arrogant ones—and the selfishly doting mothers and the second-guessers and the Romeos and the weed beaters and the reformers and the hypocrites and the pseudo intellectuals and the "everything has a price tag" boys—these and all their kindred breed I can take—not with a smile or a song—but I can take them and laugh them off—and go on.

And I can take the low salary which somehow can never quite keep its end up—and the insecurity brought on by the fact that everyone else thinks he owns you and can fire you when it suits his mood or fancy—and the additional fact that some of them can. I can take the fact that you're supposed to turn out a champion in the opinion of a lot of people even in that year when your fastest boy is ineligible—and your biggest one lacks the heart for the fray.

I can take it all—and love it all—because most of the boys who play the game are worth it all. They give me my kicks and they give meaning to my existence as the days go by.

I feel sad when they come to their last game—and they do too. We both know that next year somebody else will be around to take their place. But I know that no one ever really replaces anyone else. And my sadness—and theirs—is good.

And each year, as a new season starts, there is a thrill in looking over the eager faces of the kids who haven't yet had their turn. You know that some of them don't "have it"—and never will. Some lack skill. Some lack desire. Some lack brains—or courage—or the willingness to sacrifice or give of themselves for somebody else.

In many a boy, the strange bells never ring.

But you always have some. And that's it.

And you always know that someday another kid will stand in your office somewhere and say, "I needed somebody to care, coach. You cared."

And that's good enough for me.

GRATITUDE

Even in a season that looked bleak, the kids made it all worthwhile. I came across this story that provides a simple but great illustration of why my dad persisted for 50 years.

* * *

"First Football Practice and a Surprise Moment of Gratitude"

Published in "Something to Crowe About"
Green Bay Register
August 21, 1970

To be a high school coach must be just about the best job there is. Anywhere. I mean I know I've said it before, and I've said I would not trade with anybody—but then things happen, and you just have to say it again.

Like right now, for instance.

We've got nothing in football this year. And I mean nothing. Oh, I know a lot of the big noise boys will deny that—the all the answers breed. If we have eleven boys who can walk we should win every game as this crowd says it. They're really rather a silly lot.

We've got nothing.

One senior—and he's our captain and I don't mean he's nothing. He's a lineman and he's a good one. We had one other senior—and he was our co-captain and quarterback—but he can't come out for football this year.

Even with this second senior, who is also a good ball player, we would've been woefully weak. And I knew all summer he wouldn't be playing this year and, even though I love the darn game, I had a kind of dread about this season.

I should have known better.

As soon as I walked on the field the first night, I knew everything was all right. We may never win a game all year. On paper, we shouldn't come close. But it's all okay, anyhow. Because you want to win but you don't have to win.

What you have to do is reach the last ultimate bit that is in you in trying—and you have to be on the level with the other guys. On both counts this small squad of unknowns and nobodies and half pints and fuzz cheeks meets the test.

We will field a line that averages a hundred and sixty pounds against lines from other schools that average as high as two thirty-five. And our whole backfield is gone from last year—every darn one.

We've got some good young kids coming on—and they will be our team. But in this league, it pays to have seniors. Every coach in the conference has found that out. Actually, we do have a couple of seniors who couldn't cut it last year—but maybe they can now.

That would be nice.

But the thing is this—after fifteen minutes out there, all the apprehension was gone and the old zest for the battle was there again. These skinny young guys know the score—but they are conceding nothing. They will get knocked down, but they will get up. And they will keep coming.

The wailers and the wolves—sometimes you wish they would get lost for a while and this is one of those times—will hurt us. They will demand we do things that we can't do. That's the mark of the breed—and they can hurt. Especially they can hurt a team as young and green as this one is going to be.

But I don't think they can lick this team. I think this bunch will spit in their eye.

Anyhow, I felt great after the first night of practice, and I took a walk around town (I'd been away all summer) and the snub nose grade school gang is still around.

"Hi, Coach! Gonna win 'em all this year?"

"Gonna try."

Now that's the breed I like. You lose when you should have won—and sometimes when there was no chance—and the old guard snarls in their beer, but the freckle faced brigade bounces back with a challenge and a shout, "Next time we'll moider da bums!"

Know something, man? That kind of kick is not for sale.

And that night I took a walk along the river here—and the wind was blowing from somewhere. I read, in lots of places, that the air is polluted, and I know that's true, and I want to do something about it, too. But this night the wind was pushing the air across my face, and it felt good.

Pollution may kill us all someday. If it doesn't, something else will. And nobody wants to die. But you ain't dead yet, man!

Breathe in—and count your blessings.

Maybe you don't have as many as I. You don't have a nothing ball club, for instance, that will try to claw and scratch its way from nowhere.

But you do have the night and the stars and the wind in your teeth if you will taste how it is. What's so bad about being alive!

Sure—I miss my family. Already yet. They're still back in our summer town. And in two days, I miss 'em. But there's something to be said for being alone. Too.

A man can think. For instance. He can take time to be glad.

Just before I called it a night, I came past the big, new, splendid hotel that has sprung up in our town. It's a dandy. And parked outside it were cars the like of which you seldom see up here. Impressive. Maybe even significant.

And inside—people making a little refined noise and buying a lot of fun. Maybe. I don't know. It's not my bag—and I have no regrets.

I don't need that—nor want it. I have my ridiculous, wonderful team and my good job.

I mean—like thanks God.

My father was grateful for his talented assistants. At Marinette Catholic Central, Vendall Kaufman (mid) and Joe Oreshoski (right) directed the defense and the line play for the team.

WHY NOT?

Some men see things as they are and say, why?
I dream things that never were, and say, why not?

—George Bernard Shaw

WHY NOT?

My dad was able to quote literature from memory. He had favorite quotes. One came from George Bernard Shaw, and was repeated by Bobby Kennedy: "Some men see things as they are and say, why? I dream things that never were and say, why not?" He used the quote as a challenge to his students and to his athletes. In 1981, when his McDonnell basketball team qualified for the state tournament you could see the words "Why Not?" taped in the back window of his old blue Lincoln as he drove around Chippewa Falls.

One night, as I began to set up the room where I would sort through all the papers from his past, from the 1930s through the 1980s, I wondered if I could make anything out of it. I called out a question to the empty room, "Dad, can I do this?" The answer came back, "Why not?"

* * *

> "I took the wrong train out of St. Paul that day—and that made all the difference."
>
> *Published in "From the Bench"*
> Green Bay Register
> *March 7, 1969*

I'd been teaching and coaching at Hudson in western Wisconsin. It was my fifth year in the public schools, and I'd liked Hudson the best of them all. By far.

Then a former coach at the school came back from the wars, and under the G.I. bill he could have the old job back if he wanted it. He wanted.

The superintendent told me I could wait around and just teach there for a couple of years and if the coaching job opened up again it was mine. But I decided to move on.

I didn't know much about Catholic high schools, but somebody told me one in LaCrosse needed a coach—and that's how come I took the wrong train.

I wound up in Eau Claire.

As long as I was there, I decided to look around, and it turned out there was a vacancy at St. Pat's High School in that town. Too. That's how come I met Father Paul.

He's come a long way since those days and he's the pastor of a big LaCrosse parish now but way back then he was a young man who was the athletic director at St. Pat's—and one of the great ones I have met.

As it turned out, I had a crack at four jobs that summer. Cathedral High in Milwaukee; possibly the LaCrosse job at Aquinas; Saint Pat's. And Father Becker came up to Saint Paul from Menasha and we talked—a long time in the lobby of the old Saint Francis hotel there—and I found him to be a very fine man, too—and I almost wound up at Saint Mary's.

In the end I chose Saint Pat's because my mother was still living then and I was single, and I'd be close to home in Saint Paul. And because there was something about the rectory in Eau Claire.

The pastor was in the hospital, and everyone knew he would never leave and that first year I used to go up there to see him and he would say Mass in a little chapel there—sitting down.

Father Paul would turn the pages in the book.

It got to me after a while that old Father Dowd was able to keep on doing the thing that gave the meaning to his life almost right up to the very end—and that doesn't happen to many men in any lines or fields or ways of life.

I learned a lot watching that little old man sitting there. And raising the host when the time came.

Anyhow, maybe because the boss was away, that rectory at Saint Pat's was something. Father Hayden was there then—and Father Flad and Father Paul.

And a kind of lighthearted slant on life itself. And I lived it.

Later on, I found that all three men had a great touch with the kids and that no one I ever knew—before then and since—was able to sense and understand and reach the kids like Father Paul.

(And later on, I came to realize how vital a thing this was and how great it was for the kids to have a man like that around—and then, after that, I met a lot of priests in school work who came pretty close, and I got to feeling what a great break for high school kids to have men like that to turn to.

We have some at Marinette Central, right now.)

I even used to feel that it wasn't right that such men should only have the chance to influence kids at our school and I remember that sometimes kids from the public school would come over to share what it was.

But with a guy like Father Paul—or a lot of the others—you've got to be around them day after day to see how it is—and to breathe it all in—or something.

I used to feel how lucky the kids are to have this kind of thing touching their lives. In the grim days—and even in the good ones. And I used to feel, too, how lucky are these young priests—and some of them not so young—to have the chance to touch a lot of lives in the green years.

What better way to live your own life?

(I think of this sometimes these days when a lot of people seem to think it's all a matter of celibacy or no—or how much freedom or how little—or relating in a hundred ways.)

And all these are important, and I do not pass them by.

But the great thing for a priest is that a man turns to you not because you're the same but because you're not. He wants you to be there—and he wants to be able to reach you (communicate is the big word now)—but he doesn't want you to be just another guy.

He wants you different in a way that he can't give words to—and neither can I. But I know it's got a lot to do with his own need for God—and his belief you can help him.

And he wants you there.

This is really the first piece of a number in which I hope to be able to tell you how my life has been as a teacher in a Catholic high school. I have taught in four now. And in this first piece, I'm trying to say that one of the great things was the doors the priests were able to open. Because they were there.

And because they cared.

Oh, I've met some lemons, too. I've met some bored ones and some dehydrated ones and some ridiculous martinets.

And I've met some very small men who happen to be priests too.

But there are so many like Father Paul—although he was absolute tops—and it was a great break for a kid—boy or a girl—in the painful, uncertain years of being young—the years full of hurt and full of wonder—it was a break for the kids at Saint Pat's, for example to have men like that around. I knew I would want my own kids, if and when they came along, to have a chance to walk and talk and share with men like those I first met raiding the icebox in the kitchen at Saint Pat's rectory in Eau Claire more than 20 years ago.

And that was how it all began—and God willing, I will write down here, from time to time, how it went on from there. Story of a life. Mine. And you may rightly not care about that. But it entwined with a lot of others because that's the way it was.

And that's worth caring about. And I would never have traded it for any other kind.

A man knows little for sure on this planet.

This I know.

THE FIGHTING IRISH BASKETBALL TEAM OF 1947

"The Fighting Irish Basketball Team of 1947"
Published in "From the Bench"
Green Bay Register
March 21, 1969

Do you want to know how many kids there were at Saint Pat's the first time we won the state championship in basketball?

Three hundred and fifty. Co-ed.

We were known as the Fighting Irish of Saint Pat's—and our best player was a boy named Pavelski. Beautiful Bruce Pavelski.

The first time I ever met with the squad—in that little grade school-sized gym in that side of the road school—I told Pavelski:

"I hear you were on the sauce during the summer. In five minutes, we are going to join hands here and say a short prayer for the season coming up. If you walk out now—no hard feelings. But if you pray with us—and then sell out—hard feelings is not the word to cover it."

He looked at me for quite a long moment and then he said, "You don't have to worry, coach. You don't have to worry."

And I never did...

I carried one boy on the squad whose name was Sonny. Sonny Stolp. Later on, when Helen and I were married, Sonny was our best man. But back then he was out for basketball—and it wasn't his game.

He was short and very muscular, and he was valedictorian of the school and captain of the football team. He used to play football with a big grin on his face—and I have pictures to prove it.

He was the toughest torpedo I've ever had back up the line for me—and he tackled like there was no tomorrow—but he didn't play basketball worth a darn. I kept him on the team because sometimes it pays to have a kind of guy around.

Let me tell you how it was with Sonny by remembering his girlfriend, Jeanine.

Now, I don't like my players to go steady, and anybody who ever played for me will tell you that—and the fact made some of them more than a mite unhappy.

But I figure when I want five yards over right guard, I don't want my halfback mentally pulling leaves off the daisy. Or composing poems. Or hearing mystic violins. But with Sonny and Janine it was somehow all right. (They're long married now—and Sonny is a doctor somewhere.) He used to bring her to a school dance. The first one with her, and then he'd give her the grin and say, "See ya for the last one. Have fun."

And Jeanine would come back in kind, and she'd say, "Don't worry, lad."

And they'd dance the night away with everybody else—and the place would light up because they were there—and they'd be back together for the last one—and then they'd go home.

Together.

That's the kind of going steady I don't mind so much. The moody, grim, suspicious, one and only kind sort of turns me off, though.

Anyhow, we had a ten o'clock-be-home rule during the football season and Jeanine lived a lot more than a mile from Sonny's house, and at about ten you'd see him running past Four Corners on his way home.

"You gonna make it, boy?"

"I'll make it."

He did—and you could believe in him—and I kept him on the team. The other guys wanted him there.

Well, when we beat Eau Claire High for the first time in the school's history, everybody knew something was in the wind. The team was coming on.

But I remember how it was that night. The devotion. The identity. The wild laughter and the tears. The cheerleaders rolling on the floor in an ecstasy of disbelief.

They loved the school and so did I. The word is not too big.

Well, anyhow it finally came state tournament time, and we were going to the gym at Saint Norbert's College to play in it—and we were still the nobodies from nowhere—and on the bus the kids started to sing. Sonny Stolp started—and they all joined in—and, so help me God, they were singing the old sodality song!

I'd never heard it before, but it was kind of stirring—and that's what they were singing. And they sang it again on the way out for the semis—and for the finals—and then we were, incredibly, state champions.

"Eau Claire!" one old timer said to me in the hotel, "that's up in the timber country, ain't it?"

I guess maybe it was.

And we came downstairs after the title game, and there was a place in Green Bay then called the Spanish Villa, and it was jammed with our kids and when I came in the door they came tearing over—and half of them were crying and still half delirious—and one of them was very pretty, and her name was Mary McInnis, and she spoke to me first.

(Mary McInnis, wherever you are, I bet you're surprised I remember.) It was my first state championship. But far, far more it was my first understanding of what a school could mean to the kids whose lives were wrapped around it.

You were a very lucky girl, Mary McInnis and all you others were lucky, too, that for such a little while you were able to be part of that nothing school that was Saint Pat's High School of Eau Claire, Wisconsin, 22 years ago.

We drove the couple hundred miles home the next day and the city staged a big parade, and it was very good to be alive and the very air was sweet on the tongue that day.

And the best moment of all came when Bruce Pavelski spotted the old priest, Father Dowd, who was our pastor but was nearing the end of his days in the hospital—only they let him off for the reception—and the kids saw him under the blankets in one of the cars—and they stopped the parade and they brought that big state championship trophy over and they put it in his lap.

He'd built our little school, you know, and now some kind of dream had come true. And he cried.

He wasn't the only one.

Parade in Downtown Eau Claire celebrating 1947 State Champions, the Fighting Irish of St. Patrick's (Photo Courtesy of *Eau Claire Leader Telegram*)

BILLY HAUGEN

My father often told the story of Billy Haugen. I have a tape of him on a call-in TV show, the caller saying, "Tell the Billy Haugen story, Marty." I had never seen it in print till I found a handwritten copy as I sorted through his papers.

"The Billy Haugen Story"
Handwritten manuscript
Date unknown

Billy Haugen was a junior in the fall of 1948. I give you the story of the boy, here, because if you can't learn something about the game—and about the cut of the kind of guy who belongs in it from this story, then I doubt if you can learn it. Period.

We had one of the best football teams I've ever had that year. But, even so, we blew our fourth game of the season. To Eau Claire Public High.

It was at Eau Claire Saint Pat's and that was the game, above all others, we hated to lose. But we lost it. We, literally, threw it away.

We drove Eau Claire all over the field, outplayed them; outgained them; did everything but the one thing that counts. We didn't outscore them.

They won it 14-6.

My team felt mighty bad and maybe I felt even worse. A team should feel that way when they blow a big one. So should a coach.

This is not being a bad loser—it's being a hard loser. Bad losers alibi or blame the referee. Hard losers blame themselves.

(Good losers? Who wants them?

Knute Rockne once started a season by saying, "If there's a good loser in the house, leave now. We can get along without you."

Good losers become very good at losing.)

Anyhow, you don't keep brooding. After a couple of days, you get back to the job at hand.

Bill Haugen came to see me on Wednesday.

"Three guys are breaking training," he said. "Weeding it at the store at noon hour."

"Which three, Bill?"

He named them and one of them was one of our co-captains.

"How come?" I said.

"They feel sorry for themselves because Eau Claire beat us."

"What do you think we should do?"

"I'd like to call a meeting of the squad."

"OK."

So Bill called the meeting, and he got up before the kids and made his accusations. One of the guys bitched about it.

"Whatta ya tryin' to do to us, Bill?"

"What are you trying to do to all of us?"

(It takes guts to put the finger on one of your peers. There's some kind of code that says you don't rat on a rat. Nobody really believes in it. But try to find a kid who will go against it.

Bill Haugen did.)

They took a vote—finally. Three choices. Kick them off for the season. Kick them off for two weeks. Or nothing.

Secret ballot.

Nobody voted for nothing. A surprising number said out for the season. But most went with the two weeks suspension—and that was what we did. The weed beaters were off for two weeks.

The girl to whom I was engaged came up to our next game and happened to sit next to the mother of one of the three. This good lady did not know my girlfriend. Helen told me later that she spent the whole game rooting for the other team.

Ah, motherhood!

But we won it anyhow and we won the next one and the suspended boys came back, and we didn't lose another game until finally we had to play the toughest team on our schedule—by far—in the finals in Madison.

Madison Edgewood, that year, without a doubt was the equal of any team in the state, public or private school. We were very good ourselves, but they were better.

I watched them warm up and they had the class of a college team. And looked like they almost had the size of one, too.

The field was muddy that November night. And it was chilly. Not cold enough to freeze the mud but enough to make you wish you weren't muddy and wet when the wind blew.

Maybe the weather and the field conditions helped us. I don't know. I do know that my kids were tough. I suspect Edgewood's were too.

In football, you don't lead the pack unless you're tough. It's an essential part of the game.

At halftime, Edgewood was on top, 12–0.

I kicked a few things around in the locker room so my kids would know I was mad. I hadn't come all the way to Madison to lose if we could help it. I wanted them to believe that.

"Edgewood made two mistakes that half," I snarled. "They missed their extra points. It's gonna cost 'em the game."

We went out and discovered that Edgewood had changed uniforms between halves. We had the same old muddy gear on we'd used the first half. It's all we owned.

"I want those fancy pants to look like we do within five minutes," I screamed.

"They will, coach," a little guard assured me. "They will."

And they did.

Anyhow, after a while we scored and missed the extra point, and it was 12-6. Just before the end of the game, incredibly, we scored again, and we had tied the super team.

We went for the point with a pass.

My passer was Jimmy Miller, who later on was to be the quarterback at the University of Wisconsin for three years, but that night he was a high school freshman, and he was fourteen years old.

Besides that, the ball was muddy. Jimmy would never mention that fact because he wasn't of the breed and besides had been trained not to. I mention it. The ball was muddy.

Jimmy's pass got away from him. It was too high.

Bill Haugen came across from the right end spot and he went as high as he could, but it wasn't enough.

What does a ball player do then?

Well, some—maybe most—come down. They settle for the praise of, "Nice try."

Not Haugen.

He went as high as he could go—and then he climbed higher. And if that sounds like a contradiction, I can only say it's because of the limitation of language.

A football man will know what I mean.

The ball hit his hand and maybe because they both were mud, it stuck. He fell in the end zone, and he held onto the ball.

We had beaten Edgewood 13–12 in one of the great upsets that high school football has known in these parts.

The point, I think, is fairly obvious.

Too much is made of the skill of a boy—or his size or speed.

Not enough of his breed.

A skillful player would have found that night, that skill is not enough. When it counts you need heart or courage or guts or whatever it is that will not let you quit when quitting seems the easy way—and even an acceptable way.

The kid who climbed for that ball that night was the same boy who had stood before the squad six weeks before and called for a showdown.

I think the ingredients that go into the kind of boy who would face up to either situation are pretty much the same.

They don't get the ink too often. And they may miss the honor.

What they do earn is respect.

And that outlasts the others.

Victory!
Eau Claire St. Pat's 13　　Madison Edgewood 12

AUSTIN PACELLI 1958 STATE CHAMPIONS

When I was growing up, Saturday was game night, which meant weekends were exciting. We went to 8:00 Mass every Saturday morning. We went to Mass daily, but on game days the team was also in attendance. Rare was the guy who skipped out. Parents might not like it, thinking their sons should be able to sleep in on a Saturday, but the players knew to be there.

In addition to the "team Mass," just prior to a game, my dad would get the players together at the school's chapel, to "make a visit" and pray together. In March of 1958, his Austin Pacelli team had earned its way to the finals of the state basketball tournament. They were facing a formidable opponent, Cotter High School of Winona, MN, the afternoon game scheduled at the St. Paul Auditorium. As the team left their hotel my dad decided to "make a visit" at Our Lady of Guadalupe Church in the Mexican section of St. Paul, a multicultural experience for the boys from Austin. He had not planned for the traffic they would encounter in their new route to the auditorium.

Back at the gym, Cotter was on the floor warming up. There was no sign of Pacelli. The officials running the tournament were asking, "Where's Pacelli?" No answer was forthcoming. As the last seconds of the warmup period were ticking away, the Pacelli players entered in street clothes. The referee ran up to my father to inform him that they had no extra time to warm up. "That's OK," was his reply.

The team dressed, came out, and played a hard-fought game. The final score was 45-44, with Pacelli the victor. They were State Champions. Our Lady of Guadalupe must have cracked a smile.

1958 Pacelli High School Basketball Team

AUSTIN PACELLI 1959
WASHINGTON, D.C.

In 1959, the Pacelli basketball team took the train to the National Catholic Invitational Tournament in Washington, D.C., a tournament that included some of the best teams in the country. In tournament play Pacelli beat Pittsburgh Central Catholic in game one. They lost in game two to a powerful Archbishop John Carroll High School led by John Thompson and Tom Hoover. In the battle for third place, they lost to West High School of Philadelphia by two points, 57-55.

ORRIE

O*rrie Jirele was part of the 1958 State Champion Team at Pacelli (#7). He was selected as the Most Valuable Player in the tournament. My father wrote about him.*

* * *

"Orrie"

Typewritten manuscript
Date unknown

He was the best all-around basketball player I ever had.

At the beginning of his senior year, I called him aside. "Look" I said. "You're really gonna have to learn to take it this year. You're my star. You know it. The team knows it. Everybody knows it—and I admit it. That's unanimous. But I'm really going to pour it on you this year. If I don't, some of the lesser lights will decide you're the precious one. Coach's bread-and-butter. Coach's little boy blue. Do you understand all this?"

"Yeh."

"I'll really be on you, therefore. And you know how I can be. Can you take it?"

"Yeh."

I was on him. All year. Tough and snarling and unrelenting. He led us to the state title in Minnesota that year, but he bore the bruises—tongue lash type—all the way.

He took it.

When the season was over, I tried to get him a deal at Marquette. At Minnesota. At Wisconsin. No deals. Too small, they said. He's good but he's not big enough. He was 5'10".

He went to Saint Bonaventure back in the state of New York and he didn't get a dime of aid as a ball player. He was a top-ranking student, and he got a few chips because of that.

He went out for the team, and he made it as a starter as a sophomore. (Frosh couldn't play varsity in those days). Still, 5'10". But brains and style and a playmaking guard. He made it. Saint Bonaventure was rated second in the nation that year (Ohio State with Havlicek and the boys was first)—with one guard that everybody knew was too small to play.

You don't measure all of a man's height with a tape. Not all of it, you don't. Like, can he take it? For instance.

Some things a tape measure doesn't know—or tell……

* * *

Orrie became a successful high school teacher and coach. He and my dad were great friends for the rest of my father's life. They got together each summer, worked together in coaching clinics, and brought their teams together for scrimmages.

Orrie was a violinist. At my dad's funeral he bid his final good-bye to his old coach and friend playing "Ashokan Farewell."

WE'RE FROM CENTRAL

In the summer of 1959, my dad moved on to Catholic Central High School in Marinette, WI, and new and exciting adventures.

This piece chronicles a memorable night for him and his team, coming off two disappointing losses in one weekend. Note the date, and after reading it, go on to the amazing story that follows only one month later.

* * *

"We're from Central, Couldn't Be Prouder"
Published in "Something to Crowe About"
The Spirit
January 31, 1964

There used to be a popular song about moments to remember. I had one of those last weekend.

Our basketball team had gone into Friday's game at Menomonee on the crest of a ten-game winning streak—longest in the history of our school. Quite naturally, there was a lot of interest in and enthusiasm for our team.

Our hopes, as the poet puts it, were running high.

Suddenly they were brought low. Menominee, a traditional and ancient rival, knocked us off, by one point in overtime. And the next night we went down to Oshkosh and got clipped again, this time by a very good team from Lourdes High School.

Our kids felt mighty down and so did I.

I knew from long years in the game, what it would be like back home on Sunday. All the well-wishers and the back slappers, so numerous and vocal while we were riding high, would be suddenly silent. Or vanished. The second guessers would be in full cry.

We had committed the one unpardonable crime in the minds of so many fans.

We had lost.

So we were headed home from Oshkosh Saturday night in the gloom of a losing team's bus. (And there are good boys on my team this year, so they are not good losers. Nor bad ones. They are hard losers. They lose hard, the only way.) It was pretty quiet.

We stopped for hamburgers at a place on the fringes of Green Bay and as the bus pulled into the parking lot, there was suddenly cheering and singing in the air.

I looked out the window and saw our "student bus" parked in the lot. We had not known they would be there, but they were there.

And these were kids in their finest hour.

These were not the fine weather fans who leave when the cold winds blow. These were the gallant gang of boys and girls from Marinette Catholic Central High School who had made the long trip to Oshkosh to see the high hopes dashed for the second night in a row and who must have been tired and worn with the long trip on that school bus—and with losing.

But these were the brave and shining ones.

Poking their heads out the windows of their bus—jumping in the aisle—with the foolish, gay little green berets (suddenly so wonderful and so precious) on their heads—they sang our song, and they shouted our cheer:

"We're from Central, couldn't be prouder!

If you can't hear us, we'll yell it louder!"

Foolish words. Nothing words. I heard them a hundred times.

But suddenly they were alive and crackling in the January air. Pride. The glorious singing pride of kids in a common cause. We stand together. We go down together. We get up again. Together.

Suddenly there was a tightness in my throat, and I remembered why I stayed in this game all these years.

This was being young at its very best. Here was the answer to the cynics. Here was loyalty and integrity and identification. The no surrender guys and gals.

Nuts to the breed of adult fan who would now give us the back of the hand. Who cares? Who needs them? Who wants them?

We got off the bus to get our hamburgers—and there was something new in our squad. Like I say—precious. And you can't put it down in words.

I put my head in the student bus, and I looked at that gang and I said we were down, but we'll get up. Because of this. And I said one more thing for that gallant singing in the night—for that moment—and I say it again now.

Thanks.

STATE TOURNAMENT 1964

"Marinette Catholic Central 1964 State Basketball Tournament"
February 28–March 1, 1964
Handwritten manuscript

I never saw Power Memorial High School of New York City play basketball when Lew Alcindor was the big man there. I guess that was one of the best high school teams of all time. They lost one game in three years, I understand, and almost always against top grade opposition.

Personally, I would have to doubt that Power was any better than the best prep team I ever saw play the game—John Carroll High School of Washington DC in the spring of 1959.

Tom Hoover, later with the New York Knickerbockers, was rated the best high school player in the country in '59. He was 6'7" and weighed about 247 pounds. He played forward. John Thompson, who afterwards played on our Olympic team, with Providence and then the Boston Celtics was the 6'10" center that year. George Leftwich, later an ace guard at Villanova, was selected as the top player in the tournament in 1959. He was a bit over 6 feet and a ball handling genius. Monk Malloy was a 6'4" forward, and I lost track of him. Somebody told me he later played at Notre Dame. He was that good, I'm sure. The other guard, who was 6'3", was the boy whose name I can't recall. He was their fifth man. He would have been my first.

That was quite a team. They were never beaten or even scared, as I recall. They licked the Georgetown Frosh and the Naval Academy Frosh—bad.

They beat my team from Austin, Minnesota Pacelli High in the semifinals of the tournament by about 20 points. Our tallest boy was a whisper over 6 feet—but we had superb teamwork. We never had a chance to beat Carroll, but we gave them a better game than anyone else down there did—and a number of the teams—most of them—were much stronger than we were.

But not one played together as smoothly or as well. We had no stars. We didn't believe in stars.

I can still see my center, Mike Donovan, 6 feet tall and 140 pounds, faking big Hoover under the basket and coming back with a reverse lay-up.

On the way down the floor, Hoover, (who was a Negro, as were Thompson and Leftwich) patted Mike on the seat of the pants with that huge hand of his, and grinned.

"Nice play, kid," he said, "but you'll never do it again."

And Mike never was able to. Again.

I've had some great teams of my own. Four of them won state championships, and the Eau Claire Saint Pat's team in 1948 was never beaten. It had size, (the only big team I've ever had) class, dedication, skill—the works.

It was, without a doubt, one of the greatest high school basketball teams in Wisconsin athletic history.

Yet, that is not the team of mine which I remember best.

In 1964 I had a gang of kids who had nothing. Except a dream and a hard, cold resolution.

They had no size. If you don't have size, you've got to have speed. Speed they didn't have. They were quick—cat quick with their hands—but they were not fast. They must, someone will say, have been phenomenal shooters, then.

They were one of the worst shooting teams I've ever had.

I had a boy on that team whose name was Danny Noonan, to whom I gave the special orders.

"You're shooting range, Noonan, is 2 inches. Fire from further out than that and you'll sit on the bench with me."

Danny was really a horror as a shot. Yet he has the highest shooting percentage in the history of Marinette Catholic Central. From 2 inches your average is usually pretty good.

Those boys never conned themselves. They said to me, "Coach, we know what we can't do. But we're gonna win that state title anyhow. We may be the lousiest team ever to win it—but we're gonna win it anyhow."

So, we went to work on defense.

(Defense, to all those who have never heard the word, is what you play when the other team's got the ball. It's nice to know how. Few teams do.)

The quick hands helped here. So did the dedication and the determination. So did the cold-blooded teamwork. From the very beginning that team, above any I've ever seen, developed the attitude of despising the very idea of anybody being a star.

When they started to come along, the newspapers, asinine as always, tried to stir up the star talk. My kids spit when they read it.

The other thing they worked on was ball handling. They developed their faking to a fantastic degree. They learned to pass the ball and catch the ball. They learned how to come to precision timing on their passes.

They became the best ballhandling team I have ever seen in high school basketball.

When you can handle the ball that well you can set the pace of the game. We set ours. Slow.

We couldn't shoot and we couldn't get the rebounds. We had to make every move count. Without being able to shoot we had to keep our shooting percentage extremely high. (It was usually above fifty percent). So, we had to go for only one kind of shot—the good one. The set up. The sure thing.

Fans booed us. Opposition fans always. Our own, often. They had never seen this kind of ball before. They were used to the run and shoot nonsense that ninety percent of the teams played. They had never seen cold-blooded execution before.

Frankly, they didn't know a damn thing about the game. So, they booed.

It never phased my boys. Not once. Ever. They were one thing more besides superlatively smooth—they were utterly cold-blooded. Basketball assassins you might say. A job to do and a plan and no one—but no one—was going to divert them from it.

Off the floor these kids were as pleasant and lighthearted a group as I've ever known. (For instance, we had a slogan: "Win this one for Frank Runk."

Frank Runk was a kid I knew in grade school and hadn't seen in more than thirty years. I thought he had the kind of name that goes well in a slogan. So did they.

"Win another for Frank," they'd shout.)

On the floor they were calm, cool, deadly. How the opposition fans came to hate them when they started to come on! Livid faces. Vile invectives.

The team ignored them.

In the final game of the regional tournament, we played a bad game. We blew layups and with six minutes left in the game the score was 29-29. We had the ball.

I flashed the order from the bench. Go for one shot.

So while the crowd screamed their fury (we were playing on the opponents' floor) the kids, with superlative passing, killed the whole six minutes, went for the last shot.

And blew it.

In the overtime, same thing. Blew the shot again. Second overtime—and this time that last second shot went in.

The fuzzy cheeked, knobby kneed, cold-blooded guys from nowhere were in the state!

The sports writers from the Milwaukee papers couldn't take the team seriously. They looked too helpless when they had their practice session on the arena floor. Maybe—for just a minute there—they might have seen something that—but no, these kids are too scared. Too helpless.

Besides they're matched against Madison Edgewood and Edgewood has an 81-point scoring average and has just breezed through a tough regional.

"It's a mismatch," scribes decided.

It was, too. As soon as the game went into overtime.

Edgewood had never been in overtime before. My kids had lived that way all year. So, in the second overtime, Edgewood cracked, and we took them 50-46.

The nothing team was in the semifinals.

Stevens point Pacelli had height and they had, in a boy named Mencel, the best ball player in the tournament. I worried a lot about that one, but the game ended in a tie.

First overtime—still tied. Nobody has scored. Second overtime—same thing. Third overtime. Smokey Anderson, one of my guards, says, "Coach, I got an idea!"

"Good," I said. "I'm fresh out."

"I think they're gonna get the jump and I think they'll tip it to number 24. If I step in front of him, I can get the ball!"

"Smart," I said. "Good thinking. Do it."

(If it worked it would make me look like a brilliant coach.)

It didn't work. Smokey cut it too fine and bumped 24. His last foul. He's out of the game. And the kid has the one and one on the free-throw line.

He makes the first—misses the second.

Now we come down the floor with the ball. Two seconds gone in the overtime, but for the first time in all the seven overtime periods, we're behind.

Always before the score was tied and we had the ball. So, who's worried? But now—behind.

The kids go into their ballhandling routine. Nifty. Neat. Smooth.

But we're behind.

At two minutes, our fans crack.

"Shoot!" They scream. "You're behind! Shoot! Shoot!"

The boys keep on passing the ball. No mistakes. Nifty.

But we're behind.

At a minute and thirty seconds the coach cracks.
"For gosh sakes, shoot the thing." I shout.

They pass it around.

A minute and twenty-two seconds left and little Steve LaCousiere, five-foot-five guard, sees what he's been looking for. The alley.

He drives. They clobber him. Two free throws. He makes them both.

Now Stevens Point is behind. They come down the floor and fire from close to 40 feet out. Miss. We get the ball. They foul us.

Two more throws. We make them both. In the last minute and a fraction, the low scoring Cavaliers score 13 points and win by 12.

Point was stronger but Point cracked. My kids had trained themselves not to crack. All the boo-birds who had been on their back all year were their best friends now. They had learned to take it. And when it counted, they could.

In the finals, we meet Appleton Xavier. They are defending state champs. They have won forty-nine games in a row. They have beaten us twice that season—though it wasn't easy, either time.

At the half, the score is 15-15. In the dressing room the smell of the incredible is in the air. My kids believe they're going to do it! Hardly a fan in all the thousands give them a chance. The sportswriters still think in terms of mismatch. Even their own rooters have nothing but a dim, grim hope.

But the kids figure it's their day. They have come too far—sacrificed too much—dreamed too long and worked too hard to let down now.

I'd been in the game almost a quarter of a century—and I can sense things in a dressing room.

But this is almost too fantastic.

We hold hands and say a prayer. I look at my boys.

"This is it," I say. And we go out.

With four minutes left in the game we're up by six and Torchy Clark, the great Xavier coach, has a decision to make.

His team is noted for its full court press. The best press in the state, it's been called. But Torchy has not pressed us. He's smart enough to know that you can't press a team which can handle the ball like my kids can.

Still—his fans are demanding it—and he's got to do it. Otherwise, he knows we'll freeze the ball.

He orders his team into the press and in a minute and a half we change the six-point lead to thirteen.

We're in!

They got a couple of meaningless baskets at the end. But we're in.

We're the state champions!

The next day we return to the north country where basketball champions are something you read about in somebody else's newspaper.

Thirty miles out of Marinette, we're met by everybody from the Methodist Church choir to the fire department. The town—an unsophisticated one, thank God—celebrates for six weeks.

This is the team and the time I remember.

I started out in this chapter to tell you about some mighty teams that have existed here and there. Mine—and others.

But suddenly I realized you can learn nothing from them. They were big and fast and powerful, so they won.

So, what else is new?

But here's a hungry bunch from nowhere—the nothing team someone called them—and because they believe in work and never surrender—they're the champs.

"Cheese champs!" someone told a friend of mine.

Cheese, hell. I've had four, and this was the truest champion of them all. Because they epitomize what the game and the challenge is all about.

Learn this, younger reader. Let the old measure the boy—or weigh him.

You check on something they've forgotten. You find how tall he stood as a man.

And then—remember.

1964 State Champions

One of the players from the 1964 state championship team recounted their first meeting as a freshmen basketball team. "Coach Crowe predicted we would be state champions. We sat there in disbelief. 'What is he talking about?' But it was like he knew. He got us to dream big and work to reach the dream."

(*Photos Courtesy of* Milwaukee Journal Sentinel)

THE PLAYERS

TRIBUTE TO A SUB

My dad did not start out to be a coach. It just happened, and then became central to his life, a life filled with the stories of all those young people whose lives he touched and whose lives touched his. Some of them were stars, but many were not. He often wrote about the ones who were not. He had great respect for the ordinary kid who contributed what he could though he never made the headline but helped make the team.

* * *

"Tribute to a Sub"
Published in "From the Bench"
Green Bay Register
February 7, 1964

This is a tribute to a sub.

In case you might wonder what a sub is, I don't blame you. He is nothing. Nobody. He comes out for practice year after year—he never quits, but he never makes the team. His name is never set up in type. No one takes his picture. Most of the fans never hear of him at all.

But that's all right. The guys on the team know who he is. And what he is and what he means to the team and to them.

And, somehow, that's enough.

When the canny and confident sportswriters—or even the august coaches—gather to select their teams of "stars," no one will say his name. No one will even know it.

But when the guys in his class gather under the streetlight for a little quiet talk in the evening in the last year of their youth, they will name him.

"I'm glad he was here when I was here," one of them will put it. "I'm glad I had a chance to know the guy."

"He didn't quite have it out there," another will say. "Short on the skill you have to have. He knew it. But he never quit trying."

"He wasn't much of a guy for quitting."

"Five years from now, when it's all long over, I'll remember all you guys. But nobody more than him. Maybe nobody quite so much."

And that's enough.

You won't understand this, sportswriters. I've found most of the time that you really don't understand very much when you get to it. Never seemed to try very much—or care.

I read a lot about hook shots and push shots and long shots and soft shots—and sometimes I read about rebounds—and once in a great, long, time, about playmaking or something you don't add on the office computer—but you never knew the sub was there, did you, sportswriter?

(Unless he got in and had a hot night. I mean he gunned a lot and scored a lot some night. Then you knew. But I mean the kid who never had that kind of a night.)

And that's the kid the guys mean too, sportswriter.

Let me tell you about one. You won't understand, sportswriter, but maybe somebody else will.

This one is a skinny one. Long and lank and lean—And he can find that hoop. But he never could quite make it around the turn which separates the boy who can do it from the one who just missed.

I knew him in the eighth grade first. And he could shoot—even then. And he had his dreams. And that funny little one-sided grin which has long since become part of my life.

I thought he might do it. Through his sophomore year I had hopes—maybe even after that. But I finally knew that this one just wasn't going to be.

He knew it too, at last. And it hurt. When a dream dies it always hurts.

So, he gives me the grin and he says, "Well, that's it, coach. I kid me not. No more. But if it's all right with you, I'll just stick around. Maybe I can help a little."

It was all right, sub. I can tell you, now, because now it's all over and it won't hurt anymore—I can tell you that when we both knew your dream was over, you took it better than I did.

So, you kept coming out. Every night. Never missing at all. Sometimes the stars missed but stars have privileges. Don't they, sportswriter? When the guys sagged off or felt the old urge for self-pity, you got on them, sub.

You wouldn't let them sell out. Even for a little while. You fought them. And because you were what you were, they listened, and you won.

I owe you that, sub. It's written down.

I could name you here but why do that?

For the ones who don't care, the name makes no difference—and for the ones who care, they can fill it in.

(Besides there are four other guys who, one way or another, fit the same dimensions.)

So—no name sub. The sportswriter never used it. Nor will I. Not necessary.

Say it this way—when the scores and the screaming are forgotten—and the glory is dead as last year's hero—I will remember you, sub.

For whatever it's worth, this I promise you.

THE NIGHT BILLY REGAN MADE THE TEAM

This story, about a sub, published in the Madison Capital Times, *caught the attention of Senator William Proxmire, who read the piece into the Congressional Record on July 21, 1975.*

* * *

"The Night Billy Regan Made the Team"
Madison Capital Times
July 14, 1975

Billy Regan was a nine-minute miler.

Every man who has ever coached knows the type. Comes out for everything. Can't do anything. But a great and wonderful kid. He will never quit. (Sometimes, for once, you wish he would.) He gives all that he has but it's never going to be enough.

Like that last night at football practice his senior year.

It's a quiet time. The guys realize, all at once, that a special part of their lives is over. It will not come again. So after practice it's a long, quiet walk in the early dark of late October into the dressing room. Nobody says very much.

The boy ahead of me was walking alone—and slow. I passed him and I saw that it was Billy Regan. I wondered how he felt that night. The four years of desperate trying, over now. The dream, at long last, finally dead.

Oh, I'd tried to play him once, but it was just no go. He was so small and so unskilled but so determined that when the ball was snapped, he began to thrash his arms around. Wildly.

"Fifteen yards!"

"Huh?"

"Unnecessary roughness!"

How ridiculous can you get? Roughness! Billy Regan was the gentlest boy on the team. But again, the ball is snapped and Billy wildly swings his arms.

"Fifteen yards!"

We had to get him out of there. And that was as close as Billy ever came to making the team. It didn't seem fair somehow. A boy with that much dedication and grim perseverance. But what the hell? Like I say, every coach has had a Billy Regan. Every teacher has had one in his class.

The guys took their showers slowly that night. And it was quiet. One by one, they finished dressing at last and slipped out the door for the final time and were gone. After a while, there were just five guys left in the room. Plus Billy, of course. He took his shower, and he was the last one. Then he began to put on his clothes.

He almost made it.

By that time, I knew something was up. The five guys—waiting around. They could have left—but they hadn't. Five seniors. Regulars. The stars of the team.

Billy had everything on but his shoes when they made their move. Without a word, they walked over and grabbed him by the arms and legs. They carried him into the shower—clothes and all—and turned the water on and left him there.

Then, still with no word at all, they came out, went through the door—and were gone.

It was quite a while before Billy came out of that shower. And it took him a while to get the wet clothes off. When he came over to the equipment cage, he held up the wet clothes—and I gave him a sweatsuit to go home in.

And the tears were shining in his eyes.

But those were tears of wonder, man. Tears of glory. Magic. Choose your word. And I was privileged to be there. As a teacher and a coach, I had the honor that night to be there when five guys on the ball club saw to it that Billy Regan made the team.

"Night, coach."

"Good night, Bill."

"And… Thanks."

"Okay."

And he was gone.

Sure, his mother called the principal that night and gave him Royal Canadian hell. And sure, he called me and passed it on.

But who cares?

I saw Billy Regan make the team…

A teacher's career is crowded with little things like that. Moments that light up his life. A guy in this profession should be grateful for that. Maybe, even, some night on his knees.

I go along with those teachers in convention in LA. I am for a better salary scale—and all of that. But a teacher can get lost if he's not careful. There's more to this job than money. There are all the dreams we all had. Once. There's a chance to help and the chance to care. There's the chance just to be there when a boy needs somebody. There.

I keep thinking of that story of the well-off businessman watching the old nun working, under incredibly unpleasant conditions, with the very sick and the very poor. The place looks bad, and it smells worse.

"I wouldn't do this for a million dollars!" the man says.

"Neither would I," replies the nun.

And I guess, in there somewhere, is something of what I've been trying to say.

A MEMOIR FROM VIETNAM

Then there was a story of another sub writing to my father from the midst of war in Vietnam. It was a touching story and I wondered what had happened to the young man. His obituary showed he had married, raised a family, and enjoyed working in his yard. I was able to contact one of his daughters and share the story my father had told of her dad. I commented on the two purple hearts and two silver stars he had been awarded in Vietnam. She said the war had been hard on him.

* * *

"A Memoir from Vietnam"
Published in "From the Bench"
Green Bay Register
January 10, 1969

You never heard of Dale Vanderfin, but now, for a little while, you will.

He sits over there in Vietnam, and he writes me letters and he tells me that I had a real good impact on his life, and I hope that is right, but I know I'm not nearly the man that Dale's letters say that I am.

It would be great to be that good.

I console myself with the realization that nobody else is that good either. And I know too well that these are the words of a lonely young man remembering some good years and seeing some of the people in them better than they were.

At Christmas time, Dale wrote to the whole school. A letter to Catholic Central. A cry out of the heart of a good boy consigned to a crummy war.

So be it. A lot of guys are so consigned.

But, let me tell you how it was with this boy and then you tell me, if you can, why it is that he remembers so much better than a lot of those who counted more and got more ink, and everybody knew their name.

Dale Vanderfin was almost nothing in the athletic program here. He came out for football and basketball and track, and he didn't have it. He wasn't big, nor fast, nor skilled, nor strong.

He was just a really good boy who wanted to contribute if he could—and he never quit trying. Not until all the four years were over.

And I guess not even then.

I remember that in grade school Dale had one great and golden moment. The Saint Joe's team, on which he was just another guy named Louie, was locked in a barn burner for the title with another grade school club—Lourdes or Saint Ann's or somebody. It was a long time ago.

Anyhow, in one of those strange twists of fate that happen every once in a while, to remind a guy that there must be Someone up there directing traffic, it all got down to the very last shot of the game—whole year's hopes—the title—the works.

And who wound up taking it?

The star? I don't even remember who the star was that year. Perhaps whoever he was, he remembers. Some stars never forget. I do though. Most of us forget.

Anyhow, it wasn't the star who flung that last, wild, hopeless, desperate shot. It was nobody. It was Dale Vanderfin.

And the thing went through.

That was it. The whistle—and the game is over and they're carrying little Dale off the floor. It was a really good night to be watching a grade school game.

You forget the stars. Some things you remember.

I suppose that all through the four years of high school Dale nourished the quiet hope that lightning would strike again. It never did.

Oh, he got in once in a while, on some field or floor, in time to tell the referee the game was over. He got in because a boy like that you've got to get him in. Sometime.

Somehow.

I remember at the start of basketball season his last year, he came to see me.

"I know I'm no good, coach," he said. "But is it all right if I come out anyhow?"

"Yeah," I said. "It's all right."

It's always all right with that kind of a boy. When you start wondering what's all right and what isn't, you always know that this part of it is as right as anything will ever be.

I think maybe Dale wondered sometimes if the more skilled players got to thinking that maybe he was in the way. They never got to thinking that, Dale. Not ever in all the years.

Neither did I.

I had to write this piece today, for Dale Vanderfin—and for every boy like him on any team in the land. The good boy. The courageous kid who doesn't have the stuff to make it nor the surrender flag to quit.

The quiet kid whose name you never hear who always hoped he could contribute.

You made it, man. Every guy like Dale Vanderfin. You made it more than you will ever understand. Or than I will completely understand, either.

Only, once in a while, I come pretty close.

I wrote this piece, also, because yesterday I had a little talk with my best players. We surely aren't loaded this year, and we aren't winning—but we've got a few pretty fair ball players, and I was talking to them about what they got from being skilled—and about what they could give.

Getting is always easier than giving, of course. For all of us. We're all takers.

But a nothing substitute who graduated years ago—and nobody said his name—sat on a box in Vietnam and wrote to me and wrote to his school because, somehow, the days he spent here are still wrapped around his life.

Learn, scrub. Learn, star.

And don't ever forget to remember, coach, that without the Dale Vanderfins in it, your own career and your own life aren't worth very much. No matter how big it looks in print.

Hey, sub—may God take care of you out there.

That's my prayer, man.

THE EDDIE DECKER STORY

My dad must have felt pretty sad the day he got word that Eddie Decker had died. Eddie never received academic accolades nor the sports headlines. He was a sub.

My father knew that Eddie Decker was a good and earnest kid who worked hard. My dad held a special respect and affection for him. He ended one essay saying, "I thank God for guys like Eddie . . . who for a little while walked through my life."

* * *

"The Eddie Decker Story"
Published in "From the Bench"
Green Bay Register
April 26, 1963

I read in the paper that Eddie was dead. Somebody else was driving the car but it was Eddie who was killed.

I got to remembering that day long ago—I was teaching English classes in Pacelli high school in Minnesota—when Eddie had come up to my desk with that old, puzzled frown wrinkling his forehead. Little old hard-rock

Eddie—he always looked like a guy who didn't have life quite figured out.

(Well, who does—when it comes to that?)

He was holding a sheet of paper in his hand. I'd given a spelling test—fifty words. Eddie had blown forty-seven.

He held the paper in front of me.

"That ain't so good, is it?"

"I've seen better, Eddie."

"I'm gonna study the list some more. Can I take the test over?"

"Sure thing, Eddie."

The next time he only missed 35. He was a proud boy that day.

"Better, huh?"

"Much better, Ed."

"I'm gonna keep poundin' that list."

Suddenly I had visions of Eddy spending the rest of his life on one spelling list.

"Look, Ed. That's enough on this list. You did a good job. Work on something else now."

(Knowing Eddie, I figured he'd already given a dozen hours of his lifetime to the list. It was enough.)

"Well, okay."

He came out for football. (The teachers passed him because he tried.) He was little but he was tough. He didn't learn easily even in football. But he did what you asked him the best he could all the way. That's my kind of guy.

And so, it came down to that one night in the locker room before one big game with LaCrosse Aquinas. It was 1954 and we had our best team that year. But Aquinas had one of their best too and they were from a much bigger school, and they always had one of the top teams in the state.

They probably were better than us, but I figured we had a chance.

I'm the wordy type before a ball game. Edgy. Not the easiest guy in the world to be around. I figured my kids were scared out by the Aquinas reputation. And I was right in that one.

"The trouble is," I snarled, "you're scared of Aquinas. Big town. Big school. Big record. You're scared out by Aquinas. We've got a ball club here this year. A good one. We could beat this outfit. But we won't. And the reason—you're scared of Aquinas."

Why it worked this way, I'll never know. But as I swung around and pointed my quivering finger, there it was dead-trained on Eddie Decker.

"How about you, Decker." I screamed. "Are you scared of Aquinas?"

The old, puzzled look came into his eyes. The frown. The lines in his brow. The desperate urge to get things right.

"Who?" he said.

The short, amazed silence was followed by the wild shout of laughter. And I was in on it. You can't be scared of 'em if ya never heard of 'em. We murdered Aquinas that night.

I'll remember Eddie when most of the rest of it is long gone.

GOOD LUCK KENO LARKIN

My dad often quoted from Portia's "Quality of Mercy" speech from Shakespeare's The Merchant of Venice. He thought it contained "some of the finest concepts of man ever written down."

> The quality of mercy is not strain'd,
> It droppeth as the gentle rain from heaven
> Upon the place beneath.

My dad believed in mercy; he believed in second chances. That belief often put him at odds with fellow staff members who were convinced students learn best from consequences. Keno Larkin, another sub, never forgot my dad's graciousness in giving him a second chance. Upon his return from a tour in Vietnam he came back to thank his coach.

* * *

"Good luck, Keno Larkin—you'll be a good coach."

Minneapolis Tribune
February 18, 1978

He came into my office that afternoon. It was getting late; practice was over, and the voices of kids hung in the air down below as they said that night's good-byes.

A thousand nights you've sat and heard it all before. All the lads who were young for such a little while and are long gone now.

Jimmy and Ted and Lefty. A hundred names drift back from the years. It is a time that is kind of sad and kind of quiet. But it is a good time.

Suddenly he was standing there.

"Hi, Coach. I bet ya don't remember me."

"Keno Larkin."

"By damn. I didn't think you'd remember."

"Why shouldn't I, Keno?"

"Well, hell—I was never much."

He stood there in his soldier's suit, and he said it true. Never much. Got in a few games in football. In basketball, strictly for the bench.

"Ya gave us a lot of yourself, Keno."

"Too slow, Coach. That was my trouble. Too damn slow."

"Where are ya been, Keno?"

"I was in 'Nam for a couple of years. Got back a week ago. I'm sort of waitin' it out now."

"For what?"

"I'll be out of the army in a month."

"Hey, that's good. What's next then, Keno?"

"Maybe you'll laugh."

"Try me."

"I'm gonna go to college."

"Sounds good."

"C'mon coach. You know I never really cracked a book all the time I was in high school."

"I had a hunch, Keno."

"I dunno. I feel different now."

"How many years since you were here?"

"Six."
"A guy changes in six years."
"Yeh. Anyhow—this'll floor ya, coach."
"Try again."
"I wanta be a teacher. And a coach."
"There are worse things."
"Yeh. Only, like, ya know—I never was no good in football and not much in basketball either."
"I was worse in basketball than you were."
"You're kidding, coach."
"I kid you not. You were average. I was lousy."
"Anyhow—I'm gonna give it all I've got."
"That'll be enough."
"Hey, coach—I was wonderin' if you remembered somethin' that happened to me in high school."
"Lots of things happen."
"I mean the time they had the cops in because somebody had lifted some wallets out of the locker room."
"I remember."
"They asked a lot of questions and finally decided it was me."
"Yeh."
"Turned out they were right."
"Yeh."
"So, I gave the stuff back and they let me off the hook. You asked 'em to, didn't ya?"
"Possibly. Was a long time ago."
"Possibly hell. Ya did. Why'd ya do that, coach?"
"Seemed like a good idea at the time."
"And ya didn't even kick me off the squad. Why not?"
"Idea didn't occur to me. I saw no reason."
"Plenty of guys did."

"They did. I didn't. It was my team."

"Yeh. Well anyhow—when basketball started a lot of 'em didn't want me on the team."

"Could be. They never said."

"Maybe not to you. The word got around."

"You came out anyhow."

"I didn't want to then. But a guy can't quit."

"He can. It's better if he doesn't."

"Anyhow, sometime halfway through the season, stuff was missin' out of the lockers again."

"I kind of remember."

"Everybody figured it was me."

"Because of the other time. I guess."

"Sure. But you said that wasn't proof."

"Once I was right."

"Some of the guys said they were quittin' if you didn't kick me off."

"Yeh, I forget—did any quit?"

"Two."

"How about that. It was a long time ago."

"They were both better than I was. How come you let them quit?"

"Was up to them."

"I coulda quit instead."

"That was up to you."

"Yeh."

He was getting ready to leave. "Anyhow, it's six years late… But thanks, coach."

"Okay, Keno."

"Believe it or not, coach, but it was the whole bit—lookin' back—that made me decide to be a coach."

"I think you'll be a good one."

He had the door open by then.

But he turned back with his hand on the knob.

"Just for the record, coach—that second time—during basketball—I didn't steal anything. It wasn't me."

"Never figured it was, Keno."

He stood there a moment with the kind of look a guy remembers.

"So long, coach."

"Good luck, Keno."

He was gone then.

And may God bless you, Keno Larkin. A guy blows a few in a lifetime. For sure I have. But I didn't blow that one.

You'll do all right, Keno. A little slow of foot. But you came along better than most.

You'll be a good coach.

MICKEY'S FIRST ROAD TRIP

My brother Mickey was a talented and well-known basketball player during his high school years, playing under our dad at JFK Prep. That all changed after graduation as he fell victim to a mental illness that he has lived with since then. The story is chronicled in the book Over and Back-Mickey Crowe: The Strange and Troubled Life of a Wisconsin High School Basketball Legend, *by Brett Christopherson. I was away during the glory years, so I only saw Mickey play twice. I was there for the aftermath, and I am there now.*

Mickey held the record for top scorer in the state for 18 years, 1975-1993, with a 2,724-point total. This was prior to the arrival of the three-point shot. Mickey was also an amazing ball handler. As one former opposing player said to me at a book signing, "You couldn't guard him."

Mickey's high school career was well covered in the media. Gymnasiums were full when he came to play. Much was written about him in local and state publications, and he even made national news.

Some stories were written in the years after, conjecturing about what happened to Mickey Crowe. Those were hard years for the family, especially for my mom and dad. It is painful for parents to watch a beloved child struggle with such a confounding condition. As a counselor, I have been there with parents experiencing that pain.

I think my dad's love for my brother comes through in this article, written when Mickey was in fourth grade, returning from his first road trip. Of all the articles written about Mickey, this is the one I treasure.

* * *

"Mickey's First Road Trip"
Published in "From the Bench"
Green Bay Register *(excerpt)*
February 17, 1967

My youngest son, Mickey, is in the fourth grade. He plays on the basketball team for his school, Saint Joseph's, made up of fourth, fifth, and sixth graders.

Some folks say this is too young for competitive athletics and maybe they're right.

Still, I had quite an experience out of it last Sunday. Mick's team played in Green Bay against a similar outfit down there. It was his first "trip."

He was all jazzed up when he came home Sunday night. They'd won and that was part of it, and he'd had a good game and that was part of it. But on the way back they'd sung songs and practiced class cheers and been wildly together in the wonderful way of the very young.

And that was most of it.

As that skinny guy that is my nine-year-old was taking off his shoes Sunday night and making ready for the sack he sighed: "I wish today was just beginning."

And I guess I wish kids could stay forever nine. Where joy is clean and clear and has no plan. Where life is good, and no one is sly.

I think we come too quickly to the blasé now. We come to the take it for granted days. Where the thrill is gone because there have been too many thrills. No peaks left.

And I suppose much of this does come from too much too soon and that's why I've opposed all-star teams for the very young and awards and honors and all that. Kids don't need these and shouldn't have them. Just to be there is enough—just to share it all in the quickly flying days.

I wish today was just beginning.

PARENTS

IT'S THE KIDS

High School is a critical time in a young person's life. It is the time when an individual develops from a child to an adult, and the role of the parent changes. Sports can facilitate that transition. My dad understood how hard it is for a parent to step back, but how important it is to the kid to take responsibility for himself. He knew parents who were great supporters of their own kids and the team, but he and the team were also undermined by some who were disgruntled, feeling their child was being shorted. Unfortunately, the child was also hurt by overinvolvement from a parent. It was an issue my father wrote about.

* * *

"When the Dust Settles, It's the Kids and Not the Score that Matters"

The following letter, first written and published in the Austin Herald, *Minnesota, in the 1950s, was later reprinted in other publications, including:*

The Bethany Tribune Review *(Bethany, OK), 9/13/1962*
The Green Bay Register, *9/3/1965*
Times Review *(LaCrosse Diocesan paper), 8/30/1990*

Though I'm beginning my 17th year as a high school coach, this is the first time I've written a letter of this kind. I write it now because I'd like to establish a vital point or two before the football season begins.

I've had a lot of teams—some of them were outstanding, some not. Two won state championships. One never won a game. But they all had one thing in common—they were made up of pretty good kids.

During football season, those kids practice and drill and scrimmage in hot weather, cold weather, in dust and in rain. They get knocked down often, they get hurt a little sometimes, sometimes they get bawled out, and sometimes they lose. But the good ones never quit. Even when the cause seems hopeless, they go on—wet, dirty, kicked around, weary—but they go on.

And they deserve the praise and never the raucous condemnation of anyone worthy of the name of fan.

So does a coach, by the way and that is part of my point.

I am a coach. How good? Well, in years when I've had great teams, I've been voted a wizard. In bad years I've been voted a bum.

I guess I knew just about the same amount of football in the bad years as in the good ones.

I didn't get into coaching because I wanted to get rich. I left an advertising agency at a big cut in salary. But that was all right, because I like to coach, and I didn't like the agency.

I begin my teaching day at 8:30 in the morning, and I get home from football practice at 7:30 in the evening. On game nights I go to the game. On scouting nights, I go to other teams' games.

On other nights I sit up until midnight or later trying to figure out which plays to develop and which ones to drop—which ball players to push and which ones to pull—and how.

It's a long workday—and not an especially easy one—but I like it. I work at it hard, and that's the way it should be because my kids work hard, too.

But frankly, I'm fed up now—and have been for some time—with that breed of loudmouth who doesn't work at it at all—who wouldn't stand in the mud at a rainy practice for five minutes—but who has plenty to say and always says it with the volume turned on all the way.

He lays into the boys—or me—or both. He isn't really interested in the team. He's rooting for himself. He wants to seem smarter than the coach. Maybe he is, too. Anybody is smarter with the second guess. Even a coach can second-guess himself—in fact, all do. But for the coach, the second guess doesn't count.

For example, when a pass is intercepted, few coaches need the strategist in the third row to tell them they'd have been better off if it had not been thrown. But this bright kind of lad will tell them anyhow—very loudly—and not because it will help the team—the damage is done—but because it makes the bright boy seem brighter still. As far as that kind of fan goes, I've had it up to here. I think most of the coaches feel the same way. I'm saying it.

This afternoon one of my players came to see me. He was almost in tears. He had a problem a good deal more serious than how to gain three yards off left tackle. I didn't know the solution to his problem. I don't think the curbstone quarterbacks would've known it either.

But the point is that the boy came to see me as many others have—and as they've come to coaches and teachers throughout the land. He came to me for help, and it's my job to try to help him and I shall try.

That's the best part of my job—although by far the hardest.

Any coach worthy of his position is called upon to try to guide his boys toward manhood. It isn't easy—and it never was easy—but many of the answers come harder right now than they ever did.

The point is that it's a good deal more important for the coach to guess right on this kind of thing than on a matter of whether to pass or punt. The loud ones can argue the point if they want to, but they can't change it.

Any coach can do that part of his job best when he has the respect of his boys, and he can keep the respect of his boys best when he isn't assailed with the kind of bombast which tries to picture him as a simpleton or a fool.

We open our football season tonight and I hope a large number of the good people of Austin come out to the game because we have, once again, a mighty fine group of boys who've been working hard to get ready.

My boys will try to win. So, will I. We may do it. But if we don't I wish the wise ones would stay out of what hair I have left.

My main job is still to try to make decent men out of good boys—in a world where that outcome is by no means guaranteed.

I'd like the chance to get at it.

DADS

My dad knew that his father had big dreams for him when he was a young athlete. He often wrote about his father's enduring hopes with affection. Reflecting on his father helped him to understand and appreciate the fathers of his players.

* * *

"Thoughts About Dads"
Published in "From the Bench"
Green Bay Register
December 31, 1965

Seems like every Christmas season I get to talking to my classes about my old man. Seems, somehow, the memories of Christmas past and my dad kind of go together.

Incidentally, I hope you don't mind my calling him my old man. It all depends on the tone of voice. (The old lady was a great gal, too).

Anyhow, the reason I'm writing about him here is that when I got to reminiscing in front of my class the other day it occurred to me that some of the things I was saying then deserve to be said here.

The thing is the old man cared.

Like in summer, I'd come home from the 11 o'clock Mass on Sunday and my arm was pretty well shot by then and I was getting by on bloopers and soft curves and controlled slow stuff—junk—but I was still managing to line up a pitching assignment for some town or other almost every Sunday afternoon. And anyhow, my dad would have my uniform packed and, in the car, and my gloves and spikes and all that and he'd be ready to go with me to the game of that day.

I was about 24 then and my dad was crowding 70 but he still figured, back somewhere, that I'd make the big time yet. A big league pitcher.

That had been his dream for me from the beginning and he never gave up on it. Even when my fast one was gone and wouldn't break a window. He still thought the day would come.

Anyhow, we'd go out to whatever town it was and I'd pitch—either start the game or come on in relief. And whether the crowd numbered 200 or 2000, the point is there was one guy in it who cared.

After my dad died there was none.

I think this is the thing for a boy to remember. As a coach, dads wear me out. They haunt me. They're on my back. They overrate the kid. They make excuses and they make demands.

They push too hard. But they care.

Sometimes I have to remind myself about that. Sometimes when I come home and slam into the house and hurl my problems at Helen (that's my long-suffering coach's wife) I snarl that I've had it up to here with some parental so-and-so.

But, ultimately, every time I get back to remembering that old guy who was my own dad. He's been dead for darn near a quarter of a century now, but he's brought me back from the silly side of rage a lot of times.

I remember the time I was 12 and my mother was very sick, and my dad was in a bind and there were no presents that year, only a note from Santa Claus in that careful hand that was my dad's.

What did he think a 12-year-old believed in anyhow!

Do you know something? I started believing in a lot of things that year. Again.

The dreams and the hope and the trust. And the quickly gone years. I don't want to preach a sermon in this season of sermons, but I wish I could convince a lot of young ones that they are lucky indeed to have the old man pulling hard on their side. Even if he sounds foolish sometimes. Even if he embarrasses you sometimes.

You won't find his like again, lad. No one else—anywhere—will care like that again.

If you're lucky, it happens once. Never twice.

JOE DONOVAN

My father's reference to Joe Garagiola below was because in August of 1970, Garagiola, in his nationally broadcast radio program, had read excerpts from an article my dad had written about the relationship between two well-known sports figures, Gale Sayers and Brian Piccolo (see article in the "Sports and Society" section).

This article is about Joe Donovan. He was a man not known by many but respected by my dad. He was a father to four boys who played football for him. The next is an article written upon Joe's death.

* * *

"Joe Donovan/Dad/Good Man"
Published in "Something to Crowe About"
Green Bay Register
October 16, 1970

Joe Garagiola won't be using this piece. Neither will any other broadcaster on the big time. It's not the kind of thing that would evoke national interest. It's not about important people and no big names show up here today.

THE WRITINGS OF MARTY CROWE 2.

This is a piece about a good guy.

Recently, I have been pretty vocal in this space—and, maybe, sometimes, a little bitter—about the kind of fan—or the parents of players—who don't give us the time of day when the team is losing. I noticed, though, after our homecoming game, which we blew by two, that quite a number of considerate people are still around.

This is about one of them—but this one is really special.

What brought it to my mind at this time was this. We had our team Mass in the school library on the day of the game. Saturday. Our cheerleaders were there, and they should've been, only lots of cheerleaders never show—but we have some dedicated girls in the green and gold this year.

A couple of others, besides the team, were there—and this man I'm writing about was one of them, and his wife was there, too.

When I first hit this town 11 years ago, I had one of his sons on my team. That was John and the marks by which you knew him were cooperation and courage.

He was a quiet boy who went out on the field, in practice or at games, and gave it all he had. Every time.

Now I have the last of the sons, Terry. The marks are still the same. He is quiet and he is brave, and he gives a coach no sweat nor trouble. You can trust the boy. You can believe in him.

In between these two I had Larry and I had Joe. Quiet guys. No big statements about what they were going to do. Nor what they had done. No boasts nor threats. No talk at all.

Only a lot of performance on the field.

Larry made the Associated Press Allstate team. It's unusual for the big city crowd to pick a boy from up this way—and especially from a little Catholic high. No one but Larry ever made it from our school.

He gave it no mind.

A man wonders about that. In a time when almost everyone puts on the big mouth act—in sports or business or whatever—how come a boy who is the best just does his job and keeps the peace? How come all the brothers were like that—and most of them were pretty close to Larry in what they could do—and did.

I think the answer is in the dad.

We push our kids. I push mine. I have a son in the eighth grade who shows some promise and I have to grab myself to keep from pushing. I have an older boy in college who has done some things pretty well and I want to shout about it. I guess that's natural. But I try to cool it. In my better moments, I do.

So, I can understand all the dads who come on so strong about their sons. They feel as I do about mine. I can understand it and I can repeat that that is natural—and maybe that's why I marvel so much at Joe Donovan.

He came into Mass and the advancing years have left their mark and he has a hard time getting around now, but he was there.

In all the time I've had his sons—and like I say, there were four of them—he's never given me any guff or any heat. I'm sure he did not agree with my field strategy at times. Sometimes it was really bad. Sometimes I second-guessed myself from here to Fargo.

But not Joe Donovan.

I'm not blaming the other guys. Like I say my impulses are like theirs. We are dads but so is Joe. I have never seen a family in which the bond is closer. The kids grow up and go away, but they come home. There is a union there—and a great love. They don't have too much of worldly wealth I'm sure—and they've had their share of trouble and tragedy, too.

But they go on.

There is a kind of strength there. Or maybe you can see what is strong because there are no speeches to distract you.

Or get in the way.

Every coach on our staff rates Terry Donovan at the top. Every coach we ever had rated all the brothers the same way. There has to be a reason for something like that.

I think the reason is that man who knelt beside me at Mass Saturday. And that good woman kneeling beside him.

I like to coach the boys because they are like their old man.

In a time when many are concerned or even desperate—about things like generation gap and the crumbling of family ties, and many others—including some pretty positive big men of the cloth—come on strong and clear and much too loud and certainly much too long—about the answers in the psychology books—I'd say take a look at one farm family out there.

There's so much more than sports involved here. And there has to be an answer to the question why.

I think we know what it is—you and I. But we may ignore it and continue to beat our chests like Tarzan and shout our boastful cry down the wind. And wind up simply loud and surely pathetic.

And teach our thousand sons to be the same.

* * *

"Joe Donovan, A Tribute on His Passing"
Published in "Something to Crowe About"
Green Bay Register
February 27, 1976

The man had class…

Mara was home alone when the phone rang and whoever it was said: "Tell your dad his good friend, Joe Donovan, is dead."

My good friend?

Say it better that Joe Donovan was one man I admired and respected above most I've met in this life. I only ever talked with him about half a dozen times during the 12 years I was in Marinette. I have not seen him since I left.

But I sure miss him.

I guess Joe Donovan epitomized for me what a father can really be. I don't think the family ever made very much financially. I suspect it was a struggle through the years.

But Joe Donovan spent no time on the self-pity trip.

I never visited at the Donovan home out there in the Porterfield area. I guess you could say Joe was just a farmer who fought the good fight all the way to the end. I know tragedy touched the family several times. Seared it but did not destroy.

I coached four of the Donovan boys. They were among the best football players I ever had up there. Often, well-intentioned parents seem to feel you owe them if their sons play for you. Joe was not like that.

He used to come to some of the games, in my final years up there, when it was obviously an effort for him to climb up the steps in the stands. But he made it. Sometimes, when I blew a game we should have won, I'm sure Joe must've felt like at least asking: "How come you didn't…"

He never did.

Joe Donovan and his wife were an inspiration to me through all the years up there, although I doubt they ever knew that. I never met a man for whom I had more respect.

Respect and downright affection.

I think that Mick—and most of his peers and most of the rest of us—believe that wealth or achievement or prestige or power keeps that from happening. Only that isn't what it is. Powerful men die and I do not care. Whatever it was that Joe Donovan had—and was—that makes a man more than a number.

He won't be bending the ear of God very often. Not his style. He will listen well. And when he does say something, God will know it is worth His while to listen, too.

Joe had class…

MOTHERS OF ATHLETES

"Praise for Mothers of Athletes"
Published in "Something to Crowe About"
Green Bay Register
December 19, 1975

A couple of weeks ago I wrote a column about a young man named Dave Lefeber who played football for JFK. I said the all-state selectors should've taken a look at him and that they have not done so. I said I was writing a piece so that his mother, who is gravely ill, would know, if she were able to read the column, how I felt about Dave as a boy and as a football player.

I don't know if she ever got to read the column or not. Mrs. Lefeber died during the early hours of Wednesday morning.

I thought today (I came back from the funeral a little while ago) would be a good time to write about the mothers—and the dads—of the boys who play the game. Anywhere. Because what Dave Lefeber's mother was like is the way a good many mothers of athletes are—and somebody should give them the time of day and few of us ever do.

As a coach, I can tell you that the worst times I've ever had have been with some of the parents of the players. (If you see me walk by sometime, take a look at my back. There are scores of parents still there from long ago.) I used to resent that fact very much until I began—after a while—to understand it.

The dads and the mothers on any coach's back are the ones who care. Too much. All right. I grant that, and that sometimes is the trouble. But in a time when a lot of parents care too little or not at all—well, I'll take the ones who do, no matter how inconvenient it may be sometimes.

I've had three Lefeber brothers here at prep—Danny, Dave, and Doug. All had athletic talent, and all were first rate human beings. And their greatest fan—by far—was their mother. She was sick for a long time, but she managed to get to every game to which the doctor would possibly let her go.

And her eyes were on her boys—in pride and joy and hope—and above all love. Years ago, long before there was a JFK prep, in other places far away, I used to resent mothers like that.

I was a fool.

I remember a line from some of the talks I used to give: "I quit going to little league baseball games after a while because there were so many mothers around second base that I couldn't tell who was playing shortstop."

A clever line. Oh, clever. Always good for a big laugh.

And true. Everyone has seen it. Everyone has deplored them. Others have made other wisecracks about them. Some have written sarcastic essays attacking them.

Once I would have said "amen." Now I say, "forget it."

That woman they buried this morning made me realize—more than any other—that this kind of devotion and dedication—Most of all, of caring—is much too rare in this old world right now. I have seen so many examples—right here at Prep—of kids whose "old man" or "old lady" do not care at all. Of some who think all you need to do is slip the lad a few bucks and all is well.

No way, man. Ask such a kid about it sometime. No way.

So today, because of the way Marian LeFeber was, I salute all the mothers and dads who go overboard on the side of their sons out on the field or on the basketball floor. It would be nice if you could cool it just a little sometimes, because a coach does have feelings, too—but keep that loyalty and that love alive. The thing is—you care.

In a world grown tired with sophistication and cynicism there are not many others who do.

Thanks, Marian Lefeber, for bringing me to remember that.

SPORTS AND SOCIETY

JACKIE ROBINSON

Sports held a central place in my father's life, from his youth playing with neighborhood kids, to competitive sports in high school and college, and dreams of playing professionally. When that dream was over, he discovered the reward in being a high school coach for nearly 50 years. My father observed and commented on sports at all levels, professional, college, but had a special affinity for high school. He also always enjoyed what he called "the freckle-nosed brigade" who would hail him on the street to talk about the season or a game. He admired the coaches who found time to work with young players.

My father knew that sports could inspire us to become our better selves, but he was also aware of the insidious tendencies in our society that plagued sports. He called out racial bigotry and praised those who stood up to it. He addressed the issue in his weekly radio show.

* * *

"Jackie Robinson"
WEAU Radio Show Script
May 27, 1947
(found handwritten in pencil)

Every now and then something happens in this world that makes you proud to be a member of the human race.

More often it's the other way around, but this week it is with a real, deep down, feeling of admiration and gratitude that I offer orchids to Ford Frick, president of the National League.

As most of you know there's something different under the sun this year in the National League—and it's Jackie Robinson, the first baseman for the Brooklyn Dodgers—and what's different about Jackie is that he is a Negro.

He's a lot of other things besides: A darn good ball player; a clean training, clean living, clean talking, clean playing gentleman on and off the field; a graduate of the University of California at Los Angeles, UCLA, where he was an All-American football halfback—all in all he's a great credit to the game.

He is also a Negro. And despite the fact that we have recently finished a war dedicated to the proposition that race prejudice and religious prejudice and nationality prejudice is an unnatural and a vicious thing—despite the fact that one of the great charges against the Nazis is that they were guilty of such prejudice and hatred—despite all that, there are plenty of people here in America who are denying a man his rights as a man because of the way he spells his name—or because of the color of his skin.

Be it said to the credit of the Dodgers that they accepted Jackie as a ball player and teammate and let it go at that.

And be it said to the disgrace of baseball and particularly be it said that the St. Louis Cardinals and a few others have been responsible for the snake of race bigotry raising its ugly head.

The Cardinals recently let it be known through the behind-the-scenes grapevine, that they were going to refuse to play at Brooklyn if Jackie Robinson remained on the team. I don't say all the Cardinals took that stand because I choose to not believe that all the Cardinals are either that arrogant or narrow or un-American. But enough of them felt that way to make an issue of it.

Ford Frick, as one magazine editor points out, could have done three things in this crisis.

First of all, he could have done nothing—which is getting to be the popular response from pussyfooting cowardly leaders in many types of situations.

Secondly, he could have told the Cardinals, privately, that they'd better not go through with their plan.

But Ford Frick chose a third course.

He issued a point blank, public ultimatum to the Cardinals and everyone else who might feel the same way that if they went through with the plan, those involved would be suspended from the National League. That anyone pursuing similar tactics—no matter from what team he came—would also be suspended. That this policy would be followed no matter, to quote Frick, if it meant wrecking the National League for five years.

So, I say bravo! Ford Frick. Would that we had more men in high places in sports and everywhere else—with the courage—we have a shorter word for it in the sports world—with the courage to take such a stand.

And if the players concerned don't like it, then I suggest they lump it. And I suggest further that baseball—and athletics in general—would be better off if they pulled out of it.

So good luck, Jackie Robinson. May your success or failure be determined in the real American way—by how well you can or cannot hit and field and throw—rather than by how you would look in technicolor.

Marty and Terry on the front steps, c. 1950.

BLACK BALLPLAYERS

In 1950 Eau Claire was home to a minor league baseball team, the Eau Claire Bears. That year the first two Black players arrived in a predominantly White community that had mixed feelings about their presence. The team was searching for housing accommodations for them, and knowing my father had a large rooming house, contacted him. He said, "Sure send them over, and send a couple of other players, too. It's a big place." So, they lived at our house. My mom sometimes made breakfast for them as restaurants were not always welcoming. My family enjoyed hosting them, especially my big brother who was just a little kid then.

I found two pieces my dad wrote about that year. The first, written in 1951, was published in a national magazine, Catholic Digest. The second written in 1953, was a typed copy. I don't know if the 1953 piece was ever published. I am including both here.

* * *

"Our Town's Negro Ball Players"
Catholic Digest
May 1951

The Northern League is a Class C baseball setup in the upper Midwest. The cities represented are typically American. The Bears, one of the teams in the league, signed two Negro players. The Bears represent a city of 40,000. A tire manufacturing plant is its industrial backbone. I live in this city, and it's a pretty city. Many of its people are friendly, and I like it here.

The sports page in our newspaper announced last spring that the two Negroes would play for the Bears. Contributors to a department called *The Voice of the People* started a heated discussion. Some professed alarm at the arrival of two colored players. They said the two Negro boys might like it in our city. Then they'd pass the word along, soon other Negroes would wish to come, and before you could say Jackie Robinson, property values would begin to fall.

Other voices pointed out that we had never had a racial problem in our city and said that we should beware of importing such a problem. On the other hand, voices proclaimed horror that our city should even dare to consider the practice of discrimination. Many letters were written. Some got rather heated. But after a while, the team came to town and the two Negro boys came with them.

One of the Negroes was a tall outfielder from Philadelphia; the other was a short, right-handed pitcher from Texas. The pitcher was very quiet and very black. The outfielder was sort of brown in color. He was also handsome. Further, he had fine manners, and a nice smile with flashing teeth.

The secretary of the Bears called me the day the team hit town. She said they couldn't find a place for the Negro boys to room, and asked whether they could room at our house. We have a large house with several vacant rooms. I said they could come over. I also asked for two more players, as we had room for four. So, the two colored boys and two white boys roomed at our house last summer.

The Negro boys roomed together because somebody from the board of directors said that was "preferable." But the room occupied by the white boys adjoined that of the colored boys, which was "permissible," and they were in and out of each other's rooms all summer. This was also permissible.

The outfielder with the splendid teeth became the star of the team and of the league. Late in the season he was voted "rookie of the year," and he set a new league record for stolen bases. Also, he could cover more ground defensively than any other Class C outfielder I ever saw. He was very good.

He was so good that a lot of people were able to forget he was a Negro and called him Bill. They would shout, "Steal, Bill! Steal!" And laugh when the opposing pitcher got nervous trying to hold Bill on first.

Bill really had a good personality, and considerable education. He also had a girlfriend, Negro, and her picture was always on the table in his room. Quite a few girls from town called him up and tried to date him, but to my knowledge no one ever succeeded.

Roy, the little pitcher, was not so smooth as Bill. He was very lonely and sometimes almost forlorn. But he had a mighty fastball, and for a while he was the best pitcher on the team. The girls started to call him up, too, and since he didn't go steady, he would talk with them and even kid with them a little. Sometimes a girl would walk with him from the ballpark all the way downtown.

Someone told me to tell him he had better cut out walking with white girls like that, so I did, and he did—but one girl was in love with him, I think. And I think he was in love with her, too. Or maybe he was just lonely because he wasn't nearly so popular as Bill. Anyhow, she used to come to the house after the games were over, about 10:30 at night, and they'd sit on the porch steps and talk. And they laughed a lot.

One night, in one of the Dakotas' cities, Roy almost beaned a batter. He was pretty wild, most of the time. The player came after him with a bat and said no black so-and-so was going to dust him. But all the Bears rallied around and insisted that if the irritated young man was going to attack a black so-and-so, he better pick somebody besides Roy, because Roy was a Bear.

I almost forgot to mention the kids. Our neighborhood is full of kids, and their favorite ball player was Roy. Maybe it was because he had more time for them than anyone else on the team since he had more time anyhow. Whatever the reason, the kids liked him, and they almost wore out our doorbell ringing it and asking, "Is Roy home?"

My son Terry liked Roy, too. Terry was only a year old last summer. He and Roy had some great times together. I think Roy was happiest when he was with Terry.

Roy hurt his arm early in the season, and before the summer was over the Bears had to let him go. He was downhearted the morning he left for home. Roy really loved baseball. I suppose I'll never see him again. He left an autographed ball for Terry, and someday I'll tell Terry about him, and about color and all that. Terry hasn't got to words yet, though and when I tell him, I hope the words won't get in the way.

Well, that's about it. The summer ended, and Bill the outfielder went home, too. We rented the rooms to someone else. Property values stayed about the same.

Our town is pretty proud of the way they treated Bill and Roy. I've heard it said that "for every guy that was agin' 'em there was ten who wasn't." And I guess that's right. Lots more heat was put on manager Andy Cohen, "that dumb kike," than ever was directed at the Negro boys. Of course, now that Cohen has been moved up to manage Class A Denver next year, most of his critics "always knew Andy had it in him. For a Jew, he was some guy, Andy was."

But in its pride over the way it treated the two Negro ball players, I hope our town understands that it took Bill in because he was the great star, and because his personality and his cleanliness and his good looks overcame the obstacle of his race. In other words, it accepted him in less essential things. But it should know, too, that there was a fine, fierce pride in Bill which would have survived anyhow. Bill's contempt for the crude and the callous was strong enough to ride out any storm, I think.

It was Roy we hurt because he was vulnerable. We liked him in my town. We liked the "swift" he had on the ball, and the courage he had in his heart. But we never quite took him in—except for a girl who laughed softly in the late evening quiet, and a lot of kids who choose their heroes their own way, and a year-old boy named Terry.

SUMMER 1950

"Summer 1950, Two Young Men Shared a Room"
Typewritten manuscript
c. 1953

Two young men shared a sleeping room in Eau Claire, Wisconsin in the summer of 1950. Both were professional baseball players—both had ability—both had dreams.

One went on to the mountain tops—one disappeared somewhere along the trail. Billy Bruton is in the major leagues today. His roommate is lost in oblivion.

I knew them both during that summer that seems long gone now. I lived in the same house.

Bill Bruton wore the cap of destiny from the beginning. He did everything right. He was the fastest outfielder probably, that the Northern League ever had. He made the countless, incredible catches all that summer in every park in the league. And although he occasionally had trouble getting to first base, he didn't stay there long once he made it. He was the most exciting base runner most of us had ever seen.

Besides that, he had a way with him. A grin and a flair and a bounce and a vividness that made any crowd come alive.

Off the field, he was quiet but obviously educated. He was independent and wore no man's collar—yet he was friendly, too—relaxed and easy-going.

He was chosen rookie of the year that season. Name the rookie of the decade and it would still be Bruton.

His roommate was a little guy, and though he was very black in color his name was White. Roy White.

It is a name and a man I shall remember forever.

Roy didn't have much to recommend him except a fireball that hopped all over the place—and a great, courageous heart. The fans liked him, but he was never an idol like Bill was. Roy never was meant for a hero's garb.

He'd stand on that mound and the swift in his arm and the joyous jump in his fast one kept the batters loose and cagey. And because Roy was very small and slightly built, the fans found a surging glee in watching him mow down the opposition strong boys.

Yet Roy was—and remained—a lonely man.

Off the field he said very little because, I think, words didn't come to him so easily. He'd been around but his education in schools had been pretty limited.

Talking came pretty hard for Roy.

Maybe that's why he had so much time for the kids.

I mean, maybe it was because he was lonely and alone—and never quite sure of himself except when he stood on that mound facing the bats of the enemy—maybe that's why he had the time to be with the kids—and the inclination.

You don't need personality nor oratory nor an English tweed coat to rate with kids. You need, instead, a belief that kids are important. Not many believe that—not really. And the kids know it and remember it. Roy did believe it—and the kids knew that too.

He was their number one guy.

They liked Bill Bruton because he leveled with them too (a lot of ball players don't do that). But Bill was a part of many people's plans. Roy wasn't.

Roy belonged to the boys on our block.

They must have nearly worn out the doorbell that summer. And they must have been tough on Roy too. But the doorbell lasted. And so did Roy.

He'd play catch with them—and bring them a ball once in a while.

I remember it was a short time after the team in Sioux Falls had threatened to "get that black so-and-so" because he accidentally rocketed his fast one close to the head of one of the Canaries big stars that I saw Roy playing catch with Red and Al.

The Bears—that's the Eau Claire team—had rallied round when the Sioux Falls gang turned on the heat. Roy was their boy, and no bunch of hotheads was going to give him the business because he happened to be the wrong color. Not while they were around to make sure it didn't happen.

Of course, when they came back they did continue to buy their dinner in the restaurant that drew the color line on Roy and wouldn't let him cross it. But that, of course, was a different matter. That was business—and a man's business was his own. And the steaks, when they were in the chips, were better there.

I couldn't help the feeling when I watched Roy tossing that ball back to Red and Al—Red the tough guy and Al the poet—both nine-years old—I couldn't help but be sure that they wouldn't have eaten the best steak in the house in a place where their buddy wasn't welcome. Kids have big eyes and big appetites—but most of them also have a code for living that most of them lose later on. One part of it says you never welch on a pal. Another part says you never play the angles.

Maybe someday Al will be able to quote Wordsworth about all of us being closest to Heaven in our infancy. But for right now neither he nor Red need any quotes or references. Some things are right and some "ain't right"— and that makes it pretty simple after all.

I like to remember how Roy took to my son who wasn't quite two years old in those days. And how Terry had an evident and vocal appreciation of Roy.

They had some great times together. Or maybe good is the word. It's a better word anyhow.

I think Roy was happiest when he was with my son. He was relaxed then. He didn't have to worry about modes or meanings or angles or arrangements. Terry didn't like him in spite of his being a Negro. Terry liked him, period.

Someday I'll give my son the autographed baseball Roy left for him when he went away. By that time Terry will have learned words. I hope they won't get in the way.

Roy's arm went bad late that summer and the team let him go.

He was pretty "down" that last day. I talked with him while he waited for the bus to begin the long ride back to Texas. He knew, I guess, that for him the dream was over.

He'd been pitching in semi pro or professional baseball since his thirteenth year, he told me once, and he had feared his baseball days had about run out. Now he knew.

"Thank your wife for all she did for me," Roy said as he got on the bus. "I won't forget it—or you either."

We had, of course, done nothing. Except to live with Roy as we lived with Don Easton, the grocer—Or Fred Skinner, the garage mechanic. In other words—offhand. Man-to-man.

Like a kid.

We got a letter from Roy later on. Just one. The spelling wasn't good—and the grammar no better.

But it carefully told us that Roy was in the army—and thanked us once more for whatever it was Roy was grateful for.

That was still the fall of 1950—and there have been some bitter days between then and now for ex-baseball pitchers—and others—in the army.

We've never heard from Roy again.

I got to remembering this now as Billy Bruton's first fine year in the Majors ends.

I learned a lot from Bill that summer. Most of all I learned what it is to have the clear courage of knowing you're doing right and thus to be shielded against the twisting darts of the petty and the perverted ones.

Bill had that.

But I learned more from Roy because from him I learned that it is easy to wound the vulnerable—and that is the greatest crime of all. People who clung to the trailing clouds of greatness which so obviously followed Bill Bruton found it easy to turn the other side of their hand—or their door—to the little guy headed nowhere who shared Billy's room.

There is something shameful in hitting the helpless ones—God knows it is a popular pastime.

Anyhow, maybe Roy White, wherever he is, would like to know this. This summer when the Braves came to town Bill Bruton and Harry Hanebrink stopped in to see me. I wasn't home so I missed them but Helen, my wife, mentioned to some of the neighborhood kids that Bill Bruton had been in.

"Gee," said one, and his eyes were big because Bill has had a lot of ink in Eau Claire this year.

"You mean the real Bill Bruton?" another said. But it was the third kid I remember. "Did Roy come with him?" he asked.

Like I say, kids choose their heroes their own way—and they name their own dimensions.

Roy White & Bill Bruton
(Photos Courtesy of *Eau Claire Leader Telegram*)

GALE SAYERS AND BRIAN PICCOLO

In 1965 Gale Sayers and Brian Piccolo came to the Chicago Bears as rookies. They were both running backs. Coach George Halas decided they would also be roommates, the first time in the NFL that a Black player and White player roomed together. They became great friends. Piccolo helped Sayers work his way back to health from what could have been a career ending knee injury in 1968. Sayers was at Piccolo's side as he battled testicular cancer. Diagnosed in 1969, Piccolo died on June 16, 1970. Only a few weeks before Piccolo's death, Sayers received the George Halas Award for Most Courageous Player. He accepted the honor at a ceremony that night but said that the next day the award was going to Brian Piccolo.

My dad wrote about these two men and their remarkable friendship.

* * *

"Gale Sayers and Brian Piccolo"
Published in "Something to Crowe About"
Green Bay Register
June 26, 1970
(Joe Garagiola later featured this story on his nationally broadcast radio show.)

I first saw Gale Sayers in a movie of the college football season—on television—a number of years ago. I had never heard of the guy before but when he came on the screen, running the ball for somebody, (Kansas?) I said to the young man sitting watching the show with me, "that's the greatest running back the game has ever seen."

I don't know whether my friend agreed with me or not, and I know it was a pretty big statement to make. But nothing has happened, since, to change my mind.

When Gale came up with that twisted knee late in the 1968 season, I figured he was through. I've seen that kind of injury before—and I've rarely seen a man come back from one.

Sometimes the knee heals pretty well but the memory of the tremendous pain and the extensive damage to cartilage and tendon remains. A guy can't forget—and so he's through just as surely as though the injury had never healed at all.

So the award they gave to Gale Sayers in New York a few weeks ago as pro football's most courageous athlete went to the right man. That's for sure. I had watched him all season as he went up against those huge, aggressive tackles and linebackers. Maybe a bit of the old quickness was gone. I waited for him to hesitate—to flinch. To quit.

He didn't quit.

Before that, I had admired Gale for his blazing speed and drive and agility. I admired him much more last year for a much rarer quality.

Bravery.

But the finest hour for Gale Sayers came on the night they gave him the award. This is what he said:

"You flatter me by giving me this award. But I tell you, here and now, I accept it for Brian Piccolo. Brian Piccolo is the man of courage who should receive the award. It is mine tonight. It is Brian Piccolo's tomorrow."

I had watched Piccolo fill in for Sayers in the latter part of the season of '68. He wasn't Gale but he was something to see. Nobody had drafted Brian out of college because he was too small for the pros. He wasn't too small when I saw him play. Some small men are bigger than other men the same size.

In November of 1969 they took Brian Piccolo out of the game, and he did not come back. Ever. I'd heard he was ill. I didn't know how bad.

"I love Brian Piccolo," Gale Sayers said that night of the white man who was his roommate. "and I'd like all of you to love him, too. When you hit your knees to pray tonight, please ask God to love him, too."

Well, that was three weeks ago, and Brian Piccolo is dead now. He was sicker than we knew.

"He was so young to die with a future that held so much," George Halas said. "But Brian made the most of the brief 26 years allotted to him, and he will not be forgotten."

I'm not sure about that, George. We forget pretty easily. And Brian Piccolo was never the big time name. Even tonight, as I write this, there is a copy of the Minneapolis

Star in front of me and there is a notice of Brian's funeral. It will be Friday, the paper says, and the Mass will be said at Christ the King Church in Chicago.

But the note is a small one—and it's on the third page of the sports section. I don't know if Brian Piccolo will be very long remembered.

But maybe he will be—because of you. Gale Sayers.

For one thing—the idea that a black man and a white man can room together and that the black man can say, (and I suspect Brian would have said it the same of you) "I love Brian Piccolo"—that's something, Gale Sayers, in this time of hatred and of small and mean people—of all colors—who say this cannot be.

I will remember this. I think a lot of us will.

And then, Gale, you said there, "Please ask God to love him too."

You knew he was dying, didn't you? We did not know—but you knew.

I think God will love Brian Piccolo, Gale, because I think God loves the brave heart and a special breed of men.

And I think God loves the kind of white man who will room with a black man and not give the whole thing a second thought. I think God will love Brian, Gale.

Eternally.

But there is something else I will remember, Gale Sayers. And that is the fact that your mind and your words turned to God. You must not know—or you must not believe—that sly and clever men have said that God is dead.

Or that there never was a God to begin with.

And then you said, "When you hit your knees to pray tonight." Those are your words, Gale Sayers.

Don't you know that prayer is out of date—and the picture of a man on his knees is from some forgotten time or age. We have come so very far since then.

But you knew Brian was dying didn't you, Gale Sayers? And you knew that, in spite of all the clever people and the brittle dialogue, that there comes a time when there's nowhere else to turn.

And a man goes—then—to his knees.

Hey, Gale—I hope that you have a great season next year. I hope you run wild against them all—even the Pack.

But no matter what happens or what you do or what they write about you or what awards they give you then or how many thousands stand to cheer your name—you have already known the greatest moment of your life.

"I love Brian Piccolo," you said.

That was your finest hour.

ATHLETES AS ROLE MODELS

My father believed athletes at all levels had a responsibility to serve as positive role models for the youth who looked up to them. He spoke to that issue on his weekly radio show.

* * *

"Responsibility of Athletes as Role Models to Kids"
WEAU Radio Show Script
c. 1948-50
Handwritten manuscript

I am going to talk for a while tonight about the responsibility which an athlete has to the fans—and particularly to the kids who happen to believe that their heroes can do no wrong.

It seems to me that a very large number of great and not-so-great athletes are wearing that responsibility very lightly these days. A lot of them are going in for a type of drinking and carousing and personal disaffection to which, frankly, I don't think they have any right.

I realize that this is a free country, and I realize, too, that a man has a right to live his life as he chooses to live it.

An athlete, it seems to me, has to make a choice. If he chooses to be an athlete in the public eye—and a hero to a lot of kids—then he has to give up the right to violate the standards of decent human conduct which he might otherwise insist on.

If he hasn't the willpower and the courage and the forthrightness and wisdom to give up such a right, then he should give up athletics. It's that simple.

When our high school team came back from winning the state championship at DePere, a father in this city brought his son over to meet me.

Now, I am not a great athlete. I just happened to be the coach of a good ball club, but in the eyes of this eight-year-old that made me something special—and he wanted to meet me. I shook hands with him very solemnly—and talked to him very seriously. And it is more of an honor than either you or I would be likely to deserve that that was a great day for that boy.

All right then.

Do I have the right, then, to let that kid see me as a drunkard, or to let him hear me sounding off with filthy or blasphemous language? Do I have the right, having accepted my little place in the athletic sun, to violate the moral laws by which that boy should, in all decency, live?

The answer is certainly no. I do not have that right.

And neither do you Mr. High School halfback or Mr. College high scoring forward or Mr. Bears hard-hitting outfielder.

The hero's role is pleasant to play—but no man has the right to introduce his own ad lib lines which don't belong in the part.

It is no excuse to say that you fought a war—and your bad habits are a consequence of that fight. It is no excuse because there is no excuse.

If you aren't willing to play your role according to a script which will make the boys who have taken you for their idol or model or hero—which will make them better boys—or at least not make them worse ones—then get out of the game. Let a better man take over.

If you don't, you're fundamentally not much of an athlete—and certainly not much of a man.

Babe Ruth used to get out of line but when he grew up, he realized his responsibility and he got back in again.

Jack Dempsey did, too.

Knute Rockne never forgot it for an instant. Neither did Amos Alonzo Stagg.

Neither, for that matter, has Joe Louis, for the most part. Nor Bob Feller, say, nor Hank Greenberg. And I like to remember Bruce Smith when he was as great a back as Minnesota ever had. And do you recall Iowa's Nile Kinnick? And say—does the name Lou Gehrig mean anything to you?

These men were great athletes. They were also great men. They knew it was better that they should have failed on the field of competitive sport—than that they should have gained a victory there—only to betray those who kept them on a high bright pedestal, by their actions later on.

I know a lot of college coaches who have told me that it's more unpleasant to coach a college team today than ever in their memory before. Their reason, the athletes want the glory without the sacrifice. Too many swelled—heads and headline hunters over-conscious of their rights—blind to their responsibilities

A professional athlete has the same duty.

I've known too many very swell guys who played professional ball to become one of those who sneer at those who play for pay. If you, for instance, can name me a finer man than the great Walter Johnson, who died a few months ago leaving behind a clean, shining legacy for every kid who will ever want to pitch a baseball fast, I'd like to know who he is.

Recently, however, the pros, like their college, and some of their high school brethren, have begun to fly pretty high.

The boxers and the football players have begun to listen to the siren call of the quick and easy dollar. The gamblers have begun to move in.

And there are other things.

There is Leo Durocher, for instance.

I have always liked Durocher from the time he was a cocky kid playing shortstop for Saint Paul. He had courage and a flaming spirit and color and in my book he rated high. The Leo Durocher of the St. Louis Gashouse Gang belongs among the few who will never die in my sports memory.

But the blatant Durocher of the Dodgers, talking too much, too loud, and too often—dragging his love affairs across the pages of the nation's press—sneering at judicial opinion—making a mockery of the pretext of those who still see the family as a somehow sacred thing—such a Lippy Leo is not the Durocher I want to remember. Such a Durocher has, in my opinion, no right to be manager of the fabulous Dodgers—and the idol of millions of kids from Flatbush and The Bronx to the sunny slopes of California.

Some objector well might argue that an athlete is an entertainer, and that Hollywood has shown that entertainers have a code of conduct uniquely their own.

Hollywood, may I point out, is a stench in the nostrils of the world—and Hollywood stars are hardly the idols of American youth—the male end of it anyhow.

I'd like to tell Leo Durocher—and others in high places—a little story.

It's about a big broad-shouldered guy who used to play ball for Columbia University. He was an easy-going guy with a big grin, and he could hit that apple a country mile.

The fabulous Yankees brought him up as a rookie, but it didn't look as though he'd ever get in that lineup until one day the star New York first baseman Wally Pipp got hurt. And that was the day this big, raw rookie took over on that first sack. He stayed there for 15 years. Through good days and bad—through hitting streaks and slumps—through charley horses—smashed fingers—sprained wrists—bumps and bruises—all the ills to which baseball flesh is heir to, he stayed on. He became one of the greatest hitters of all time—and along with the Babe and Lazerri and the rest, he made the Yankees perhaps the most powerful ball club ever to take the field.

In the process, he made a million friends. His name became part of household conversation—and across the nation dirty-faced kids with a ball glove slung in their belts dreamed of the day when they might be like him.

He played hard. He lived clean. His was a shining kind of courage—and somehow no one ever was quite so much the real American as this big son of Dutch parents was.

Then suddenly in 1938 he slowed down. He couldn't get to those grounders anymore. He couldn't tag that ball. The sports world was startled. But gamely the big guy fought on. Then one day—May 2, 1939—he came to manager McCarthy and asked to be taken out of the lineup. After 2130 games in a row, there were the Yankees without him.

He never came back.

Finally, the word was passed down the line. He had some strange disease—a sort of chronic polio—and his muscles were drying up.

He was dying.

On July 4, one of the greatest spectacles in sports history took place in Yankee Stadium. Babe Ruth was there. Earl Combs. Bob Meusel. Joe Dugan. Tony Lazzari. Herb Pennock. Aaron Ward. All the fabulous names that had made the Yankees through the years had come—to say goodbye to—Lou Gehrig. His Mom and Dad were there too. And Eleanor, his wife.

And Lou stood out there on that old familiar diamond with all his old teammates around him—and he brushed his hand across his eyes—and he said, "With all this, I consider myself the luckiest man on the face of the Earth."

That was Gehrig's farewell.

On June 2, 1940—he died.

And everywhere on earth where men follow the game, there was a strange new sadness that day.

Something that was great and good and fine and clean had left the world.

No man in sports history was ever loved more than Lou Gehrig was.

No one has ever worn his old Number 4 since that day—and his locker remains sealed. But he'll always live on in the hearts of his friends.

And all the great names of our day might do well to profit by his example.

Marty recording a radio broadcast on WEAU, a local station, c. 1948-50.

ADVOCATE FOR GOODNESS

LYNCHING

My dad was introduced to politics, as a six-year-old in 1921, campaigning with his father in his run for office. As an adult he spoke up for morality and justice in his writings, and as a teacher he informed students about the world and encouraged them to be good human beings.

My father spoke against racial injustice and challenged it in the sports world. He talked about it to his students, and he wrote about it.

I found this piece in the archives of the student newspaper The Aquin, at the College of St. Thomas in St. Paul, MN. My father wrote it when he was a young man of 23. It is a first-person narrative that describes a lynching at a place called Sandy Hill. It is not a factual account, but rather it is one of a series of articles he wrote in narrative style to focus attention on real problems in our society. Though the account is fictional, lynchings were real.

* * *

"Lynching Usurps Authority, Puts Brute in Power"
The Aquin
December 3, 1937

I say to you, America, that I was at Sandy Hill. I saw what happened there.

They lynched this man because he was little and frightened and black and because they were many and he was all alone. And they were savage and bruted and blind. They said to him, "Have you anything to say, you murderin' skunk, before we string you up."

And that little black man whose name was George Washington Jones had known there was no hope, and he said, "White man, you did not understand. White man, you did not try."

And so they hanged him—that blood hungry mob. They sated their hate and their lust. And then they licked their foul lips and went home and to bed. And America did nothing about it. America let it go by because America was too busy patting itself on the back as the land of the free and the home of the brave; too busy reconsecrating its constitution and dedicating it to liberty eternal. May God have mercy, America, on your smug and selfish little soul.

For I say to you that the fact that that Negro was innocent is unimportant. It intensifies the crime, but what matters most is that at Sandy Hill, America gave its government back to the brutes—surrendered itself to a gang of bums and tramps and "respected citizens" with minds that were warped and twisted and inflamed. It allowed its courts of justice to be laughed to scorn; it's protective laws to be trampled upon. And there have been a thousand Sandy Hills.

In every case America should have acted. It should have sent those shrieking mobs of madmen crashing into the oblivion where they are so long overdue. If ever man has forfeited the right to free existence, those lust-ridden wretches have. But they have piled outrage on outrage, and nothing has been done. Drunk with their own power, they have come to fear neither God nor man.

And yet they are cowards of the rankest sort. Skulking in mobs, their courage is flaming and loud. Alone, they gibber in terror. But America has allowed them to continue in mobs because America has been busy making Fourth of July speeches proclaiming to the world that it is the cornerstone of world freedom, the foundation of true democracy.

But the accusing finger of George Washington Jones, like those of countless other martyrs, comes pointing from a forgotten grave. "White man, you did not understand. White man, you did not try."

Will America continue the hypocrite? Or will America send its resounding answer thundering to the long awaiting skies.

WHAT COLOR IS DEMOCRACY?

I found this composition handwritten on yellowed paper with a title page, neatly folded in the files. The piece appeared to have been written in my father's early teaching years and probably was never published. The cover page had his mother's return address so clearly, he was still a bachelor.

The essay contains some racial slurs in the dialog, so I hesitated to include it. I decided the content was too important to omit.

* * *

"What Color is Democracy?"

337 Iglehart Ave.
St. Paul, MN
Handwritten manuscript, c. 1943-44

It is important, first of all, that you understand that Lucille is patriotic. She sells war stamps in the factory where she works, and great is her vocal scorn for those she feels are not "digging deep enough." She has a "boyfriend" in General Bradley's army, and she has known from the beginning how low down the Germans are.

She also hates the "Japs" with complete dedication and obvious enthusiasm.

No, there can be little doubt of Lucille's patriotism. She shows all the accepted signs. Among other things, she dances with the boys at the USO. To "bolster their morale."

It was in connection with this latter of Lucille's patriotic contributions that the discussion of the Nisei came up. There are a large number of Japanese American soldiers from our city stationed at the front. Many have been overseas for a long time and have only recently returned.

"A Jap's a Jap," says Lucille. "Here and anywhere, you can't trust them."

"The Army trusts them," answers Joan who is ordinarily a rather timid girl. "The Army puts them in uniform."

"Yeh? You notice they don't use any of 'em in the Pacific though." Lucille is very sure of her ground on that one.

"Of course they do," Joan replies. "Last night's paper had pictures of a bunch of them just back from India, or Burma or somewhere. They'd been wounded."

"I don't believe it," says Lucille. "Anyhow, I, for one, won't trust 'em and nobody can make me. Talk to the boys who have been fighting 'em. They'll tell you."

"Our boys haven't been fighting the Nisei. They've been fighting right alongside them."

Lucille ignores this and makes her point. "I went to the USO last night and three different Japs asked me to dance. Catch me doin' it!"

"Aren't you supposed to dance with anyone who asks you?"

"They can't make me dance with a Jap. Not me."

"They won't make you, I guess. But why don't you stay away from the USO then? So many Japanese American soldiers go there now. Why don't you just skip it?"

"No Jap's gonna tell me where I can go! And no Jap's gonna dance with me. They're repulsive to me."

The formidable adjective surprises Joan. But only for a moment. Then she says, very quietly, "I wouldn't let it worry me if I were you, Lucille. You know—you may be repulsive to them too."

With that, Lucille flies into a vicious rage. (She has not spoken to Joan since—and she is busily engaged at present in loudly and frequently voicing her doubt of Joan's loyalty to this country and what it stands for.

Joan, opines Lucille, is not a true American.)

I want you to know that Grace is a patriot too.

Grace teaches in the same high school that I do. She has been in charge of our salvage drives. She has been responsible for our "welcome home" dinners for boys when they return. She has taken up collections for flowers for the families of our boys when we find out they are never going to return again.

Grace is patriotic for sure.

The other night Grace said to me, "One thing for sure—when the boys get home, first thing they're going to do is get the Jews."

I was surprised.

"What do you mean—'get' them?" I asked.

"Well, put 'em in their place anyhow."

"Why?" I said. "Are they out of their place? I didn't know they had one."

"Any boy in service will tell you," Grace assures me. "They get all the breaks. Make a lot of money out of the other guy. Gold brick. Wait'll the boys get home. You'll see."

"In other words, after we lick Hitler, we'll take over his techniques," I said. "Seems like a funny kind of war aim."

That gets Grace mad. I've got to work with her, so I shut up. I shouldn't though. I know that.

A year ago last Spring, when a gang of boys in the Detroit school at which I was teaching then deflated all the tires on an automobile parked near the school by four Negro women war plant workers, they were ready for my resulting anger. They were rather surprised to find my criticism echoed, and even surpassed, by my colleague in the social science department, who happened to be from Missouri.

"I'm ashamed to believe that boys from my class would have so little sense of what America is all about" he said.

But the defense of those who admire the unnamed vandals—and of those who blame them as well—is the same.

"N*****s are getting' way out of hand around here since the war started. They think they're big shots now. Ya got to keep 'em in their place."

I point out that the tendency toward pride and "cockiness" is not confined to Negroes these days but seems to be a result of a sudden financial affluence on the part of people who'd never experienced such a thing before. I point out that such a reaction is natural and to be expected. And that it is only temporary—that the collapse will be sudden and shocking.

My words are wasted.

"It's the n*****s."

A prominent citizen in the small city where I now teach and coach athletics, tells me that I've got to "close my eyes" to a few things the boys from the north end of town might do.

"They're all wops you know. No bringin' up. You can't blame the kids."

"For what?" I ask.

"Stealin' equipment. Smokin'. Drinkin' a little. Ya got to overlook some things."

"No I don't," I tell him. "Those Italian boys aren't stealing or drinking. In fact, they go to church every Sunday and some of them on weekdays too. And they have nice manners. And they're good kids. I like them. I think their folks have done a good job with them."

He looks at me and he doesn't believe me. He knows what "wops" are like. And "nobody's gonna tell him different."

Now that I'm home for summer vacation the lady on the corner is telling me again that the Jews put us in the war to make money out of it. The old maid down the block assures me that, "the n****r kids" will steal all the apples from the trees in my back yard as soon as they're worth stealing. The girl in the bakery is angry because her landlady "won't allow a girl to have her boyfriend up to her room—but she's letting a Jap soldier move his family into the apartment next to mine."

And I realize—every day the more—that the feeling of racial superiority on which Hitler so evilly capitalized is not confined to Germany. And that the hidden little hatreds in mankind that flare out with such increasing frequency in these days, is the stuff of which fascism is made.

And I know that next year more than ever, I must stand in my classroom and teach tolerance and humanity to one's fellow man. I know I must teach the American dream in its native land because that dream is foreign to so many of America's people.

I know that the paradox will recur in which I will be accused of being unpatriotic because I insist on those things for which this nation stands—and to foster those for which it was born.

I know that a salvage chairman who hates Jews will wrap her acts and words in the flag she knowingly or unwittingly betrays—and be accepted by many who reject me.

I know that many superintendents will continue to prefer that "nothing controversial" be discussed in the classroom—will mean, though they would label it otherwise, that American idealism is controversial.

And I know that many parents will want their children to learn "facts—not a mess of ideas and theories."

And I know that many students will quote radio columnists, newspaper writers, and various other commercial sages—not to mention ponderous politicians—to refute me. And I know that many will accept the prejudices drilled into them around the dinner table over anything I can say to break down such prejudices.

And I know many students will want to know, "where all this stuff is going to get me personally, anyhow. What I'm interested in is getting ready to earn a living."

I know all that.

But that's my job. As a teacher. As an American. As a human being. As a guy who believes in God.

It's up to me.

And, by the way, it's up to you, too.

You might almost call this a postscript to this article.

A few weeks ago, on the steps of the graduate building at the University of Michigan, I witnessed a meeting between two old friends. One was Japanese, about thirty, in regular civilian clothes. The other, a service man, about thirty-five, with overseas bars on his shirt. There was genuine affection on the face of each man as they met. And only slight embarrassment on that of the soldier when he offered his left hand in response to his friend's greeting.

His right arm hung nerveless and useless at his side.

A guy can learn a lot at a university if he keeps his eyes open.

COST OF WAR

My father lived through three wars. He saw pride, ambition, greed, or lust for power often set wars in motion. His concern was always for the soldier in the field and the ordinary people who fell victim to the carnage. He was concerned about the impact of war on our humanity.

* * *

"Cost of War to Our Humanity"
(Written in Response to the My Lai Massacre)
Published in "Something to Crowe About"
The Spirit *(excerpt)*
December 5, 1969

If the recent American atrocity stories out of Vietnam should prove to be true, it will underline something we have been talking about in our classes up here for more than a year now. War brutalizes men and a long and dreary war brutalizes them more than any other kind.

Not all men of course. The vulgarity and viciousness of the war raise some men up and ennobles them. A young man visited in my classroom recently who had signed to return to Vietnam. Reason? To help the people—and especially the kids.

The same lad related how he had seen men he knew descend into a kind of mindless cruelty.

"Some were pretty good guys," he said. "Then their buddies got killed and a lot of them went crazy."

"That's happened before," I said.

"Yeah. Only a lot of these guys stay that way. Coach, we've got guys now who are just plain killers. They just want to kill somebody and that's what they do."

"You think they'll change when they come home?"

"I don't know, coach. I wouldn't bet on it."

When the recent charges were made about the massacre of civilians at "Pinkville," I got to remembering what the Nazis had done at Lidice. I have told the story of what happened in that little town in Czechoslovakia many times, to a lot of classes, through the years.

> "The Nazis killed every male adult in the town. Then they took the women and the kids and put them on cattle trains and shipped them off—in different directions. It was supposed to terrorize the world. But the result was not terror but fury. The very name of the town became an abomination in the minds of men because of what had happened there."

Stalin used terror as a weapon. The starving of the farmers in Ukraine—his own people—which was as good an example as any. Hundreds of thousands of them.

"To teach them a lesson."

Perhaps we have learned the lesson, too.

I hope not. I do not readily accept every story and every tale that now comes down the line. I just think that we had better check the whole thing out—and if it checks, we better begin to ask ourselves what we have become—or may become.

I've talked to many young men who are opposed to this war. It is assumed by some that they are opposed because they don't want to fight—or they don't want to get shot at or die.

Maybe.

I suspect there are few of us who relish the idea of being shot at or killed. I don't believe the young men I talked with are more cowardly than you or I.

Or, to put it another way, that we are braver than they.

"I just don't want to kill those people," one boy told me. "I don't think they deserve to be killed."

Well—maybe some do. It begins to look like a lot were killed who did not deserve it.

This country has been a song in the wind. People believed in us when there was nothing else left to believe in. When the brutes on the political right and on the left were out there exterminating the people—there was always America.

We were hope—and faith. We seemed like we were kind.

If this goes down the drain of history, we are done. And the world is done. If that happens, there is nothing left.

That is why we must find out whether the orders for wiping out villagers came from higher up. Or whether—if our guys did these things—they were led to believe they were expected to do them.

It won't do to say the enemy is worse.

The evil of the enemy is what makes him the enemy. If we say that we may do the things they do—after all that we have said before—then we are fakes and frauds before men.

And we will be seen to be so.

I know that war is a dirty business. No man needs to tell me that. And I know that this war may be dirtier than the others have been.

I know what war is.

The question is—what are we?

BODY COUNTS

In the 1980s we were in the heat of the nuclear arms race and the threat of nuclear war loomed over us. The Catholic Bishops formed a committee to address the threat. That committee met for nearly two years, considering responses from hundreds of church leaders and government officials. Eventually they presented three drafts to the full conference of bishops. According to the New York Times (May 4, 1983) the document "caused the White House great concern and efforts were made to modify the drafts." The final draft from the U.S. Bishops became one of their most important pastoral letters, "The Challenge of Peace: God's Promise and Our Response." The document was affirmed by a vote of 238 to 9.

My father found more hope for our country and world in these moral leaders than in military leaders. Such voices are often discounted as being unserious, not credible. He challenged those assumptions.

* * *

"Body Counts"
St. Paul Pioneer Press
January 2, 1983

A lot of critiques have been written lately maintaining that bishops, nuns and housewives are hardly experts in nuclear physics and propulsion and related subjects. Therefore, they should all fade away, or at least shut up.

The bishops, however, (and I suspect nuns and housewives, as well) are not writing or talking about explosive destruction potential. They are hardly experts in that field and certainly do not try to sound as though they were. (The experts are all those guys in uniforms and medals who tell how to blow up the world but not how not to.)

The bishops are writing about something they do, presumably, know a bit about: God, human life, the sacred quality of life, the soul of a man, the souls of all men and eternity.

I doubt the planners of mutual destruction capability give a heck of a lot of thought to any of these things. They seem to regard life as something that could be thought of in terms of relative numbers, like in body counts.

GERALDINE FERRARO

In 1984, Geraldine Ferraro became the first woman nominated for vice president. She was the running mate for Walter Mondale, the Democratic candidate for president. There were those who thought having her second in line to be commander in chief would be risky. My dad had a different opinion.

* * *

"Macho Men Have Failed"
Milwaukee Journal
October 17, 1984

One of your syndicated columnists recently told us that he would be "frightened" to have Geraldine Ferraro in the big chair in Washington during a time of international crisis. He said it was because of her lack of savvy about military matters, but I could not escape the impression that he meant that, because she is a woman, she would not be "macho" enough to measure up.

Well, we've had a lot of macho men and macho statements coming from all sides for a long time now. I don't see that they have made the world a safer or more peaceful place to be. Maybe a few ideas from a woman might be the order along about now. It would be hard to be more absurd than the male warriors from a lot of nations have been.

If one does want to be "frightened" though, I would suggest that he remember that it was George Bush, our present vice president, who was quoted during the Republican presidential primary in 1980 to the effect that he felt that a "limited" nuclear war was possible and perhaps even feasible.

A man like that is scary, indeed.

SLAUGHTER OF INNOCENTS

My father cared about the innocent victims of war. He wanted us to care as well.

"Slaughter of Innocents"
Minneapolis Star Tribune
January 8, 1980

Only on rare occasions do I hear a homily at mass that really reaches me. One recent morning was an exception. The speaker at our parish in Eau Claire was a young man studying for the priesthood. He is, I understand, a deacon in Minneapolis. The day was, in the Catholic calendar, the Feast of the Holy Innocents, and he talked, briefly, about that.

He said the slaughter of the innocents has gone on. He said it was at Hiroshima as it was at Belsen and Buchenwald and as it was in Vietnam and is now in Cambodia. He concluded his little talk by saying: "The slaughter of the innocents must end." He was right, you know.

The belligerent disc jockeys recently calling for death and destruction on Iran are wrong. We go one way or the other. Not both. Meanwhile, the God that both Islam and the Christians give lip service to looks over the situation. He's been patient as all the innocent ones went down—at our hands or those of the enemy. Could be he will run out of patience. Then what, jock?

A PRAYER FOR MY DARLIN'

When I was born in 1951, during the Korean War, my father wrote a piece for me about what he hoped I would become as a person. The article ended with the story of a little Korean girl, an innocent.

* * *

"A Prayer for My Darlin'"

Catholic Digest

November 8, 1952 (excerpt)

And finally, learn from that five-year-old girl in the cold November rain on the bleak cobblestones of that Korean town, ripped from everything a child of such an age has any right to know, ripped from home and warmth and soft laughter and all the tender words and songs, by the trigger men from the east and from the west. As she stands there in her thin, worn dress to watch the trucks rumble by in the night—from her learn patience.

And from the sergeant who sees her and groans and turns his head away and prays for her, from him learn love and hope and faith. And an anger that sings in the air toward every evil man and deed that God allows to inherit the Earth.

Be a tough cookie, darlin'. Fear no one but God. Remember that even the Korean child standing in the rain is not lost to God. He will find her out, and those who brought her there, or left her there. He will find them too. Learn from these models, then my darlin'.

I could have given you all the models fashioned in one—a woman whose name was Mary. But that name embarrasses so many—scares so many away. And you will find her anyhow, darlin'. And who knows now—maybe, so will they.

* * *

During the Vietnam war my father's writing was often criticized for siding with the young protestors. Though he did not always approve of their tactics he was with them in their cause.

In 1967 my brother Terry went off to college at UW-Eau Claire. It was the height of the Vietnam War and students on college campuses were at the center of the debate on the war. In those days, when you passed the TV room off the university union, during the 5:30-6:00 pm time slot, it was filled with students watching for the latest updates on the evening news.

On Terry's first visit home he had much to share with our dad. I remember us standing around our parents' record player in their bedroom and listening as Terry introduced us to one of the protest songs of the time. I think it was Bob Dylan's "Blowin' in the Wind," sung by Peter, Paul and Mary. My father listened intently. He liked it. He liked Peter, Paul and Mary.

My father became an early fan of Joan Baez. In the winter of 1994, Baez was scheduled for a concert at the State Theater in Eau Claire. My dad was 79 and in a wheelchair by then, but I thought we could not pass up the opportunity. I decided we would surprise him. My husband and I devised a plan to get my dad into the car and drive him down to the theater. I wheeled him in, secured an aisle seat, and he and I sat together and listened to an evening of song with one of his heroes, another longtime advocate for goodness in the world, Joan Baez. I am glad I followed through on that plan and I smile today to remember our concert night.

HUBERT HUMPHREY

Politics can be a dirty business. Many of those involved are driven by ambition and self-promotion. Some are sincere public servants. My father knew that his old friend Hubert Humphrey was the latter.

* * *

"Humphrey—as we knew him"
(Tribute on his passing)
Chippewa Herald Telegram
January 18, 1978

Will Durant wrote this once: "A good man who is not great is infinitely more precious than a great man who is not good."

I believe that. I have used it in my classes for years to tell the kids that though their own dad may go to work with a lunch pail and may not speak the King's English very well that he may be and probably is a good man and that, if that is so, then he is better than so many of the so-called great men who have cluttered up the stage of our history in recent years. We have had it up to here with great men who are not good.

Hubert Humphrey was a good man who happened also to be great. The fact that he was good is the one that I remember.

I first met Humphrey when I was teaching adult education classes at night for the WPA in Saint Paul. HHH was our supervisor. I was young and brash in those days—just one more hot one fresh out of college with all the answers. Humphrey and I got involved in the locally famous Crowe-Humphrey debates. He was an all-out Roosevelt man and I had been that way too, but I had cooled a bit on FDR as we drifted closer to war and the president kept saying that wasn't so.

But Humphrey never doubted his man. Maybe he was more right than I was.

Anyhow, when he was mayor of Minneapolis after the war was over, I went over to see him one day and a young man who was politically ambitious went with me. This lad, I remember, did not think it was possible that we would be able to get in to see the remarkable young mayor whose star was very obviously on the rise. He didn't know Hubert Humphrey. Of course, we got in and the meeting was informal and a lot of fun. Humphrey had a way of making everything seem like fun. I remember that I sat for a bit that day on the corner of Humphrey's desk and the formal young man who was with me was horrified. I would not have done that with another man. But Humphrey was not another man.

A bit more than 10 years later, after a lot of forks in the road had been met and followed one way or the other, Humphrey was a United States senator and I was coaching a high school basketball team in Austin, Minnesota which got invited to play in a national tournament in Washington. (We had won the state championship the year before and that was why. The team we took to DC was really rather average.) Humphrey and I had corresponded through the years—off and on—and he invited me to come see him when I hit town. With a lot of men such invitations are form and no more. With HHH they were real.

When I got to his office that day, he was in conference with some important looking guys who were, I'm pretty sure, from one or the other of the countries of the mid-east. Now I never did lack for self-confidence in a situation like that—except that once. I think I would have skipped our meeting. But Humphrey would have none of that. He moved the big wheels along pretty fast and then he came out and we had half an hour or so to remember how it had been once upon a time when we—and all the world—were younger and maybe a bit more innocent than we had become by 1959.

That was Humphrey. A big man who did not believe in bigness. Not in those terms anyhow. He believed, instead, that every man counted because he was a man. Bankers, lawyers, laborers—even coaches. He lived his public and his private life that way all the days until the end.

Maybe that was why so many did not have to fake they felt bad last week.

A couple of other things along this line....

Humphrey believed in and preached the "politics of joy." Some folks made fun of that, but Hubert meant it. He loved the battle and the competition, but he was not a bitter man and not a man who hated other men, regardless of what they believed or stood for. There was real joy in all of it for Humphrey.

I think sports should be that way, too. I believe you play to win and that is why they keep the score. But I reject out of hand the kind of grimness that a lot of coaches introduce into the picture. They make it a business and when you do that the fun is gone.

Humphrey would have liked being a coach. I would've liked having him around. But we could ill afford to not have him where he was.

A second thing is this—the young war protesters misread the man in 1968. I was against the war, too. (I even headed the Gene McCarthy campaign in two Wisconsin counties that year). But I never once said that HHH was a war man. He was trapped where he was as Lyndon Johnson's VP. I knew how he felt about that war and any war. The protesters never gave him a chance. I am convinced, as some of the senators said on TV the other night, that if Hubert had made it in 1968, we would've been out of Vietnam years sooner than we were and a lot of guys who died there would be alive now.

The third and last thing is that I don't always agree with Jimmy Carter but when he took Hubert Humphrey with him to Camp David a few weeks before Christmas I thought that showed the president at his very best. It was incredible to me that no one had ever invited this tremendous man down there before.

I have a picture which I cut out and saved—and talked to my classes about at the time. It shows Hubert returning from Camp David and Muriel there to greet the helicopter when it came in. The greeting is warm and tender as it always was with Humphrey and the girl he married. In the background, Jimmy Carter is standing. You can tell that he is deeply moved by the scene as this man who has but a short time to live comes home. All politicians, I guess, learn to fake things when it counts. But no man could have faked the look on Carter's face that day. I, not always before that a real Carter man, will not soon forget how that all was.

The man who never became president was responsible, in a way, a few weeks before he died, for the finest hour of the man who did.

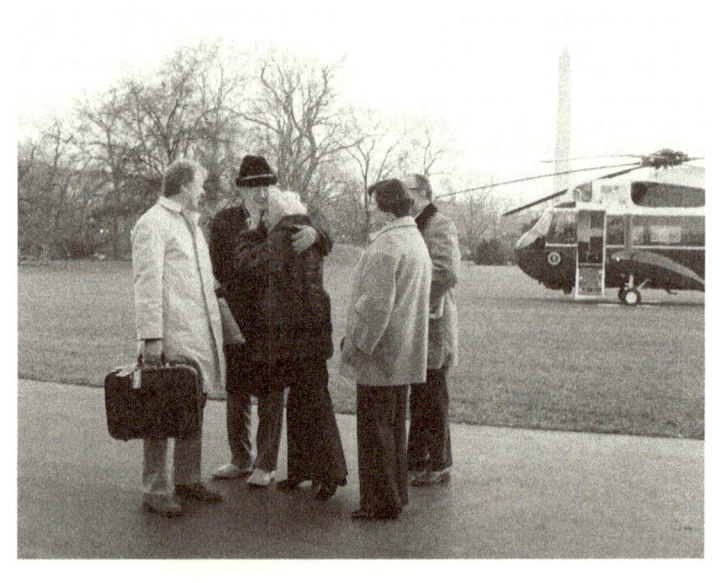

Sen. Hubert Humphrey, D-Minn., is greeted by his wife, Muriel, as President Carter looks on at the White House, Dec. 11, 1977, in Washington D.C. (*AP Photo/Peter Bregg*)

CHRISTMAS 1950

I always knew my mother loved Christmas. Each year we had blue lights on our Christmas tree because it reminded her of "Silent Night."

My youngest sister was born on December 10, 1962. Before my mother left for the hospital, she gave me one charge, "Go down to Woolworth's and buy Harry Belafonte's new Christmas album." The record was "Harry Belafonte: To Wish You a Merry Christmas," a 1958 album which had just been reissued. I still have the LP.

I was surprised to find in my father's writings that he loved Christmas, too. Certain Christmas stories from his youth are told and retold. His fond reminiscences of our "growing up years" in Marinette evoke Christmas memories.

My father empathized with soldiers away from home at Christmas, especially those in combat. He wanted us to remember them, too.

One day, searching through a box, I found an old envelope. Across the face was written, "Christmas Script." Inside in faded pencil, were the fragile pages for my dad's Christmas radio show, 1950.

That December night, our soldiers were fighting the Battle of the Chosin Reservoir in the northeast part of the Korean peninsula, an especially bloody fight in bitter cold over tough terrain. Many lives were lost. On another Christmas, just six years earlier, 1944, World War II, another group of soldiers fought in frigid weather, the Battle of the Bulge. In the six weeks of that battle, 19,000 American soldiers lost their lives. That night my dad was thinking of the soldiers from both of those battles.

* * *

"Christmas 1950"

Radio Script
December 1950

We have now come to the Christmas season in the year 1950.

It is possible that in the 2000 years that have gone by since first there was a Christmas, we have lost something.

Oh—we have gained things too, of course. Some of us have gained fine homes—fine clothes—fine cars. Some of us are now the rather proud possessors of a good deal more of the earth's goods than a lot of the people used to own.

Mary and Joseph, for instance.

But something is gone—a little.

A song in the air—or maybe it was a kind of quiet. A goodness or a peace or a sense of reaching out.

It is not gone entirely. It never will be. It is only gone—a little.

Maybe we shouldn't be too big at Christmas time. Not too important. Not too rich. Maybe we were closer to something a long, long time ago. Way back in 1944.

Do you remember Christmas that year?

We were all a little scared—and a little lonely—and our wealth seemed a little helpless, then. We had a kind of perspective in 1944.

Maybe we're getting it back a little now at that. 1944. That was the winter of Von Rundstedt's counteroffensive in Belgium. A lot of boys were cold that Christmas—like a lot are cold right now—but they're easier to forget this year—it's easier—and more convenient—not to remember.

A lot of boys died that Christmas.

I wonder if it's all right if I dedicate tonight's little story to all of them who didn't quite last until December 25, 1944—or for whom that was the last Christmas they ever knew.

And I think I'll dedicate this—tonight—too, to those guys who didn't quite make it all the way back to Hungnam last week. A pretty tough 25 miles over the mountains. A lot of them stayed there.

In particular, may I dedicate this to one boy you didn't know but I knew. A boy named Al. You can substitute if you want to. He was a good guy—Al was. Yeah. A good guy—

(Song up-"White Christmas"-fades under)

Al:

"Well—Mom—here it is Christmas again—and I couldn't let tonight go by without writing to you. It ain't so easy to write up here—but ya can do it.

Don't seem much like Christmas out here. Joe Kallas got it a while ago—and he was my best friend—Joe was. Don't seem right they should be killin' your best friend on Christmas Eve. Or anybody's friend.

Don't even seem right to be killin' your enemies, Mom. Somethin' we learned in school a long time back about lovin' your enemies. Seems kinda like a laugh out here—but tonight you sorta remember it. And you don't feel like laughin' tonight. Maybe they had it right back there in grade school, Mom. Maybe a lotta important people kicked things around between then and now. Maybe we got too many important people in the world, Mom. Everywhere.

Anyhow—I know one thing for sure—Christmas never was meant for killin' guys.

How is it back home, Mom?

Is the air still kinda quiet and waitin' like it used to be? Are the hills all white? It ain't so white over here Mom—but it will be again someday, I guess. If people let it be.

Did Dad still hunt all over town for a Christmas tree like always—and still wind up buyin' it at Tony's like always?

Remember when we used to go to church, and it would be kind of snowin' soft and easy—and nobody said very much—but ya felt good inside—and when ya were almost there ya could hear the choir singin'?

I used to like that, Mom. I never really knew how much till I came out here.

Remember the time I wanted boxing gloves for Christmas, and you didn't want me to have them because you thought they were too dangerous—but you gave in anyhow like you always did. Gee how I wanted those gloves. I was only 12 then, but I was going to go out and lick the world. I was gonna grow up and be like Jack Dempsey and go out and—yeah.

Thanks, Mom. Thanks for a lot of things. Boxing gloves don't seem very dangerous anymore, do they? Not—anymore.

And remember that sled? King of the Hill they called it. Doggone sled sure could travel. Remember the time Fred Kelly and me were slidin' down Chilkoot Pass and the runners caved in. Yeah. Have you still got it, Mom? Old King of the Hill.

You were sick one Christmas, Mom. Remember? That was the year I wanted that fielder's glove. Dad didn't get around to buying any presents that Christmas—and when I got downstairs Christmas morning all I found was a note sayin' Santa Claus didn't bring things to houses when the mother was sick, but he would be back later. The note was signed Santa Claus, but I recognized Dad's writin'.

I was nine years old by then. What did Dad think?—Ya know somethin'—Mom. That was a pretty good Christmas. I wish I still had that note. I never told him that I knew.

Later on, when the fielder's glove and all the other stuff was there, I made off I was sure glad Santa was good at rememberin'. I've still got that fielder's glove somewhere, Mom.

Tell Dad thanks too, sometime—when you think of it. I guess maybe there is a Santa Claus at that.

Remember the year we took Julie out to Aunt Kate's for Christmas dinner?

That was my first year in college and Julie was so small and dark and shining—like an angel. I know you don't like Julie anymore, Mom. I know you're sore cuz she took up with Dick Crane when I was out here. But don't blame her too much, Mom. She's young—and the years go by fast, and Dick's a good guy—so, if you see her, just tell her Merry Christmas from me, Mom. Like the song says—May her days be merry and bright. And may all her Christmases be white.

Save the picture though, Mom. The one of Julie and me out to Aunt Kate's that Christmas. Don't throw it away.

I get to rememberin' so much tonight, Mom. Ya do out here.

But most of all I remember—and most I miss—the closeness we always had.

I once read something that somebody wrote where they said, "Home is where you hang your childhood."

That's close.

And some poet we studied in school wrote, "Home is the place where when you have to go there, they have to take ya in."

That misses it a little.

In that vase on the buffet—among all the things you clipped out of the paper through the years—there's one by Edgar Guest. "It takes a heap o' livin' in a house to make a home."

Maybe you wonder why I remember all these sayings so good, Mom. And maybe I wonder myself. I guess it's because that's the thing you gave me most of all—you and Dad. You gave me home. And nothing in my life has been more to me than that.

It's what a guy remembers when he's away. And it's what makes a guy half full of laughter and half of tears when he gets back there. It's what you hang onto, Mom.

And tell Dad he doesn't have to worry anymore because he never could get enough money together to do the things he wanted to do for the house. Tell him he did all that was necessary by being inside it—and being like he was. It isn't the house, Mom—not the roof nor the yard nor the paint—maybe ya have to get a long ways off to see it isn't those things. Anyhow, I see it now.

A guy should be home for Christmas—Yeah.

Funny when you think about it—how the guys we killed—most of 'em had a picture or two in their pocket. And it never was Betty Grable, Mom. The papers got it wrong. It was always their wife and kids or their dad or mother or sister or somebody like that. Maybe the girl they wanted to marry. When a guy goes out to take a chance on dyin' he carries a decent picture with him—he carries the ones with the good memories attached.

And I guess it don't make much difference whether he's a German or English or a Russian or me. Somethin' about us all that's the same—and stays that way.

Remember the crib we used to have, Mom? I saw one kind of like it in a Belgian town last night. And some of the hymns were just the same.

I wonder if I'll find a crib in Germany.

Well—Mom, I guess I've sounded off a little long tonight. Sorry. But a guy gets feelin' that way sometimes.

We'll be moving up pretty soon now. Don't worry, Mom. I'll be OK.

I sit here and I look at the stars—and I see the one we used to call the Christmas star. It's still there, Mom. And anyone can see it if ya look. Even over here.

Funny thing.

Same star above me in Belgium is above you back in Wisconsin. Makes a guy feel kind of humble—and quiet—don't it?

Same star was there when I was a kid—same one was there when Julie and me—same star.

I like to think that's the one who's light first broke through a couple thousand years ago, Mom. You used to tell me how the wiseman followed it then. Remember? Maybe if we were wise, we'd follow it today. Maybe the trouble is our Christmas got earth-bound somewhere along the way. Maybe we ought to—look up—for a change.

I'm not trying to sound like a poet or a philosopher or somethin', Mom—and I can't say it like I want to—but a guy gets thinkin'.

Same star's been there for 2000 years. It's seen a lot of shootin'. A lot of killing and a lot of pride and plenty of big shots have come—and gone.

It's outlasted warriors and kings—and it will survive Hitler. And you and me and all of us.

People have ignored it and sometimes mocked it, and even tried to tear it down.

But it can take it—the Christmas star. It can take it.

Well—so long, for now, Mom. We're ready to move. I feel very close to all of you tonight. Very close and very grateful. Thanks again for everything—and Merry Christmas

Merry Christmas.

BELIEVER

RULES

My father was a faithful Catholic all his life. He often challenged the church, but never left.

He questioned the onerous rules and some of the mind-numbing rituals that persisted over decades. Church politics could be a concern for him. His father left the church when my dad was young because the local priest said that anyone who belonged to the Farmer Labor Party should be excommunicated. The priest claimed they were communists. My father challenged the silence of priests and bishops when the ambitions of the powerful led to war which victimized the innocent.

But my father never left. He thought Jesus Christ was the greatest man who ever lived, a man who showed us how to live. He often referenced Jesus in calling on us to pursue goodness over greatness. The leaders in the church might fall short, but Christ did not.

My father welcomed the changes ushered in with the Second Vatican Council, and he hailed Pope John XXIII who led the effort to reform and "open the windows of the church." He thought Pope John was one of the greatest men of the 20th century.

* * *

"Rules—'Father is it all right...?'"
Published in *"From the Bench"*
Green Bay Register
January 17, 1969

"Father, is it all right to brush my teeth before receiving communion?"

"Yes. If you don't swallow the toothbrush."

This was one of the early dialogues in the church, some forty years ago. The participants were a conscientious lady from old Saint Michael's in Stillwater and God's right-hand man on earth, in the early days of my youth, his royal nibs Father Charles Corcoran, chief high priest of the good and ancient parish.

Another went something like it.

"Go ahead and tell your sins," Father Corcoran snarled in the confessional one night, as some pious soul set the stage for his revelation with all the careful preliminaries the nun had always taught us were an absolute must.

(The priest's shout rang through the church that night—and a buddy of mine, Noah Bibeau, who played centerfield in his bare feet because he always misjudged flyballs, but he could pursue the errant ball at great speed with his shoes off, was next in line for confession. I always figured Noah had his penance in before he ever entered the confessional.

He was a nervous and unhappy lad that night).

Many years later, when I was married and with part of my family in the car, I was hurtling through the night faster than I should have been because I wanted to get to Faribault in time for a sandwich before midnight, on account of I intended to receive communion the next morning in Austin.

The road turned left, and a branch went straight into a roadside cemetery as it turned out. I must've been a bit foggy for sleep and I followed the straight road just for a moment. I say my speed was too great because of that communion fast.

I hit the stone wall around that graveyard. Was lucky no one wound up living there.

Actually no one was hurt much but the car was a real smash. I never did make it to Faribault for the pre-midnight snack. Heck, I might not have made it anyhow.

Later, that fast period was cut to three hours and now it's one. I figure there shouldn't be any at all. Receiving your God inside you is the idea—not whether a graham cracker was there first.

I still find some of my boys on the team who don't receive because they can't remember whether they were chewing gum within the hour.

Good grief!

We have gone very deep in nonsense for sure. It is hard to shake the hangover.

Another thing that's happened is we are not ordered to be terrified of the host anymore. (In at least one parish in our town you put the wafer in your own mouth.) Once upon a time, if the priest dropped the host, it was like you were going to have to replace the floor—and bury the first one in hallowed ground.

On the other hand, these new look lads who want to make it all so casual that the only thing you're doing when you receive is eating, leave me way out in the cold.

It's not an oatmeal cookie, Cal.

Also, a lot of the lads get really sweated about some little old lady fingering her rosary over in some dark corner of the church. Like a tribal rite, they scream. Away with her!

Rend the rosary! Shred it! Tear it apart!

Oh shucks, man. It ain't all that awful. Five will get you ten, that if you ever do crash them pearly gates, little old Miss McGillicuddy will be sitting there waiting for you—smiling a little and making you the old offer of tea and cupcakes.

Anyhow, you've been a bit inconsistent.

For instance, you get rid of litanies. Thank God for that, say I. I was very tired of asking St. Ruby to pray for us, or from tempest to be delivered.

I grant, as you maintain, it was very much routine and a long way on the road to dead.

But you've substituted for instance, the offertory petitions. And, in some churches, they say, "The response this week is, "We beseech you to hear us"—or "This we ask of thee today"—or "Grant us this we pray today."

And listen, buddy, don't use last month's response for this month's petitions.

Pray for rain or sun or our soldiers (how about theirs?) or wayward clergymen or astronauts or deer hunters (how about the deer?)

Man, this is as routine as the litany to Saint Leotardia. The people respond by rote and wait for the list to end. Some good ideas, but we are being drowned in a sea of words.

Just remember, Harry—if you didn't swallow the toothbrush, you're home free. Make your move to the rail.

POPE JOHN XXIII

"Reflecting on the Renaissance in the Catholic Church Under Pope John XXIII"

Published in "Something to Crowe About"
The Spirit
April 19, 1974

I guess what used to bother me the most was the pomposity and arrogance, and I guess the main reason was that so many of my friends quit the church because of the way it was. And the pompous and arrogant ones did not seem to care.

"Let 'em go. Who needs 'em?"

But the point was that if the church did have answers to what life is all about and was the key to what eternal life might someday be, then we all need it. And for a priest or a bishop not to care when even one man is needlessly lost, is to make pomposity and arrogance seem even more repulsive than they already are.

And, like I say, they didn't care.

I grew up with the idea that when the priest in our town spoke it was like God speaking. That was bad enough, as I look back, when I believed it. It was far worse when the priest began to believe it, too.

Maybe, to be fair about it, few of them ever quite made that mistake, but some of them seemed to come pretty close.

Bishops, as I recall them, were regarded as the friends and associates of the very rich. And most of the time that is the way it was. A few held out against that kind of identity, but they could not change the way it at least seemed to be.

Sometimes one or another took a stand on things like the matter of race and the question of the desperately poor—and who was to blame and why. Here and there, somebody came out against the whole bloody business of war—and even against a particular war.

But mostly, they just went along.

One of the main jobs of a bishop was to raise funds and underwrite building programs. They needed rich friends, I am sure. I'm not so sure they needed them quite as desperately as they seemed to think they did. Nor am I sure the price they paid was not too high.

The picture is different now, of course. That's why many of the old, powerful friends of bishops across the land are startled and confused by what has happened. The conference of Bishops now comes out with stands that would not even have been dreamed about some years ago.

"The bishops ought to stick to religion."

The powerful people never used to say that when the politics and the economics and the sociology of the bishops matched their own—or was totally controlled by them.

John XXIII broke all the ancient rules. He opened the windows to let the fresh air in. He rocked the status quo, and it has never quite got its old balance back.

Like the time he visited that jail in Rome. No pope had done that before. And John told one of the prisoners there not to feel too bad about being in the place because he, John, had had an uncle that had spent time in stir. For stealing a horse, or whatever.

John turned the world around.

You don't, for instance, hear nuns very often, who are prophets of doom. The devil will have you by the hair if you don't watch out. The floor will open up and you'll be gone.

March the kids to Mass every day and then nary a one of them show up all summer. March them to the stations. March them over to say the Rosary. Herd them in on Friday for confession. Make it all as dreary as you can.

Say your morning and evening prayers. Don't swear. Don't lie. Don't steal. And above all else, beware of sex. Sex is dangerous and usually evil. The worst possible sin is that of impurity. And impurity is always tied in with sex.

Racism? What's that? Bigotry? That's what other religions feel toward Catholics so don't go near the YMCA. And don't dance with a Lutheran girl—or a Baptist—because she might fall in love. And that would be very bad indeed.

Don't talk in church. Don't laugh. Don't be joyous. Just be there and shut up. Church is a place to be grim. Religion is a pretty grim business. Hell is very hot. Just ask the Baptists. They've got their faults, but they really know about hell.

Or ask the priest when the next mission hits town. Those missionaries can make you so scared you're afraid to walk home in the dark.

How many times did you sass your mother? How many times did you have bad thoughts? Bless the battleships. Bless the tanks and the troops.

When I think back about it all, it almost suffocates me. It did kill the faith of a lot of my friends. They grew up and they got out. They shouldn't have. I know that. But they did.

They're gone.

And then John came along, and the fresh air came in—and the light—and the sound of music. And it was good. Long overdue—but sweet and bright and good.

But then the new arrogance came in, too. And about that another time....

THE EUCHARIST

My father believed in the Eucharist, that the bread and wine are transformed into Jesus Christ by the priest at Mass, and then we receive Christ at communion. He went to Mass every day and often stopped in church during the week to "make a visit," kneeling in the dark, alone, with God.

* * *

"Spinning Along on Spaceship Earth"
Published in "Something to Crowe About"
The Spirit
April 26, 1974

Recently, Eric Sevareid, the CBS philosopher, reminded us that we are all together, inescapably, on a ship in space and that our supplies are running low.

It was, I thought, a pretty vivid and true picture of something that all of us are, in our most lucid moments, quite aware of, but which most of us, for whatever the reason, don't think about very often.

We really ought to give it some thought. Or maybe, just as well, we ought to think about those words uttered by Paul Newman in the movie called "Hud."

"Nobody gets out of this life alive."

All this fits in with what I've been writing about in this space recently—the old and the new look in religion—because I think maybe the one thing the new breed theologians have steered away from is the sense of mystery.

Rachel Carson called it the sense of wonder.

Disgusted with a thousand years of "pie in the sky" preachments in which important clerics, themselves obviously well fed, told the poor to forget their troubles—or simply accept them—because all would be made right "out there" someday—having had it all the way with that kind of self-serving hypocrisy, many of the new look lads have overreacted.

Badly.

They have seemed to be content, sometimes, to let God really be dead—or to question that he ever lived. I'm pretty sure they didn't mean to go that far—but that's how far many of them did go. And they left those who believed in them stranded.

On a spaceship with the supplies running low.

Because religion needs God or there's no religion at all. Religion, by its very nature, needs mysticism and mystery. Simply because a man's mind, new breed or old, cannot comprehend the idea of God is not reason enough to deny it.

A man's mind cannot comprehend the idea of no God, either. I have watched a few give it a try.

So, all right, new breed. There was too much incense in the air. John said open the windows and he was right. Too much ceremony. Too many ceremonious people in charge. Too much ritual. Too much capitalizing on superstition.

Too much class distinction. Too many led to believe they could buy their way into heaven.

All right.

I have watched the young walk away from all that. Okay—run. I have been embarrassed, too, by the idea that a man can be callous and cruel and cold and, because he is a priest, that is all right.

No way.

The idea that the hands which were blessed can do no wrong—that the words of the priest cannot deceive and mislead other men—I reject that, too. It took me a while. Once we were not allowed to reject it. Sacrilegious, they said.

Or worse—if there was anything worse.

And the idea that a naked human body is somehow obscene, but a body torn apart by a grenade is not—okay, you've made your point and I see it and I agree.

But then some of you said—or seemed to say—that the idea of Christ existing in a wafer of bread was ridiculous. Or impossible. I can't go along with you there.

Hell—H.G. Wells, that once upon a time British historian, said that fifty years before you were born.

So, you—some of you—have tried to tell me that when I receive the Bread, I am only sharing a meal with the other guys. No big deal, just have a bite and then, as one priest put it, "We'll do the dishes."

For me, it's still a big deal, man. The biggest. And I'll try to tell you why I think you run from it. I think maybe you're scared, man. You said the old church tried to scare hell out of the people. I think you're right.

But you're scared, too.

Here we are on this spaceship and science can tell us we're in space but cannot comprehend space. No end. Science cannot explain no time and no end. Like God.

You're a TV baby, man. You grew up believing that if science can't explain it, then it isn't there. And that's arrogance, man. That's arrogance to equal, and maybe surpass, the incense burners and the "holy water makes everything right" lads of my youth.

Science cannot explain God in a piece of bread. So, what else is new? Science cannot tell me if there is a fence that marks the end of space, either. Nor what's on the other side of the fence.

Science can do what it can do—but you've got to keep a sense of wonder.

Man.

Meanwhile, spinning along on Spaceship Earth we......

MARY CHAPUT

"Mary Chaput's Funeral"
Published in "From the Bench"
Green Bay Register
June 23, 1967

Mary Chaput died the other day. She was eighty-five and it was time. You never knew her and that is all right, too. She was just another old woman who had lived a good life and come to the time for dying.

Twenty-one years ago, this coming fall, I took my first job at a Catholic high school—in Eau Claire. Old Saint Pat's High. (Now Regis, a bigger and more imposing place.)

I was single then and I used to eat breakfast at Mary Chaput's house. She was only in her sixties in those days, and she had an easy way with words. We used to talk football a lot because our team at Saint Pat's that year was one of the best there was, and it was fun to talk about it.

But you wouldn't care about all that anyhow, except that it explains how I happened to be at Mary's funeral the other day and how I happened to hear Father Brady's sermon.

Because that is really what this is about.

Father Brady came to Saint Pat's a short time after I did, and he's been there ever since. Twenty years as pastor there. He's a good priest I think, with culture, class, and a sense of humor.

He is a good man, too. I have liked knowing him and have been reached by his words before.

This day he talked about holy communion.

Toward the end of it he pictured Mary Chaput as a woman who found joy in the Eucharist and found a good reason "to climb the hill from her home to the church" to receive Him.

I guess that Father Brady's words got through to me so clearly that day because I knew he was saying it true about how it was with Mary Chaput.

And about how it is with communion.

Recently, I've read so much and heard so much about participation. Reading, responding, singing. The liturgy. The works.

Good stuff. I believe it. I've said here before that I like the new look. Especially the priests and nuns on the line for justice and decency and kindness. Overdue.

But I am—honest to God, am—a little bit tired of the emphasis on talk. The "people of God" stuff. We are the people of God. We stand a lot. We read. We respond. We sing. Watch us. The old ways are dead. Sentimental goo anyhow. Watch us. Hear us.

Oh, I don't miss the novenas. (Although reading Mary clean out of the party isn't quite necessary, I should think.) Never cared for them anyhow. Goo was the word, I suppose. Sentimental.

(I used to sneak in for benediction at the end—amid many hard looks—and also be there, in some discomfort, for "Good Night, Sweet Jesus"—or the like. It was goo, all right.

Still—I mean should we sneer and all that? Isn't the sneer stuff, itself, a bit overdone? I mean.)

The rosary, I'm told is neglected.

I say it though. On my own, once in a while. Sorry about that, man. Can't explain it either.

Do I have to?

Well, anyhow, some of the moderns, lately, seem to be taking a dim view of holy communion. I mean, one lad in that paper that has all the answers seem to be saying that maybe we should look at the Eucharist as just symbolic, really. A representation.

Some Dutchman called it trans-signification—and how about that. Nothing is anything anymore if it doesn't have significance. Right?

(Maybe these chums are influenced by that science type who wrote a song, "The Vatican Rag" or something. How do those lines go....

Two, four, six, eight.

Let's all trans-substantiate.

Clever, you know. Only H.G. Wells, among others, came up with all that stuff—oh, years ago. Decades, really.)

Well—let him look his way and I'll look mine. I always say.

But I do get the feeling that a good many now, are upgrading reading the words and downgrading what "some" have always called "that Catholic wafer."

So, thanks, Father Brady. Glad I was there the other day.

Like I heard one boy in our ball club say once, "I hate going to mass. It bores me.

Well, son—you're not alone. Bores me too. Always has. I've tried to get there just about every day for quite a few years now—and it's bored me. Every day.

Or maybe boring is the wrong word. Say it never really got a hold of the cockles of excitement. Or something.

The words. Repetitive. Automatic. The Kyrie. The Gloria. The Creed. The Responses. Even the Epistles and the Gospels. (Except for the Sermon on the Mount, for instance. That was exciting enough. World shaking. Only everybody gives it lip service and nobody tries it out.) Taken alone—as words—it's pretty boring stuff. I agree with my player. Many do. Many who come to mass every day do. Only most won't say so, of course.

One part I never found boring.

The communion.

You don't believe, you shouldn't be there. You do believe—no bore.

Me—I believe. So, if the science types want to feel sorry for me in my innocence and ignorance, that's all right. Do them good to feel some compassion for a change—no matter the cause.

But I believe—and the communion is not boring, man.

When father Brady pictured Mary Chaput coming out of her little house and heading up the hill, I remembered that.

You had a good funeral, Mary.

YOUTH AND RELIGION

My dad was concerned about the increasing disinterest and diminished participation of young people in the church. "Boring" seemed to be the explanation from the youth. My father understood their dismissive excuse, but he did not accept it. He felt the church needed to work to better understand the youth and come up with responses to engage them.

* * *

"Youth Finding Religion Dull"
Published in "From the Bench"
Green Bay Register
May 27, 1966

Recently I got to talking with some of the kids from a Catholic high school in this part of the state. Somehow, I asked them which class they liked least in school.

Almost everyone said religion.

Now, if this were a unique experience would be one thing. The fact that other students other places have come up with the same answer to the same question makes it something else entirely.

I asked them if they would take a religion class if it were optional and most of them said no.

Later on, we got to talking about extracurricular activities and especially clubs. The clubs they liked the least—and many had not joined, and others had quit—were the religiously oriented ones.

They said they were the dullest and most pointless organizations in school. More than that, they called them silly.

Well, by this time I was a bit irked, I guess. I asked them if there would be any point in having Catholic high schools if you did away with religion classes and all clubs with any kind of religious base.

I said public high schools had classes in English and science; had pep clubs and Latin clubs; had the band and dramatics and the chorus and the football team.

I said what would be the point in sacrificing to keep a Catholic high school going (something I'm convinced is worth it all) if you made them simply into carbon copies of the public schools.

Some kid said it would still be worth it because students learned to behave better in a Catholic school. I said if you wanted simply good behavior I would recommend a private school, like Blake in Minneapolis for instance, which was not Catholic, but which turned out young men who were models of good behavior and deportment.

(I mean if you eliminate the religious base as a reason for behaving right, then I'm not sure if some of these other schools might not have us beat.)

Some kids said it would still be worth it to have Catholic high schools because simply having nuns and priests around had a salutary effect on students.

(I wondered if having them around after all traces of religious teaching has been removed wouldn't be a travesty—and, perhaps, hypocrisy.)

Some said that while they didn't believe we should have religion classes, as such, they thought that religion should be introduced into studies in other fields—history, sociology, science, literature.

(I once wrote an article explaining why I, then a social science teacher, had changed from public schools to Catholic—to give me the chance to teach with integrity.

But I'm not as sure as I was that to project religion into "the other" subjects doesn't, on occasion at least, post dangers even greater than the obvious virtue such a procedure contains.)

Anyhow, all these things can stand more detailed discussion than I'm prepared to present now. But one thing stands out clear to me—religion is not dull and should not turn out to seem dull to the students.

We have optional mass at our school. You can take it or leave it. About five percent of the kids—sometimes ten—take it.

I thought this was a pretty small turn out until I happened to visit a Minnesota school, recently. From a student body of about 700, there were five kids at Mass—all girls.

You rarely see high school students at a parish mass on Saturday. You rarely see them at special things such as rosary services or benediction.

Many regard all these as pretty dull. And, I suppose, in a way they are. Sometimes it seems as if a special effort is made to make them so.

(Recently, of course, an attempt has been made to make the Mass less dull by getting the people attending it involved. Still—the number that shows up remains small.)

I don't know the answer on Mass attendance or any of the rest of this. Or the answer as to why all of it—and religion classes and clubs—seem to bore the kids.

But I do know Christianity is not dull.

I do know that the Man who stood on the Mount and said: "Blessed are the clean of heart for they shall see God" and "Blessed are the meek for they shall inherit the Earth" was not a dull man.

His words still come through loud and clear, and they can kick a guy harder than any politician's platitudes—here or anywhere.

They barked at Him, snarled at Him, lashed at him, but they couldn't snare Him out or make Him quit.

They killed Him but he lives on. They buried Him and He kicked away the rock and walked free.

They tried to destroy His teaching, but His words live on. Theirs are forgotten.

"Love your enemies," He said, "Do good for them who persecute you." We've never understood such ideas but they, for sure, aren't boring.

When Pope John XXIII echoed them, he wasn't boring. When Paul VI stood before the UN, he was quiet, but what he had to say was not dull.

The priests and the nuns on the line for the lonely and the forsaken and the dispossessed are not boring and they are not dull.

Countdowns at Canaveral may someday be boring because they've happened too often. Trips into space may become common place.

But the trip into eternity—the last countdown every one of us has to face—someday—well, I guess few welcome it, but it's not dull nor boring.

Religion, in or out of the classroom, should not be the dull part of a Catholic high school education. Nor should the introduction of a religious concept be greeted with sardonic smirks, limping wisecracks, or looks of weary resignation. If these things are happening, we should try to find out why.

And soon.

THINK OF THIS HOMILY

My dad advocated for changes that he thought might encourage all people, but particularly the young to engage in the Church. He recommended shortening sermons to one minute. This was not well received by some, and he heard from them. He quoted from one of his old oratory professors from St. Thomas, "Have something to say, say it and sit down." The length of homilies continues to be an issue in today's Church. Pope Francis has spoken on it.

Though my father thought most sermons and homilies needed work, there were some that touched him and moved him. He wrote about them.

* * *

"When You Want to Get Even, Think of this Homily"

"In My Opinion" column
Milwaukee Journal
September 24, 1984

Recently, I went to mass at the college up here and the priest gave a homily (we used to call them sermons), which has stayed in my mind ever since. That's unusual because

I don't like the homilies most of the time—and almost never remember them.

Anyhow, here is how this one went.

"... I have an uncle and aunt who are Mormons and close to my favorite people of all those I know. Today's theme for my talk—based on the readings we just heard—is suffering and pain. Just how does this tie in with these relatives of mine?"

"They have known deep pain."

"Things were going along so well for them, and they had a daughter they loved very much, and she was married and the mother of three fine children. One morning they got a telephone call informing them that their daughter had been murdered."

"Shortly after that, the shock became even more intense, when it was evident that the man who had killed her had been put up to it by her husband."

So far this is just a story much like scores of those you read in the daily newspaper. But the priest knew where he was going with his homily.

"It is hard for me to comprehend this," he said, "but for years now these two people have driven more than a hundred miles, every once in a while, to visit their son-in-law in prison."

"I told them," the priest said, "that I couldn't do something like that. The injury was too great and the pain too deep."

"My uncle said to me, one night, that while the hurt in both of them was deep, indeed, that the pain inside the man in the cell who had been responsible for the death of their daughter was greater still—and more intense and more inescapable."

"So, we go to visit him when we can."

I can't shake the impact of that story. I don't want to. I know the pope went to see the man in prison who had tried to kill him. That was remarkable, too—but that was the pope. These are just two people whose beloved daughter was wiped out.

In a time when the Russkies won't let us "get away" with anything and we treat them the same way—and the people of Israel swear vengeance on the Palestinians and vice versa—and a smart click slogan of our time is: "Don't get mad—get even"—in such a time in such a world the story of these two ordinary folks somehow rocked me all the way to the ground.

Our world could learn from them, I think. Maybe if we could and would learn, we might yet be saved from the shadows that every day close in on us just a little more.

And maybe I'll listen to the homily from now on.

SOMEONE MUST GIVE IN FIRST

Sometimes the lesson of a homily helped my dad to help a student.

* * *

"Someone Must Give in First"
Green Bay Press Gazette
April 3, 1977

I went to mass in the hospital chapel and the gospel was the story of the prodigal son. Now I will rarely get into subjects like this in this column, but that story has a lot of impact and a lot of meaning for our times. Father Crane, who is the chaplain here, gave a good sermon. He said the point of the story is to make clear the forgiving quality of God and to let the worst sinners know they can always come home if they want to.

I agree with that interpretation of the story. I think there is an additional one, however, and it's that one I'd like to talk about, because it fits our lives today so closely that it is almost startling. I think the message is: "Father, forgive your erring son (or daughter). Welcome him home if he returns no matter what the provocation no matter how wrong he may have been."

And here I am speaking of earthly fathers and wayward sons.

One of the grim signs of the times has been a breakdown in family life. A young man will not abide by the "rules" at home, so he packs his bags and takes off.

"If you leave, that's it."

"So be it."

And he (or she) is gone.

This happens so many times right now that when I write about it you may feel I am talking about somebody in your own family. Well, maybe I am.

I recall the first year I was at JFK, one of the boys on one of the teams had a fearful showdown with his father. It began with words and ended with blows. And then some final words.

"Don't you ever set your foot in our house again."

"You don't need to worry, man."

At our school, every teacher is supposed to be, in a sense, a counselor and a guidance man. Our official guidance counselor, Joel Mukavitz, once said to me: "That makes my job so much easier. Each teacher—or almost everyone, anyhow—is willing to give it a whirl."

That is why I got to talking with this lad who had fought so bitterly with his dad.

"You really ought to back off and start over. You don't really want things to be this way."

"Why should I back off? Why not him? He's in the wrong as much as I am. Maybe more."

"You're here. I can talk to you. I can't talk with your father."

"No way."

Well, if nobody gives a little, nothing is given and nothing changes. And the wall of silence and separation grows ever stronger and ever colder.

(Is this what you really want, young man or old man, who has had this kind of thing in your family? Do you really mean it to be forever? It will be, unless one of you gives a little. Who first? Why not you?)

`I don't know when this young man I write about made his decision, but I know he did go home for Easter. (JFK is a boarding school and he lived a number of miles away). And his dad saw him coming "while he was still far off"—and he was glad.

There was no fatted calf but there was an open door. And a happy mother, too, and a family again.

Somebody asked Jesus one time: "How often must I forgive my enemy? Seven times?"

"Yea—verily I say, seventy times seven times."

That kind of thing is not easy for us. It was never meant to be easy. It is much easier to hang onto a stiff-necked pride.

But the price is high. Like in loneliness and heartbreak, and a sense that what we are doing not only hurts us and hurts the other guy, but it also is very wrong.

Is there too much "coddling" in our time? Sure there is. Too much permissiveness? Sure.

We have made mistakes because no one has all the answers. But it is true and certain that cold anger is no answer. Frozen face and frozen personality. The cold vendetta.

So, give a little, young man, old man. You will be surprised how little it hurts and how good it feels. And you will be surprised how happy and warm you will be with the result.

Up above there, somewhere, I said that no one has all the answers. Well, that isn't quite right, I guess. One Man did have them all. Only we must listen to what they are.

And he said: "The old man saw his son coming from far off and he ran down to meet him…"

That's one of the answers.

IS THERE A GOD?

My father's faith was at the center of his life. In 1972 the world seemed to be going in a different direction, enthralled with science and skeptical of the divine.

My father believed that what we did with the time of our life mattered, that in the end, we well might be held accountable. The world seemed to toss aside considerations such as that, but he felt there might be a little doubt in people.

* * *

"Is There a God? The Final Interview"
Published in "Something to Crowe About"
The Spirit
October 20, 1972

Recently the church announced that it would be spending a good deal of time during the next year in trying to convince its people of the need to pursue "peace and justice."

One lad said to me: "What's the church monkeying around with stuff like that for? The church's job is saving souls. Leave peace and justice to the politicians."

Well, we've been doing that all right. And the politicians of both parties, have come up with no peace and very little justice. As to whether souls are being saved—that's a question clearly up for grabs.

For instance, last Sunday the sermon I heard dealt with "respect for life." It struck me that the topic was well within the limits of religion's concern. Certainly, the politicians—and the generals—have shown little interest in it.

Some years ago, we used to be told that if we did the right things, we'd ultimately get to heaven—but if we made out with the devil, we'd wind up in his hot domain.

We have studied a lot of books and looked through a lot of microscopes and tested a lot of tubes since then—and we have come up with the conclusion that there is no heaven and no hell and that old debbil was just a scare story thought up by nuns to keep bad boys in the fourth grade from throwing spitballs at the good little girls.

Well—could be.

And I remember, once, being mighty concerned when I read something by a protestant minister about "the big interview." He meant the final conversation with God in which the review of our earthly deeds was made and our sentence—good or bad—was arrived at.

Didn't seem like the sort of interview anyone would look forward to.

But now I am assured there is no interview, and there may well be no God and if there should be, there wouldn't be any tough sentences handed down anyhow because that would suggest that God is an old meanie and that would be out of character for God.

If there were a God, that is.

Well, this is all mighty encouraging because I definitely had a negative feeling about that old interview, and it is nice to know that the smart money men have found out the whole thing is just an old wives' tale.

(Old wives have taken the rap for tales for quite some time now.)

The trouble is, I am not totally convinced. Oh, I know these men are learned men all right. And I know that Russky cosmonaut said he didn't see any God when he was floating around—and I suppose that should be pretty convincing because a cosmonaut has to have 20-20 vision and all that.

But somehow a touch of doubt remains. Like maybe that Russky didn't know just where to look.

And the point is that if there should be that doggone interview after all, how am I going to explain napalm? Fragmentation bombs? Villages wiped out. Farmers decimated. Kids roasted in the classroom.

My explanation is that I wasn't there? No, God—I was playing golf that day.

Just on the off chance that there might be an interview after all, is that answer going to satisfy God? I just don't have that old confidence anymore, I guess.

Because I say no.

UNCLE BOB

When I was growing up our family was bound together by religion. We attended daily Mass and prayed the Angelus. My dad wrote a family prayer that we said morning and evening. We routinely dropped into church during the day to "make a visit," to say a short prayer and light a candle. I am grateful for our family rituals, and even more so for the depth of my father's thoughts on God. Poring through his papers has been deeply moving for me. I laughed and cried reading his stories, but also have been impacted when contemplating his beliefs about God, the Church and eternity, and how those beliefs permeated his thoughts in all facets of his life.

I had an unusual opportunity to return to my role as daughter on a spiritual journey with my father in the final years of his life—laying his brother Bob to rest. I wrote it all down to preserve the record of that day.

* * *

"Uncle Bob's Funeral"

"Uncle Bob died," my mother announced as I walked into her room.

"Dad wants to go to the funeral, but he can't go."

My dad was nearly 82. He had problems with confusion and could not drive anymore. My mother got her license late in life, but never drove. She was working hard to just get them through their everyday life in their home.

The funeral was to be held in St. Paul, a simple service at the funeral home, arranged by one of Bob's friends. Bob was my dad's younger brother, his only sibling. For most of his adult life, Bob lived simply in an apartment building in St. Paul. He never married. I sometimes heard inferences that something had gone wrong in Bob's life, but never had a clear explanation. I know my dad made sure to stay connected to Bob.

We drove over to visit Bob every summer when we were in Eau Claire. My dad would pick him up in St. Paul and bring him to Pioneer Park in Stillwater, the town where they grew up, went to high school and had their glory days as brothers. My mother would have the picnic lunch spread out on the table. After we ate, my dad and Bob would sit and talk, looking down the bluffs to the St. Croix River and downtown Stillwater while we played.

Every year, in the week before Christmas, a package would arrive from Bob. It was the one gift we were allowed to open on Christmas Eve. Inside there was a present for each of us, wrapped separately. I remember one year getting a little manicure set in a red leatherette case. I was quite taken with it. Bob apparently understood what would appeal to a little girl.

My dad was loyal to Bob and he to him, though at times they had differences. They shared a common history only they could know.

I told my mother, "Dad must go to the funeral. I will get off from work and I will take him."

So it was that on March 27, 1996, I helped my dad into my Buick, my 15-year-old daughter in the back seat, and we headed out on Interstate 94 to the Twin Cities.

My dad had been an English teacher and a coach. He was a great communicator. He had the power to evoke in his players strength and courage they did not know they had, and to inspire students in the classroom with the power of language and the wonder of literature. He was a great listener, someone I sought out for answers as I wrangled with troubles or explored ideas. But the years had taken away his gift. The ideas were locked away, words were gone. Now as we drove down the highway to St. Paul we talked in circles.

"Nice car. What kind is it?"

"It's a Buick."

"When did you get it?"

"Three years ago?"

I continued talking to him with little response, then a few more miles down the road,

"Nice car. What kind is it?"

"It's a Buick."

"When did you get it?"

"Three years ago."

I took the conversation in a different direction; he just let me talk. Then....

"Nice car. What kind is it?"

"It's a Buick."

"When did you get it?"

"Three years ago."

I looked over at him. He was looking straight ahead and smiling. Was the joke on me? I thought it might be and smiled. We continued our journey.

We arrived at the funeral home, a lovely old Tudor style stone building in downtown St. Paul. I helped Dad out of the car, into his wheelchair and pushed him inside where a handful of people gathered. The man who made the funeral arrangements greeted us at the door. He seemed surprised to see us. My dad's cousin from Duluth waved to us from across the room. A priest from St. Thomas University, a singer and the three of us rounded out the attendees.

We found our seats. My dad signaled that he wanted to go up to the casket and see his brother. I wheeled him to the front. Uncle Bob was well dressed in a brown suit with a white shirt and lavender tie. His friend joined us at the casket. He handed me a black folio. He said it contained items from Bob's apartment. He and another man had cleaned the place out. He thought the family should have the memorabilia they found. I thanked him. He told me Bob had told him he wanted a simple funeral, and specifically said he wanted "nothing strange," a curious request, I thought.

I stood for a while with my father as he paid respect to his brother. "Goodbye, kid," he said. He handed me a round Merle Norman make-up container indicating he wanted me to put it into the casket. I knew what it was.

An ardent Catholic all his life, but an independent one, he believed in the presence of Christ, of God, in the consecrated host. Late in life, when he could no longer get to church on his own, my dad kept pieces of the host in the house. He wanted to be close to God.

Those little pieces of the host were in that round container, now with Uncle Bob in his casket. I signaled for Bob's friend to come over and simply pointed and told him, "My dad wants Bob to be buried with that." He nodded. I quietly apologized to Bob for this "strange" request, and we took our seats.

Some Catholics, some priests, may be disturbed by this. They might view it as irreverent handling of the host. I think Jesus would approve. He Himself was not rule-bound, that was for the Pharisees. Jesus preached love. This was an act of love, one brother to another.

It was a simple service. The priest from St. Thomas University spoke. He began by recognizing my dad, "The great Marty Crowe is here." I flinched. My dad was a graduate of St. Thomas, where he'd been a star debater and a starting pitcher for the baseball team. He went on to make a name for himself as a coach for high school sports in Minnesota and Wisconsin and had quite a following as a writer, publishing human interest stories and pieces on education, politics, and religion in various newspapers. Bob was proud of him. The memorabilia from his apartment included pictures and articles about my dad, but this was Bob's funeral. I quietly apologized to Bob again.

The priest read from Bob's obituary:

Robert Crowe, age 80, of St. Paul, survived by his brother, Martin, sister-in-law, Helen, and six nephews and nieces. He was an activist in the DFL Party, a longtime member of the St. Paul Hiking Club and once its President. He was a writer, a thinker, and a rebel.

"How fitting," I thought. Their dad had run for the Minnesota State Assembly in 1921, endorsed by the Farmer and Labor Party, fighting for union representation. That group joined with the Democratic Party in 1944 to form the DFL. Both of his sons followed in his footsteps.

The singer began the opening strains of Antonin Dvorak's, "Going Home," a cappella, crescendoing until her soprano voice filled the room. I was mesmerized. It was a moving and fitting farewell to Bob. The song ended and the ceremony was over.

I talked briefly to Dad's cousin and thanked Bob's friend. I was struck by the kindness of this man who had so thoughtfully planned and organized the memorial. He clearly was a good friend.

On the return trip, we would be passing just a few miles from my dad's old hometown, Stillwater. I thought it would be good to take a detour and drive through.

Every summer of my growing up years we made regular trips to Stillwater. A family picnic at Pioneer Park was followed by a tour of the town, my dad pointing out the markers from his youth.

"There's the baseball field where I pitched ball along with my best friend, Louie Sal. He was the catcher."

"That's Phoebe Costello's house. She was the prettiest girl in town."

"There's where the Runk brothers lived, and over there, Noah Bibeau."

We would always make a stop at his old church, St. Michael's, where he had been a boy.

Next to it was the elementary school he attended. "Let's make a visit," he'd say and the whole family would pile out and go inside the church to pray or meditate for a few minutes.

That afternoon we revisited some of those places. When we reached St. Michael's, the bells began to toll signaling noon, the time to pray the Angelus. Praying the Angelus was a regular family activity in our house, a prayer we said three times a day, morning, noon and night. From a child's point of view, I thought it was kind of a long prayer. As the bells tolled, my dad said, "Let's say the Angelus." As we prayed, "The angel of the Lord declared unto Mary….," my dad pointed for me to turn left. We rounded the corner by St. Theresa's, another nearby Catholic Church, "Behold the handmaid of the Lord."

As we continued with the prayer, he kept signaling for me to turn left, circling the block. When we reached the front of the church he said, "Let's say the Angelus." Surprised, I looked over at him and responded, "No, we just said it." He was smiling. The joke was on me again.

We said goodbye to Stillwater and headed for the interstate. We reached home, mission accomplished. I helped him out of the car. My husband and brother got him into the house. I reported on the day to my mother and said my goodbyes.

Several days later I was on the phone with my sister. She reported that my father was quite upset and causing some distress for my mother.

"They've been looking all over and can't find that Merle Norman container he keeps the host in."

"Well, I know why he can't find it. He put it in Bob's casket."

"What?"

"Dad wanted him buried with it."

And there it is today, accompanying Uncle Bob on his journey.

NO MAN IS AN ISLAND

No man is an island entire of itself;
every man is a piece of the continent, a part of the main.

If a clod be washed away by the sea,
Europe is the less, as well as if a promontory were,
as well as if a manor of thy friend's or of thine own were.

Any man's death diminishes me because I am involved in mankind.
And therefore, never send to know for whom the bell tolls;
it tolls for thee.

—John Donne
"Meditation XVII"

DAN McAULEY

My father often referenced words from John Donne's, *Meditation XVII*. The words aligned with his belief about our humanity. We are here together and what happens to one impacts all.

We live in a society that promotes individual achievement, competition, "be number one." We celebrate achievement, and then look on for the next challenge.

My dad saw more important measures. He paid attention to the people walking through his life, those that he saw doing good, without fanfare, those he met along the way. He wrote about them.

* * *

"Tribute to Dan McAuley"
Published in "From the Bench"
Green Bay Register
August 16, 1963

An old man died in Eau Claire the other day. His name was Dan McAuley and you never heard of him. That's all right. He was a good man and I suspect he died well.

I know he lived well.

I got to remembering a lot of things when I went to Dan's funeral this morning. I thought it would be a very big funeral, but it wasn't really. Average size. Well, Dan wasn't rich or powerful or famous and I guess that makes the difference.

I first met him a short time after I came to Eau Claire in 1946 to teach and coach at the old Saint Patrick's High School there. Somebody had told me that his wife had recently died so when I met Dan, I tried to say the kind of things we all owe to one another but never say very well.

I didn't say them well either, but I got to know Dan a little and although he wasn't much of a sports fan—or maybe partly because of that—I got to feel a little closer to him in conversation then I did to most other people I met.

I left Eau Claire in 1950 and went to Marshfield to coach—and teach—Columbus high school there. One morning, a weekday, at Mass, I met Dan.

You know how it is when you see somebody from the old town in a place in which you don't expect to. We talked a while, and I was glad that he was there.

He told me he had a daughter living near Marshfield and that was how come. I saw Dan up there several times during the two years I worked in that town.

I went to Austin Minnesota—still as a teacher and coach—in 1952. I was at Saint Augustine's High School (it's now Pacelli) there and one morning at Mass at the parish church there was Dan McAuley.

It seemed kind of strange somehow—almost mysterious.

It turned out that Dan had some relative over there in that Minnesota town, too, and I saw him there a number of times during the seven years I was in Austin.

Summers in Eau Claire, I'd see him, of course. A few years ago his vocal cords gave out. I guess he had cancer or something—he had it for years. He couldn't talk after that, but he seemed just as quietly courageous—serene or something—as he always had.

I used to see him at Saint Pat's church in Eau Claire. He was often in there alone when I'd happen to drop in. It always seemed to me that a church can get to a guy most when you're in there alone with all the singing and the words turned off. Maybe Dan felt the same way. I never asked him. It isn't the kind of thing you ask a guy.

I used to see Dan at the library a lot, too. Seemed to me that church and the library were two good places for an old man to spend his time.

He used to walk a lot, too—alone. Even in the days when he was pretty sick, he'd walk real straight. Spunky, kind of.

And walking—and being alone, some—is good for a man, too.

Maybe what I mean most is that I meet a lot of young guys—many of them used to play ball for me—who are say, 30 years old, now, or a little more. They seem awfully anxious to impress. They tell me about their job or business—cement or feed or their law practice or something. Some of them drive some pretty fancy cars and some have homes with gosh-knows-how-many levels out in the suburbs. They tell me their kids are fast or big or clever or good looking, or all of these. They tell me they may go on vacation to some island or another.

They seem to be trying to prove something.

And I get to thinking about old Dan McAuley—in church or the library or walking. Straight and brave.

Proving nothing much, I guess. Not trying. Not working up a sweat about it.

A really good guy—but not great. Letting it stand that way.

Well, that's the end of this little piece—and looking back, there isn't much in it.

Except one thing, maybe.

To use the sports writer's kind of cliché—when I step up to that old dish and take my last cut of the ball—I'd rather be Dan McAuley than the guy who owns the bank.

Yep.

LONELINESS

M*y father paid attention to the people who get lost in our society. Sometimes, as with the woman in this article, he would find them on page five of the newspaper.*

* * *

"Loneliness: One Disease Penicillin Will Never Cure"
Published in "From the Bench"
Green Bay Register
December 17, 1965

Recently, I read a piece in the paper, way back on page five, about an old lady in a little town in mid-Wisconsin who hanged herself one Tuesday morning. No one answered the door when somebody knocked so they broke it down and she was hanging there.

She was 71 and she lived in that furnished room in that little town, the paper said. It noted, too, that her husband was five years dead, and she had a son who lived in Ohio and a daughter in Albuquerque, New Mexico.

She had moved to the furnished room in that town from another little Wisconsin town where she'd lived with her husband once. And watched her son and her daughter grow up.

Once.

But that was long ago and now the son was selling hardware in Akron and the daughter had four children of her own and was active in civic affairs in Albuquerque.

The piece, which told about the end of the story of the little old lady in the furnished room was on page five of the paper and the people who put the paper together obviously didn't think it was much as stories go.

Maybe they were right.

Gemini some number or other was taking off that week for somewhere and the Packers were playing somebody who had big tackles and a tough pass rush.

Besides, there were rumors that Fuzzy Thurston or Barry Goldwater or Hubert Humphrey or Cassius Clay or somebody had stomach flu.

In addition, Mr. McNamara was analyzing Southeast Asia and doing away with B-52s and replacing them with new, faster bombing planes. Bankers were concerned about a possible change in interest rates. Some guys were worrying about dying in the jungle.

So, one more little old lady bit the dust—and nobody cared very much. Oh, maybe a hardware merchant in Akron had a twinge of regret and a young matron in New Mexico society circles had a hurting conscience for a minute or two.

But it's Christmas time and maybe that's why I know more surely than otherwise that the story of the suicide in central Wisconsin is a greater one than the tale of Gemini 6.

Because our affluent society, in the midst of all the getting and spending is attacked by one disease which penicillin will never conquer.

Loneliness.

Across the land tomorrow morning a thousand little old ladies will watch for the mailman in vain. But they will watch.

And old men will sit and stare out the windows of warm and comfortable homes for the aged and wonder if anyone remembers or anyone cares.

Oh, Christmas is the busy season. I know that. It's the time of the running people—the shovers and the scramblers. Short tempers and thin lips. Sometimes.

And, when we remember, the time for nostalgia, too. And wistfulness.

Every man, I used to think, will come home for Christmas. If he can. No matter how far. No matter if he has to crawl all the way on his hands and knees.

The kids in Vietnam won't be home this Christmas, of course. Seems the season, sometimes, is also meant for killing people.

But some day—sometime, if they live, they can come home. And so, they mark the dates on the calendar. And they wait.

Home, someone has written, is where you hang your childhood.

Home, said the poet Robert Frost, is the place where when you have to go there, they have to take you in.

Where is home for the old woman in Mankato I used to see going to the cafeteria every night at five? Or the old man who waits until it is mealtime again at the Holloway House?

I remember my own mother standing on the porch waving goodbye.

Wave goodbye to grandma, kids. We've got to get going now. We've got so much to do. Wave good-bye to grandma.

So many times. So long ago.

She used to like fudge, I remember. Divinity. So Helen used to send her some each Christmas. And we always got up there during the season. At least for a little while. In those years.

But we were younger then. And the family, you know. And it was never long enough.

So, this has been a sentimental piece. And so what else is new? Push a button, somewhere, lad, and come back to reality again.

But grab a pencil first. Or phone for the bus schedule.

There's no penicillin for loneliness, friend. There's only you.

THE LOST SON

Spending summers in Eau Claire meant picnics at Pioneer Park in Stillwater, MN. We would often pick up Uncle Bob, my dad's only sibling. They grew up in Stillwater and enjoyed sitting in that park, with its scenic view, high above the St. Croix River of their youth.

My dad would often take our family on a tour of Stillwater, always stopping at his old church, St. Michael's, to make a visit and winding up at the ice cream shop for a cone before heading home. The best part of the excursion was driving past the homes of the people that populated his youth.

I remember his tour guide voice as he indicated landmarks. "We used to ride our sleds down that hill," pointing to a steep street climbing out of downtown Stillwater. "That's where the Runk brothers lived," and "Noah Biebeau," and "Louie Sal," and "That's Phoebe Costello's house, the prettiest girl in town." Sometimes the tour would include little anecdotes.

There was one house we only saw occasionally. I remember the melancholy in my father's voice, "Those people lost their only son in the war and rarely came out of the house again." My memory of the words may not be exact, but the sadness was tangible. I believe the lost son is the young man in this column. Today I wonder if what I heard in my father's voice in that tour of Stillwater may have been due to the regret he expresses in this column—the lost opportunity to tell the soldier's father how much his chance encounter with the son just before graduation meant to him long after.

* * *

"I Wish I Could Have Told Him...."

Published in "From the Bench"
Green Bay Register
May 22, 1964

If you ever visit my old hometown you might ask somebody where Dutchtown is (or where it was, anyhow, when I was a boy). In case you're shy about asking directions, I will tell you that you head out the main street going north and after a mile or so you're there.

Well, right at the end of Dutchtown, where the road turns down toward the river, there used to be a white fence under the streetlight. Maybe it's still there.

Anyhow, one night in May long ago, just a couple of weeks before graduation, I headed out to Dutchtown to see a girl in the junior class who lived out there. She was a very pretty girl as I remember it.

She wasn't home that night, as it turned out—but a guy in my class, whose name was Al, was there. He'd come out to see the girl too (let's call her Brenda for no particular reason) but she was out with a third guy that night. Never did find out who it was.

Anyhow, Brenda's mother was feeding Al some kind of hot pepper pickles she used to make, and she invited me to come in and have some too, which I did.

After a while, when we had run out of words, which doesn't take long when you're a teenager talking to a grown-up, we took off together. Al and me that is. (Pardon the grammar, teacher).

I don't know why we went over and sat on that fence under the light. Maybe we were trying to kill time in the hope that Brenda would come home early. Which wasn't very likely.

This Al was no real close buddy of mine, see. He was second base on the ball club, but he was strictly no hit and not much field. And he didn't even go out for the other sports.

Anyhow, sitting there on the fence talking to Al and chewing on a weed or something, I got to feeling that sad way you do, sometimes, toward the end of your last year. In school, I mean.

It's kind of happy-sad, actually. And you feel kinda old and kinda nice.

I don't remember what we talked about sittin' there. Not much, maybe. Except, toward the end, Al said, "When you get down to it, Mart—We live with ourselves as long as we last, and that's what makes the difference."

Well, Brenda didn't show, and after a while we headed home, and I never had a chance to talk privately with Al again and in a couple of weeks we were graduated, and the class broke up and our family moved out of town.

I heard, years later, that Al got himself killed out in the South Pacific fighting the Japanese.

By that time, he had finished college and was supposed to be a promising young man. Whatever that means. In the old annual at home it says that Al was voted, "The boy most likely to succeed." Like I say, whatever that means.

A long time later I went back to the old town to pitch a ball game and I saw Al's dad. He'd been the banker in our town, and he liked to take constitutional walks and he was a big, rugged guy—and he looked terrible. Sort of shrunken. Somebody said he got that way after Al was killed.

I wish I could have gone up to him and told him how it was that night sitting on that fence and what Al said. But how do you say something like that to a boy's dad four years after the boy is dead?

I wish I could have told him that of all the things ever said to me in high school by the teachers or my buddies or anyone, what Al said lasted the longest.

For me, anyhow, that second rate second baseman was a success. And underline it.

I wish I could have told that old man how it was.

MOMENTS THAT MATTER

We are busy people. We value achievement, efficiency, hard work, but what do we miss in life and in the people we live with every day? Last night I saw a poignant demonstration of this in a movie, Driveways, starring Brian Dennehy, his last movie, a fitting and touching final act. My dad was keenly aware of the price we all pay for our busy lives, including him. He wrote about it.

* * *

"The Time of Our Life and the Moments that Matter"

Published in "Something to Crowe About"
The Spirit
December 8, 1972

Way back in 1958, when the world was much younger than it is now and cynicism as a way of life was not yet in style, I was coaching at Pacelli High School in Austin, Minnesota. Our basketball team won the state championship at the auditorium in Saint Paul.

A few weeks later, when the sun of early April was on the land, a photographer from the *Austin Herald* happened to see Helen and our three daughters (we had only three, then, and they were very young) sitting on the grass along the shore of Austin's little artificial lake. Apparently, he figured the championship was still news because he snapped a picture, and they ran it the next day.

I'm glad he did that because now that more than 14 years have hurried on into history, the picture of how it was that April afternoon—and how Maureen and Mary Aileen and Kathy were then—is very precious to me. (Two of them made it home for Thanksgiving this year. Older and smoother now.)

Long blonde hair and innocence and joy—a time in a life that is too soon gone. You know how it is because there are pictures in your book, too, from some long forgotten afternoon. Somewhere...

Kathy, Mary Aileen, and Maureen on the shore of East Side Lake, 1958 (Photo Courtesy of *Austin Daily Herald*)

Mickey, our younger son, is playing on the basketball team at JFK now. He's only a sophomore but he is playing pretty well and the other night he was hot and broke the conference scoring record (or so they tell me because I am not much for records and don't know—or really care)—and I am proud and glad. Naturally.

But my memory goes back to the morning I saw him pitch a baseball game when he was eight. I don't remember how well he pitched but I recall that suddenly, at the end of that summer in Eau Claire, I realized that I would never see him pitch again while he was eight.

All at once, I was sad about that...

Or that afternoon when my team from Pacelli had stopped at my mother's house in St. Paul for a little while. As we were driving away, I looked back, and she was standing on the porch in the cold winter air with her shawl and that ancient sweater. She was very small and old. And alone.

I remember that suddenly I knew that she was just about out of such moments. That I would not be able to look back and wave goodbye very many more times.

That is long ago—but I remember how it was, like it was really yesterday....

And that night so long before when I was 19 and coming into a Wisconsin town I hardly knew then—my folks had moved there for a while, so that strange town was home because the old man and the old lady were there—and I had been away too long.

I was huddled up on the back of the locomotive on which I'd hitched a ride out of Milwaukee when the cops weren't looking because I was broke and the yearning to be again with somebody who gave a damn was a deep burning inside me. I crouched up there by the coal car which used to be part of the engine on any train—and it was raining and cold. I saw the lights of the town ahead and I knew I was almost home. I wanted to leap from the train and go racing through the night ahead.

If you've ever been away, you know how it was to come home.

Or the Sunday afternoon in Milwaukee in March of 1960 when I met that young priest I'd known in Minnesota. I'd heard he had come on bad and trying days—there was a girl or something and so what—and I met him in the lobby at the tournament there. He looked bad and I stopped to talk with him for a couple of minutes—I always liked and admired the guy—but he believed when you are down people always have an appointment somewhere.

Only, damn it, I really did. And the next time I heard about him more than a year after that he was dead. I could have made my players wait. They were young and they had time and their problems, if they had any, were minor ones. Appointments, sometimes, can go to…

Because sometimes, somebody needs you—and you've got to be there. Man—you've got to be there. Then….

You know something? All our lives are little snatches, little moments—and pictures. Whatever meaning there is in life is in there somewhere. We'll never understand exactly. But that's all right. As long as we keep looking.

And as long as we remember.

FAMILY

WHAT IS IMPORTANT?

This column was in such poor condition when I found the clipping that I nearly threw it out. I changed my mind. A resolute session at the ironing board saved the article from oblivion. The print was worn thin, almost unreadable, but as I continued to decipher the smudged letters, a simple yet important message appeared. Penned by my father in 1967 the piece is now digitally preserved in 2024. I think my dad would be pleased that it didn't go out with the trash.

The column has a message of what he valued in the world. Our lives can get complicated, and we can become anxious, fearful, sometimes hostile. Simple gratitude can be a great antidote.

My dad often dropped by church to make a "visit" in the middle of the day. I think it helped him reflect on what was important. This article identifies what mattered most to him.

* * *

"What Is Important?"

Published in "From the Bench"
Green Bay Register
January 6, 1967

As the year ends a man can list some of the things that count for the most. First—as for any man, the family. For me it is Helen and the six—four of whom are girls. The youngest just finished with being three, and the years go by too fast.

But for me, as any man, the first gratitude and the greatest meaning is there in the family.

Second—there is the job.

Too many of us get lost here, maybe. Too many want too much too quick. I will admit to having listened to that kind of siren song, too. Once.

But I am blessed with a job where a man can watch the dreams of the young unfold.

The classroom can be grim—but it can come to grace. For they come there—the gifted and the denied—the pretty and the plain. A man can watch them yearn and watch them reach.

I suppose my impatience with some assignments and my scorn for certain books is because they get in the way. Someone has said there is no way to learning save through work and sacrifice and sweat.

Well, sacrifice is a precious word with me. Yet I feel that, for many, the way must be a different way. For some the lights must come on first. The challenge. The excitement. These must be there. And they are not the same for all. A man must seek the way for each.

To teach, one must come to know compassion. One must learn to be kind. And when he forgets, he must remember that he forgot.

The greatest words ever written in a class of mine—for me—came from a below average student in Minnesota who said: I always felt that in your class I counted for something.

This is a good job.

(I have a bonus factor in my job, too. I am a coach and so I share some special dreams with some pretty good lads in some of the best years of their lives.

I have listened to the language and the laughter of the innocent—and found it good.)

Third—there is the place where you live and the people who say hello.

In a world where most people are obsessed with the need for running—and with speed—it is good to be in my town.

Someday, soon per chance, I shall try to get on to paper how it is to be here. For now, say it only that I wish everyone of you could—for a little while—taste the pace of the people here.

Some say that our town has not yet joined the century. And that could be. This town takes its time—and there are strange things here like clerks who talk instead of sell—and streets which go nowhere and end when they find it out—and sometimes—signs which brag of an event soon to be which happened three years in the past. And people who know your name and say it.

It is the kind of town a man wants to come back to if he can. A good town anytime, I think.

At Christmas, it is a town which remembers what Christmas is. Excited but never nervous.

A town which remembers. And reminds.

THE GROWING UP YEARS

Family topped the list of what was important to my dad. When we moved to Marinette, we were young. I was the second oldest and starting 3rd grade. That first year our beloved dog Aristotle joined the family. My dad wrote about him often.

I was excited for the adventure in a new town. I remember exploring the neighborhood that first day with my two younger sisters. We got disoriented and lost. Up drove Mr. Zahorik who taught with my dad. He recognized our plight and pointed us in the right direction.

Years later Mr. Z was my freshman English teacher and directed our drama group, the Windsor Players. I spent many a Saturday up at the school gym, working on the stage crew and oversaw props for our three annual productions.

My father referred to our 12 years in Marinette as our "growing up years." It was a precious time for him and my mom, for all of us.

* * *

"Marinette: Remembering the Growing Up Years"
Published in "Something to Crowe About"
The Spirit
November 4, 1975

A line at the top of the feature section of the Journal said: "You can buy anything on time except time itself."

Makes a guy think a little. Like that story in the book by Lin Yutang where the American grabs him by the arm and races him through the New York traffic—twisting and dodging—to catch a subway train.

"Why?"

"If we catch this train, we save 15 minutes."

"What do you mean, you save it?"

(Like, I mean, do you add it on? At the end?)

Anyhow, it all got me to thinking about some of the best years of my life... So today we'll skip the sports. You've got to forgive me once in a while....

When we came to Marinette back in 1959, Terry was in, I think, the fifth grade at Saint Joe's. He was our oldest. Then Maureen and Mary Aileen and Kathy. And Mickey was like two.

Then.

Mara hadn't gotten around to being born yet.

That first year we drove out into the country toward Coleman or somewhere and bought a dog. A collie pup. We named him Aristotle and he was an important part of the family until he died twelve years later—which was the year we left the north country and came down here.

Anyhow, those were the growing up days for the kids—and of being there for Helen and me. The best years of our lives. Yours or mine. When Harold Zahorik put on the play, "Our Town" (Terry was a junior at Central by then and he had a good part in the play) that's what the message was.

The days and the years go by, and we never quite know the wonder of them until they are gone.

(What is it the TV ad says? Phoning is the next best thing to being there.

But not the best.)

The house we lived in for most of those quickly fled years was just an average house on Carney. Nothing splendid. Nothing fancy. Somehow, though—precious.

"It's the house I care about" Mickey says. "The best years I ever knew were right there."

(He's had his share of ink and fleeting fame, and it was exciting, and it was fun. But the years with his friends at Saint Joe's—and the neighborhood there—the best years.)

We'd pile the whole tribe in the old car and head out for somewhere. Usually Henes Park. It was so—desolate—out there in the late fall. End of October. Early November. No one else there. Nothing. Except the echoes of summer laughter. The empty swings. And the lonely bay beating against the shore.

We'd have the whole place to ourselves, sometimes, and we'd race through the trees (I was younger then) and the dog choosing whom to chase and his wild joyous barking lighting up the night.

A good time.

"You coached the teams there. Weren't there some bad times too? Weren't people on your back?"

Oh, sure.

You come home some night and you'd lost a tough one and the world was suddenly an onion. And then the dog would meet you at the door and he didn't give a damn about the game. He was just wildly glad you were home.

And after you got over your self-pity and your gang was all around, you started to get your values straight again. And you walked down the street next day and some towhead kid yells, "Next time, Marty, we murder 'em."

A good place to be. An easy-going, no hurry kind of life. Never quite enough money to quite get by. But you get by. Never going to be rich or very famous either. So, what is rich, man?

What is rich?

Terry and Mickey with Aristotle, c. 1960

CARS AND THE FAMILY

Six kids and a dog necessitated a big car. Finances sent my father shopping for pre-owned vehicles. Though he couldn't afford an expensive car, he was always drawn to the luxury line. In my youth our cars were mostly Lincolns, a challenge for the novice 16-year-old driver.

I remember our annual moves from Marinette to Eau Claire as the school year ended. Our "luxury" car packed just short of the ceiling, kids lying on top with our collie dog, Aristotle. Not comfortable, but excited because we were headed to Eau Claire and our summertime friends.

In mid-August it was back to Marinette. My mother usually stayed behind to finish setting up student renters in our house for another year. (That additional income was vital to a family with six kids, on a Catholic school teacher's salary). The riding accommodations were the same, car packed to the gills destined for the practice field to begin the football season. Because my father was usually wheeling in at the last minute we disembarked at the field, with our dog, and walked home, excited for the new year ahead.

* * *

"Looking Back at Cars and the Family"
Published in *"From the Bench"*
Green Bay Register
July 26, 1968

I bought a new car.

Well—not a new one exactly. It's four years old. It's a 1964 Lincoln and I'm hoping the motor is in as good shape as the upholstery. The looks of a car I can judge. The quality of its innards—it might as well be beans in a jar.

I've never owned a new car. That fact had not bothered me very much. I have six kids and a big dog—and a wife named Helen—and I need a big car. A new one therefore has, for a long time, been out of the question. I got my '64 Lincoln for less than half the cost of a new Chevy, plus my 1960 Lincoln which I had for 15 months, and it was kind of a lemon, and it went out on me all of a sudden and had to be towed in.

Even as a trade-in, it had to be towed. It was a little embarrassing.

My new car has been well cared for and it looks pretty good, and a lot of people say wow and think it really is a new car or close to it. I would wager there isn't a schoolteacher in America driving a new Lincoln—unless he has a sideline like bookie or something. Or married a gal whose father owned the bank.

If you want to drive a new Lincoln—or Cadillac or a big Olds or Chrysler, don't become a schoolteacher. On the other hand, if you want a life with a hundred happy times, you might give teaching a try.

I say this to any young man who might wonder what street he wants to walk down with his life. This one has its compensations.

A guy doesn't really have to have a new car.

Well, anyhow this piece isn't actually about schoolteachers. It's about used cars.

A car can tie into your life. Sometimes, when it goes, even if it's all worn out and has been giving you trouble and grief, a door closes somewhere.

What car in your own life do you remember the best?

For me, there was that model T in my high school days. For instance. Remember the three pedals on the floor? The brake, clutch and reverse. You stepped halfway in on the clutch, and you were in neutral, and you could shoot down a hill like a bat out of—like fast, man.

Push the clutch all the way in and you were in low. For up a hill. Clutch band wear thin and there wasn't any low and you'd start sliding back down the hill. We used to swing it around then—step on the reverse and go up the hill backwards.

Disconcerting to somebody coming the other way.

Or there was that 1946 Plymouth I had once. The Blue Goose. Newest car I ever owned. Two years old and new to me the day I got married and Helen and I took off into whatever life might be ahead.

How was it with you that day? How did your car hold up?

Or the big Chrysler I had once and Terry, our first born, opened the back door one day near Owatonna and fell out—and we were doing fifty-five. Would've been more but it was raining.

Thank God.

A kid falls out of the car—again the good break, the shoulder side—and you don't expect to see him walk again. Ever. And when Helen screamed, and I stopped the car and started back up the highway and I saw that three-year-old of mine get up and come running down the road—crying but alive. A good day, man. A very good day.

We used to play tricks on him a lot. The first one. You remember how it was.

And as I held him, he sobbed because he figured another trick, "And that wasn't funny either!"

A good day.

I will remember that Chrysler. It gave me some bad times, but I will not forget....

Or that '36 Ford.

I bought it in 1939 and I was on my first job. WPA. Teaching adult education classes in St. Paul at night. A smart punk, fresh out of college and having a heck of a good time on the job.

My dad was in the hospital, and I went down, and I bought that 1936 Ford. Then, a couple of days later, my mother and I drove out to Ancker and they released my dad and I helped him down the stairs and I knew he wasn't going to last a real long time (but he made it for two more years) and when he saw that good looking Ford, which was the best car we ever had in the family I grew up in, my old man was glad.

He felt really good that such a fine car was ours and I felt good because I knew how it was and we got in that old Ford, and we drove home.

That was a good ride.

Almost 30 years down the drain since that afternoon, but I remember how it was. I remember that life was beautiful and a sweet taste on the tongue.

My old man never owned very much in this world, but he sure owned a big chunk of me. For whatever that was worth.

A car can wrap itself around some days you don't ever want to forget.

Yep.

GOOD-BYE TO A CAR

"Good-Bye to a Car Triggers Memories"
Green Bay Press Gazette
March 20, 1977

Our old car came to the end of the road the other day. It was a 1964 Lincoln and we got it in '67 or '68—and it was going up this hill and all at once decided that was it. It never made it to the top.

I guess I could have had it repaired enough so it would go again for a little while but that would have cost a couple of hundred bucks. I think the old car was telling me it wanted to rest anyhow.

Permanently.

What I want to write about is how it is that something like a car can take on an identity and a life of its own. When we said goodbye, it was like saying it to an old friend.

I guess that's because a family car wraps itself around much of your own life. Like Aristotle—our old dog who is dead now—used to get so excited when we were going for a ride in the car that he could not contain himself but would go into squeals of sheer ecstasy.

And he would ride along with his head hanging out the side of the car and little kids would see him and shout, "Lassie!" because Aris was a collie, and most collies look alike. Now he is gone and the car he loved is gone.

So are the days when we would get the kids together for an expedition to Henes Park in the cold of November—or up to the Menomonee River or somewhere. Or our annual summer jaunt to Eau Claire. There wasn't room in that car—or any car—for such a mob of people and dogs.

But no one cared.

Now the kids are gone, too. Or just grown away from the days of being young.

We don't taste this life deep enough while the good things are here. Thornton Wilder made that point in his play, "Our Town," which Mr. Z. put on at Marinette Central once. Terry was a junior in high school then and he was in the play, and it was a great and good night in his life.

The '64 Lincoln was almost new then and I don't know who owned it nor where it was.

You don't have to be rich.

I know it's a cliché and sophisticates will curl their lips—but it is as true for them as it is for you. Or me. You don't have to be rich—or important.

(Who's important, anyhow?)

What you have to be is aware. Because the sweet and precious moments are quickly gone—and they do not come back. Not the way they were. Never the same. You've got to taste them while they're there.

Maureen used to drive that car her senior year in high school. And with her long blonde hair blowing in the wind—to the people who didn't know the car was a long way from new, she must have looked a little bit like a debutante or country club.

And her old man a schoolteacher!

But that car had flair and style and verve and class—and a kind of zest for life. Until the rust started to come on and it began the long slow descent which ended the other day.

Those were the days when Mickey was practicing layup shots on the basket on the garage and not a photographer was around. And Mara was eating cookies and napping on the rug in kindergarten.

You can never buy back the way it was, rich man. Put your wallet away. There are things which are not for sale. And those are the ones we really yearn for when we remember.

So goodbye now, old car.

You will not return on a summer day to climb the steep hills of Stillwater, that quiet little town in Minnesota where I was a boy once long ago—and to which you carried me back to those happy times.

You will not—ever again—come tearing into Marinette up Highway 64—loaded to the gunwales with our family things because I was racing back from summer for the first day of football practice—and I was always late.

I don't know where they'll take you now, old car. Nor what your material destiny may be.

EATING OUT

My dad had two favorite destinations for family outings during our time in Marinette, the Menomonee River and Henes Park along The Bay. His favorite time to go was in the chilly days of early spring or the dark cool days of late autumn. My father found wonder in the solitude of the off season and valued time spent with family in the quickly passing days of our youth.

* * *

"Eating Out"
Published in "From the Bench"
Green Bay Register
May 16, 1969 (Excerpt)

Some of you will recall how Helen and I took what's left of our home gang—what with Terry away at college and Maureen and Mary Aileen grown too tall—out to one of our favorite lonely spots along the river last fall—when the summer crowd was gone away.

You breathe in deep, the air is crisp with promise and quiet for remembering. It is a good time.

We went back the other night.

The summer people have not come yet. The tables were still piled and upside down. But the lonely swings were waiting. And Mara is six now—and wildly ecstatic—and so she rushes pell-mell to greet them once again.

And the night is filled with the sound of laughter and the shouting and the barking of our old dog, Aristotle, who forgets how old he is when the night and the woods are around him—and a good part of his family is still there.

Because Mickey is only 12 and it is an age when some kids have walked away—but he hasn't. And Kathy is 14 and caught between the desire to hold on and all the demands that she let go. We were going to leave her home this time. She wasn't happy about that. She senses that that will come and when it does it's final. So she came along—and because she believes—yet anyhow—that it is better to be joyous than to try to be impressive—she had a shouting good time.

I walked away—alone—for a while and watched the fire under the hamburgers and the friendly smoke rising—and listened to the words and the laughter caught for a moment and suspended in the air—and I knew—that most of the reason for why I was born was right there somewhere. For a man to see if he will take time.

I guess I'm sorry I never made the big time in something—like the hometown predictions once said I would. But if I had to give up any of this, I would not trade. Let those who need it fancy go on looking and trying.

The river slipping so silently in the night says the same thing now it said on a night like this late in last October. Says don't sweat it man. Says hold to this because it is sweet and true and very precious—and because nothing lasts forever.

It was Kathy, while we were eating, who shopped out the capper.

"The Crowes are eating out again," she shouts. "Marty Crowe says let's eat out tonight—so we all get dressed—and here we are!"

I wonder who lives in that tri-level that advertising agency man once told me I would someday own if I would stay on writing those cake commercials—and live in Minneapolis. You know—that was a real nice house.

Whoever lives there now, I hope he "eats out" once in a while.

And takes some time to listen.

HENES PARK 1970

"November Night: Henes Park–1970"
Handwritten piece found in files

We packed up two of our kids—Mickey and Mara—and our old dog—that's Aristotle—and drove over to Henes the other night.

Henes is a park along the way up here and in the summer there are many people there, but now that the cold winds of November have come, the only ones around are the parkers and the lovers—and they'll be gone soon too, and the park will be closed for the winter again.

It's the best time there is to go out there I think. A man should be alone once in a while anyhow—and I walked the shore alone for a while that night and looked up at the stars in the sky.

Eternity, man.

We sweat and strain a lot—and get mad a lot—and worry—and count our money if we have any and balance it against the bills—and each day we've lived one more—and one less is left.

A guy should look at the stars sometimes. For sure he should walk alone.

Besides that, I walked down on the lonely beach with the two kids and the dog. (Helen had to stay in the car because she had hurt her knee doing some of the work around the house that I should've been doing instead). You're cut off from the world out there. The sound of the water on the sand—and the kick of the wind in your face.

And way off across The Bay there, the lights of the city. In another world somewhere.

Hey, you really ought to give it a try

We cut up through the playground area and a lot of it is locked up for the winter but the slides are still there and the kids climbed them in the dark and slid down—and the dog barked a lot and ran around a little slow—and it was good to be there.

Good to be alive for every day we make it.

I got to thinking of all the kids who'd been there during the summer that was gone. You let your mind move out a little and you can hear their shouting and their laughter. Still there. Thomas Wolfe wrote once that all the little sounds we make as we come and leave—they never go away.

Maybe.

Anyhow, those kids will never be back.

They may return next summer it is true. But the boy who was 10 will be 11 then. The boy who was here last July will never come back.

And that is a much sadder thing than the fact that business was bad today.

We walked through the woods for a while and because I am not young anymore and always was a little heavy-footed anyhow, I tripped over a big log in the dark and I fell pretty hard and it hurt.

Mickey and Mara were quiet with concern as I lay there—and the dog wondered what I was up to now.

After a while I got up—a little shaken—and conscious, very vividly, of the fact that the days of yore return no more.

But who needs them?

There I was, with my leg throbbing a little from the pain, but the hard, cold wind against my teeth. And Terry was in Ireland and Maureen and Mary Aileen away at school and Kathy off somewhere with the girls of her time—but still two of them with me.

And the ancient dog.

And down there a ways is the girl—a girl no longer—with whom I have had the great privilege to share so much of my life—waiting for us to return.

And after we got back we went over by the cages and looked at the coyote and the timberwolf and the porcupine and Mara was in ecstasy because, people are OK she figures, but timberwolves and porcupines are what life is all about.

On the way home we would've stopped for cones at the Dairy Queen but it was shut down because the summer trade is gone away.

It looked a little desolate and lonely, all dark.

The kids would've liked cones because there is something special about driving up to get them together. Everybody has cones at home now, I guess. You need adventure with your ice cream.

They sang on the way home. Not me, of course. I sing like a crow. Helen and Mara and Mickey. And the dog in his fashion.

After I put the car in the garage, I stepped for a minute outside—alone—I took a final gander at the stars.

Hey, Sam Rockefeller—what did you do tonight?

* * *

Unbeknownst to my father, this was probably one of the last excursions to Henes Park. In the spring the family would be leaving Marinette.

Leaving Marinette was hard for my parents. They loved the town and its people.

My dad had great affection for the school, Catholic Central, and the students. I remember a column in which he described walking through the school at night and loving the old squeaky floors to which he'd grown so accustomed, thinking about all the students who had walked those halls, many who had become a part of his life.

He was moving on to a different setting, one in which he would again create those bonds with the people he encountered and the students he had yet to meet. JFK Prep and the Village of St. Nazianz would become a treasured time and place in his life.

THE ROAD LESS TRAVELED BY

Two roads diverged in a yellow wood,
And sorry I could not travel both
And be one traveler, long I stood
And looked down one as far as I could
To where it bent in the undergrowth;

Then took the other, as just as fair,
And having perhaps the better claim,
Because it was grassy and wanted wear;
Though as for that the passing there
Had worn them really about the same,

And both that morning equally lay
In leaves no step had trodden black.
Oh, I kept the first for another day!
Yet knowing how way leads on to way,
I doubted if I should ever come back.

I should be telling this with a sigh
Somewhere ages and ages hence:
Two roads diverged in a wood, and I –
I took the one less traveled by,
And that has made all the difference.

—Robert Frost
"The Road Not Taken"

GOOD MEN

My dad had to start over, several times in his life. I admire the enthusiasm and optimism he brought to each new beginning. The relationships he forged with young people in his classes or on his teams, and with the people he encountered in daily life mattered and that made it all good. He paid attention.

* * *

"Good Men"
Published in "Something to Crowe About"
The Spirit
December 15, 1972 (excerpt)

As you know, I don't believe in big shots. I believe in little shots who, on occasion, have big days. Of course, sometimes these little men look in the mirror after such a day and see a distorted image—and never forget it.

If there were such a thing as a big man, in this area where I live, Vic Miller would come as close as any. He doesn't view himself that way because he doesn't believe in big shots either.

But he is the newly elected head of the state bar association and that's unusual for a small-town lawyer. And he is well known in state political circles—and religious as well. I knew a lot about Vic before I ever came down this way.

(He was a mediocre first baseman, by the way. Good glove—fair hit. When he was 17. Maybe he improved later.)

Anyhow, a couple of Sundays ago they had a big dinner at Saint Gregory's in Saint Nazianz. Only small towns can do this kind of thing anymore—everybody comes and there is no pretentiousness or sham whatsoever. Unless you're watching your weight, it's a fine place to be.

I stood on the steps in the Saint Greg's school, with Vic Miller that day for an hour or so talking politics and other nonsense, and I'll bet that at least 30 times I watched him turn to talk to some old guy or gal who was painfully hobbling up the steps. Much of the time he talked with them in German.

Helen (my wife) can speak it and I really don't think much of it as a language, but these people did—and most of all they were aware that here was somebody who cared.

Because Vic did care. There was no fraud or fake in the scene. He felt good doing it and those old timers felt good being there—and I felt good watching.

It's a fine thing to be head of the bar association, Vic—but the scene on those steps was better by far. And a lot of big lawyers wouldn't have had the time for it.

* * *

"Anselm Platten is the main force behind this whole thing," Vic said. "He's spent a good chunk of his life for this community and its people, and he's never got the recognition—not half the credit—for it that he surely deserves."

So, this last is a small touch of recognition for Anselm, because I know Vic said it true. It's funny how we can come to take a man and his work for granted—year after year—until all the time there is runs out.

Merry Christmas, Anselm Platten and Vic Miller—and all people, everywhere, who have the time for others who need somebody—and all people, everywhere, who have found that a small town can indeed be a good place in which to live.

And be….

FATHER WINFRED HERBST

JFK Prep was a new experience for our family. Terry, Mary Aileen and I were away at school by then. Our dad, mom, Kathy, Mickey, and our old dog Aristotle made the move to a rural setting on a campus where they would be living in community with resident students, teachers, and priests and brothers. My father saw stories worth telling, so he wrote.

* * *

"Father Winfred Herbst"
Published in "Something to Crowe About"
The Spirit
October 1, 1971 (excerpt)

Father Winfred Herbst, a tall, gracious man of more than 80 years, just the other day observed the 50th anniversary of his ordination. Fifty years a priest. Something there in these days of quick decisions and uneasiness and uncertainty. A man who knows why he was born.

He has had quite a life. He has authored many books—edited magazines for many years. Given retreats and missions and counseled many men.

Now, in the final years of a good life, he has put many of his sermons on tape. And readings from his books. And from the New Testament. And from the recent ideas coming out of Vatican II. Some 400 tapes representing a fabulous expenditure of this man's talent and time. They go winging across the land to scores of people and groups who ask for them.

He stays here at Saint Nazianz most of the time, now. Like I say, he's 80. But his thoughts and his words continue to go out to anyone willing to listen.

A lucky man, I think, to be able to give his life that kind of meaning and impact all the way to the end. Not many can or do.

But it's not even this that stays in my mind.

I watch Father Winfred as, night after night, he walks this campus. Alone. Alone with his God, I suspect. A long lank man. Like I say—80. And yet he walks straighter and taller than most lads in the bounce of being young.

He has found the strange kind of joy and exaltation, even, that can come from being alone. The kind of wisdom, maybe, that comes to a man no other time or way.

I watch him walk among the trees on this beautiful campus—in the shadows of early evening—and I feel that I can learn or understand something subtle but significant just by seeing him there.

For me, in a time of hustle and hurry and very much ado about a great deal of nothing, to see this man walk alone is the greatest sermon of them all.

THE BROTHERS

The JFK Prep campus was housed on property owned by the Salvatorian Brothers. The Brothers lived on the campus, took care of the grounds, and some of them taught in the school. My father saw and admired these good men and the quiet work they did. He noted the impact of their contribution to the campus.

* * *

"Brother Vergil and the Football Bowl"

Published in "Something to Crowe About"
The Spirit
August 3, 1973 (excerpt)

We had a little get together for the Whittiers the other night. Larry is leaving to take a college job in Illinois. He will be missed. He started football at the school and did a splendid job coaching the team. And he was the best high school counselor and guidance man I have ever come across.

In these days, all schools need such a man.

When I came here two years ago, Larry had been here three. I hesitated to take over as his assistant in football because I had been the head man in a lot of places for almost 30 years. I figured I was a bit too much the egotist to be much of an assistant anywhere. I think that would've been a correct evaluation if I'd been somewhere else.

But the two years helping Larry (I had the defense) are two of the really fun years I've had in sports. He's quite a guy.

But this piece is not really about Larry. (I've written about him before.) Nor about me. (I've written about him many times.) This is about a man who did as much for football at JFK as either Larry or I—and who, as far as I know, doesn't know a triple reverse (my favorite play) from a fumble in the end zone. (Another good one.)

Brother Vergil is the man who keeps this campus looking as beautiful as it is. (Brother Modestos, too, because he keeps the flowers alive and proud). He runs the ancient equipment all summer long keeping the vast lawn mowed and attractive. It takes quite a touch just to keep some of that stuff going.

Anyhow, Larry tells me that Vergil is the one responsible for the fact that our football bowl is, beyond all doubt, one of the most beautiful in the state. Larry said it used to be a mud bowl and he thinks it was once a garden.

(With the current price of vegetables, the team better do something right or they may turn it back into a garden again.)

Anyhow, it was the diligence and patience and skill of this man that turned the whole thing around. Our team may or may not be worth anyone's attention this year, but our playing field is worth the trip.

I think it was Keats who wrote once, "A thing of beauty is a joy forever."

It's hard to remember that down in that football bowl on a bad day—but it is true, nevertheless. The JFK campus is, indeed, a thing of beauty and the main one responsible is a guy up there on the seat of that ancient mower.

A lot of people in this world do some pretty fine things for the rest of us and it never gets mentioned by anyone. Here's one exception....

JFK PREP

M*y dad fell in love with JFK Prep. He called the school and the campus his "Camelot."*

* * *

"JFK Prep, My Camelot"
Published in "Something to Crowe About"
The Spirit
December 17, 1976

There used to be a question raised, after John Kennedy had been dead for a while: "Can we ever go back to Camelot?"

By that I think we used to mean, will we ever be that young again? Will we ever again find the fun and the challenge and the sheer joy of how it was that glorious once upon a time?

The question will come up again pretty soon now.

I think we need more right now than the "practical men" in both political parties have to offer. We need a song and a dream. We need a special kind of faith.

We need an end to envy and callousness and cold pride. And bombers over Cambodia. To schemers and planners and men with blueprints.

We need to go back to Camelot.

My purpose in writing today, however, is not to get into politics or the question of candidates or campaigns. I want, instead, to note that I believe there is a personal Camelot somewhere—for each of us. And maybe we miss it or pass it by and never know that it is there.

I have found mine.

I have always been grateful to God that he let me spend the years of my life as a teacher. It is a life of deep rewards and the kind of personal associations that a man remembers forever. I would trade my job for no other.

I've been fortunate, too, in having had the chance to teach at the great school that was St. Pat's in Eau Claire back in 1946. And I was at Columbus in Marshfield after that and then Pacelli High over there in Austin, Minnesota. Good schools both.

And still very sweet to the tongue is the remembered taste of 12 cherished years at Catholic Central in Marinette. I will have a deep affection for that old school and the people I knew there as long as I have a memory.

But my Camelot is here.

There had to be something new and good under the sun and I found it here at JFK. The place is alive with the pulse of youth, and I, who am no longer young, feel it and am glad. It is alive, too, because there's a fierce faith, here, in the future of mankind.

In the time of the cynic, faith becomes a very precious thing.

We need a particular kind of faith in the future of this school. And we have it. Like most private schools, JFK fights constantly to survive. But we are winning the fight because everybody here believes, and everybody joins in.

In a time of many battles that have no meaning at all, this one has all the meaning the mind of a man can ask for. And I find that this kind of fight has a special kind of fun—maybe magic—all its own.

Central had to battle to keep going. St. John's of Little Chute, I note, has to do the same. Many others. And the kids in the good schools—like these—do not mind. They go out and storm the barricades for their place.

But there is something extra special here.

We have no parishes to turn to for help. No city population of which we are a part. We are alone out here in the hills. The campus is so beautiful now, with the snow upon the trees, that it almost hurts to breathe.

"My God!" One girl from Milwaukee sighed as she got off the bus here Sunday night and looked across the great field in front of the administration building.

And there was a reverence in her tone.

And the incredible faculty we have here—the charismatic, young, bearded men like Tony and Bruce and Greg and Dan—the brilliant Melvin— the philosophic—and shaved—older (of which I am the oldest by far)—all these hurl themselves into the battle to make do.

No holding back. A recklessness and a kind of laughter that has a surge of life all its own.

"Right on!" The kids cry—and they join in.

You ought to come down and see us sometime. I doubt if there is a better way of teaching and of learning in all of this state tonight. The drudgery is gone. The grimness. The stifling, boring repetition—the picayune penalties ("Write this sentence five hundred times!")—the monotony of routine.

A bunch from the faculty met the other day to decide what to do about a boy who was a problem, and we decided the problem was us for not coming up with the answer sooner.

"I don't think we ought to kick him out," I said.

"Nobody ever thought we should."

"We don't intend to solve our problems by sending them somewhere else."

Hey, man. A guy can wait all his life to hear that kind of music in the air.

REMEMBERING ARISTOTLE

Our old dog Aristotle made the move to JFK Prep. He lasted a few months, but finally died that fall. Mickey told me he was coming home on a bus from a game. He looked up and saw the light was out in Aristotle's room and he knew he was gone. It was a hard loss for the family. He was a good dog.

* * *

"Remembering Aristotle"
Published in "Something to Crowe About"
The Spirit
November 19, 1971

During all the years we lived in Marinette, I used to write a good many columns dealing with our family. The kids were young in those days, and we'd have picnics out at Henes Park, for instance, in November when all was quiet and bleak and desolate— and the cry of the gulls was lonely in the night.

It was a kind of wonderful.

And always along and sharing it all—eager and quick and bouncing, once, and slower and quieter as the years went by—but always loyal and faithful and true—and always there—was our big dog.

Aristotle.

He was 11 years old this fall, and I knew he would not last forever. Aristotle died a week ago. And part of all of us—in the family—died with him.

If you've never had a dog around for a long time perhaps you cannot know how it is. Or maybe you can, even so. Aristotle lived in the house all those years. At first, so his barking wouldn't bother the neighbors. And later—because we wanted him there. He met each of us at the door when we came home, and he was always indescribably glad to see us. No one will greet any of us quite that way again. Not ever.

He was a big dog—a collie. When we'd drive along in the car (and to ride in the car was one of his greatest joys) little kids along the way would see him with his neck and head outside the window and almost every time one of them would shout, "Lassie!"

He was a gentle dog with the kids—and yet fiercely defensive of the home. We had to warn everyone not to open the door without knocking. Ever. ("We have to put the dog in another room.") If I faked it that I was mad at Mickey or Mara and bounced them around a bit, Aristotle would be there, instantly, shouting and barking and defending.

I used to come home after we'd lost a game and some of the fans had been pretty caustic and pretty blunt, and he'd meet me at the door. Maybe it had been my fault. Maybe I had blown the game. But Aristotle didn't care.

You didn't have to win to have the dog on your side. He never let a guy down. He made it all right again.

I know that collies don't have souls, but if they did, they'd be in better shape than yours and mine. Devotion and faith and loyalty and affection—Aristotle had them all. No man I ever knew could match him in this way. It's something I am not likely ever to forget.

In the last years, his quickness and awareness and a lot of his alertness were gone. And some of his confidence went, too. He became more dependent on a guy. He'd wait for the guiding word or hand. He loved to jump up on the couch and share an hour close to you.

Brother Vergil, here at Saint Nazianz, showed us where to bury him. And he suggested we get another dog real soon. I suppose he meant a replacement.

But no dog can replace one who's been part of your life for 11 years. I doubt if we shall have another one around for a long time. Maybe never.

It took him two days to die—and Terry and Helen and I were there most of the way. (At the end, Mickey was around, too—And Kathy.)

We tried desperately to pull him through—but after we took him to the vet the second time, we knew he wasn't going to make it.

Terry and Mickey and Helen and I buried him on Saturday morning. Very silent and sad—and somehow very close.

So, an era of our lives ends. It's the way time and all lives go by. We put a note in the old dog's grave—sealed it in a jar and threw it in. The note said "This was Aristotle. He was a good dog. We shall not forget him. Not ever."

So, rest well, old dog. There was something about the way you were and what you were that held much of what a man should know about creation and about existence. You had a big hold on a part of my life.

TIME AND WASTE OF TIME

TIME

My dad was a joyful man. Though faced with many challenges he did not despair and never seemed knocked down by them. Going through his papers, I have come to appreciate the courage both he and my mother showed in those trials.

My father had a zest for life. He sought out the beauty and wonder in the world and in literature and tried to bring his students to see and appreciate it. He knew time was limited so he did not want to waste it. The rub came between his concept of "wasting time" and the assessments of others.

* * *

"Time"
Handwritten manuscript, c. 1969
Article referenced is from Life *magazine, May 9, 1969*

"There is never as much time left as men suppose."

That quotation is a good one, I think. It comes from an article in a recent issue of *Life* magazine called "Requiem for Courtney Smith" and the article deals with the sudden death, last January, of the president of Swarthmore College in Pennsylvania.

It is a pretty good article. I guess just about anybody who wants to give his mind a little free rein would benefit from reading it. Courtney Smith seemed like a good man, and he died at the height of some racial trouble they were having at Swarthmore.

The trouble was minor compared with much of what came before other places—or has come since. It was new to Swarthmore, though—and some tried to imply that without it Courtney Smith would not have died.

They cannot say something about that—not really. Neither can I. But I can and I do recommend the article to your attention.

And especially the idea which runs through it that there is never enough time.

The playwright, William Saroyan, once wrote a play with the title, "The Time of Your Life."

"The time of your life," he told someone who asked him about the title, "is the time between the moment you are born and that in which you die."

The same issue of *Life* which contains the "Requiem for Courtney Smith," also has a movie review—in advance of production—of something called "Husbands" which will star John Cassavetes and Peter Falk and Ben Gazzara—and is directed by Cassavetes.

I would predict that it will be a tremendous movie because John Cassavetes is more sensitive and sharper than most men in the business and because the movie "tells the story of three men fast approaching 40. They attend the funeral of a friend and suddenly become afraid...."

"Getting old doesn't bother us," says Cassavetes. "It's still being young and not having done anything...."

There is a poem Carl Sandburg wrote once about a man who is on a train and asks another man where he is going, and the other man says "Omaha."

I don't know exactly how that fits in right here except that I know—as Sandburg knew—that no one goes to Omaha.

Or wherever....

And Thomas Wolfe entitled one of his novels, "You Can't Go Home Again" and it means that you can go back but you are never the same and no one else is ever the same. Nothing is the same.

So, you can't really go home again....

The thing about all of this that bothers me is the matter of the passage of time. No one can stop time from passing. I know that as well as the next man and perhaps regret it more than most.

I would like to freeze time if I could—Every once in a while. Not keep from growing old, I mean. Not even to keep from coming to the end of my own time. We all do that after a while.

It's more that there are such moments of terrible beauty that come along once in a while—and are gone so quickly. Sometimes we don't even quite know that they are there before they're gone.

Forever.

Thornton Wilder said all this so hauntingly in his play, "Our Town."

Do you recall the part where the girl, now long dead, is granted the chance to come back and choose one moment from her life to live over again? Or not to live it exactly—to see it as she lived it once.

She chooses her twelfth birthday.

Her dad is there, and he has brought a present and her mother is there and the other members of her family, and the whole thing is touching and beautiful and sad. Because, like she says, we never know how wonderful and precious the fleeting moments are until they are no more.

We never quite taste them while they're there.

I truly, therefore, have wondered, lately, if I have the right to talk to somebody about wasting time. Is a man planning a business deal using his time wisely and another lying on his back contemplating the stars a fool?

Somebody said to the Chinese author, Lin Yutang, once, if we hurry and catch this bus we will save an hour and Lin asked him how you save an hour.

I have never heard the answer.

There was a time when I was getting ready to pitch that game in Forest Lake and I knew I had the strength and the swift in my arm and could throw the ball very fast, and I felt tall and forever young, and I can remember kidding around with some of the girls along the street there and how it was to be confident and strong and young. I remember eating an ice cream cone before the game. I even remember the flavor.

Blueberry.

And the time when Terry was three and he fell out of the car along the highway, and we were doing fifty in the rain. And I stopped the car and started back up the road and I saw him get up out of the ditch.

That was a good time.

Or that day I was picking wild plums and because I was clumsy and also a fool I fell out of the tree and that silent, older man who was my dad came running and it looked like I was hurt worse than it was, and he held me pretty tight, and I knew something about my dad right then.

That time.

Or the night I came home on the back of the engine of the train because I was broke and I'd been away for a long, long time. And I knew my mom and my dad would be glad and I was cold and hungry and wet from the rain and that old train stopped and I got off and started to run down a familiar street....

I'm not smart enough to decide about how you waste your time—or spend it well. I only know that I think that it's gone too soon.

I know that we should see it—and know and understand—while it's there.

WASTE OF TIME

"What Is a Waste of Time?"
Published in "From the Bench"
Green Bay Register
January 7, 1966

Years ago, I used to teach in a school in which it was very difficult to conduct our baseball games. The reason was simple: The games were played in the afternoon. Most of the schools we played, played in the afternoon. Most of the schools we played against were small town public high schools; they wanted to start the games by 3:30 in the afternoon at the latest so the farm boys could get home to help with the chores.

And the good Sister in charge of our school didn't want to let our boys out in time to be dressed and ready for a game that early.

We had a heck of a time when we played out of town because we always arrived about an hour after the opposition school wanted the game to start—and everybody was always mad.

When we played at home it was kind of embarrassing, in a way, because the visiting team would always be finished with its batting practice and infield warm-up, all before our team—the home club—even showed up. We'd always have to skip one warm up and start the game as soon as we got there.

I think the Sister in charge meant well. She was convinced that there was something pretty barbaric about athletic competition in the first place, and that to let the kids out early for a ball game was very bad educational practice and probably immoral as well.

(We didn't have the problem in football and basketball because the games were played at night. It was little old high school baseball, a minor sport if I ever saw one, that caused all the trouble.)

Our entries in music, debate, one-act play contests, and such seemed to get better breaks. (My recollection is prejudiced, of course.) I suspect the idea was that there is more of an educational tie-in there.

I wonder, now, if our administration had a kind of scorn for the buffoons in charge of the schools we played. After all, they were always on the field on time.

My point, I guess, is that I'm never really convinced by educators who are forever calling attention to how superior their own intellectual postures are.

The lad, for example, who tries to prove his intellectual superiority by simply sneering at the physical and the muscular in general has not, in my book, produced enough evidence.

I heard a sermon on New Year's Day, about how precious time is and how a man should not waste his share. I doubt if the speaker had in mind that playing a ball game—or even watching one played—was necessarily a waste of time. But I suspect the administration at the school I am remembering here felt it was.

I would've liked to ask that nun what was not a waste of time. I think she would have said studying was not. For instance. And I would have liked to have asked, "Then, studying what, Sister, or studying for what?"

Is making money a waste of time?

In the philosophical sense of the New Year's Day speaker, it must be. Certainly, if a man gets lost in making money he may well get lost in wasting all the time he has. A lot of men spend all their time in this fashion.

Isn't much of studying intended, in the final analysis, to enable the student to be richer or more important? Or bigger—socially and economically? Isn't this the goal?

If not—what is?

If the average lad, for example, doesn't go to college to enable himself to come up with a better job—and if the criterion for a better job isn't the salary it commands—or its "importance"—then what criterion would you suggest as the one the average young man has in mind?

Some folks say a dreamer wastes his time.

I read a very involved book on "the world of tomorrow" the other day in which the author made the point that this is the time of the activists (the example he gave was chiefs of staff) and the contemplatives (example, poets) have no real place in it.

Could be.

I wonder if these folks who worry so much about the "waste" of time regard dreaming as a waste.

Because I want to go on record, once more, as opposing such a position. I guess I believe that maybe the dreamers and the poets and the contemplatives are using their time about as well as time permits.

Or the limitations of the finiteness of man permits.

Is war, for instance, a waste of time?

Activists always come up with answers like war. In fact, activists come up with answers for almost everything. The only trouble with the answer is that most of them don't work—or do any good. A lot of them do a lot of people a lot of harm.

In his book, *The Moon Is Down*, Steinbeck has an old Norwegian refer to the Nazi invaders as "a time minded people."

That's as good a description of the breed as I have come across. The new masters of China are time-minded, too—in a land in which men were once philosophers about time.

Blue-printers and authoritarians are always against wasting time. In the end, though, it seems to me that they waste all of it.

Right now, we have a target date for reaching the moon: 1970. As good a year as any for it, I always say.

But in the time of technology, maybe we should take time to remember that we all have (if there is a God and, in spite of the scorn of many moderns, I believe there is)—we all have a "rendezvous in space." Somewhere. Some time.

We had better be ready for it.

Say, if you have the time, take a walk tonight. Through the lonely night—and out through the trackless snow. If you can find some.

Look up, lad. At the trackless sky—the trackless infinity of space. You will find it. It will be there.

Take time to let it hit you. Take time to feel humility. Take time out for wisdom if you can. You've had enough time with wise guys.

Breathe deep of the cold winds of the dark. And listen to the silence.

This is the sound of wonder.

And if this is a waste of time—so be it.

JOYRIDE

One of my last outings with my father was a ride, but our vehicle this time was not the big Lincoln, but a wheelchair—not a venture to Henes Park and The Bay, but a meandering trip on the bike trail along the Chippewa River. I wrote a story of the day to preserve the memory.

* * *

"Joyride"

My father spent his final years in a nursing home. Not much wonder there. His thinking had grown confused and his speech was limited. One summer afternoon I decided to take him for a walk, outside, away from the facility. I pushed him in his wheelchair out the front door and just kept going. Across the Water St. bridge, down to the bike trail, along the river. As we continued my pace slowed, I began to wonder how far I could go. Suddenly I heard him speak the only words he spoke that day, "This is good for me." All I needed to hear. We continued, block, after block, after block, till we finally reached a solitary bench along the river, below street level. We sat together in the quiet and watched the river flow by. Here was wonder. This was good for him, and for me, too.

As we began our return trip, the journey seemed daunting, with all the hills on the trail. I opted to go to the street level, which took us through the Water St. Business District. He lit up as he recognized its landmarks. Finally, we were in front of Kerms, his grocery store, a place he visited daily over many years. He signaled for me to turn in, so I did.

Just inside, off to the left was his favorite stop, the bakery. I tried to rush by, but he saw it. He hung out of the wheelchair, leaning toward the bakery, one arm reaching out. Sweet treats he loved so much were no longer an option. Late onset diabetes had taken that pleasure away. I pondered what to do. I didn't want to end our day together disappointing him. We headed toward the freezer section. Ah, ice cream bars, a favorite treat, and with a sugar-free alternative. Only sold in packages of six, we bought the whole box.

I handed him his ice cream bar as we left the store. We continued down Water St., across the bridge, back to the facility, ice cream bars melting in the bag, content.

EPILOGUE

I began this project in the spring of 2021, with no plan for where I was headed. I began with sorting. I am familiar with sorting; I do it well. My project evolved into something different.

The sorting became discovery. I came to know my father as a young man having to abandon his dream of playing professional baseball, discovering the wonder of literature, finding joy and purpose in becoming a teacher and coach. Through it all I saw his abiding commitment to fostering goodness in the world. Though he was tested, he never abandoned that pursuit.

I saw my mother as his girlfriend, and then his wife and partner. She was with him through the challenges and the triumphs, understanding his purpose.

I saw them as parents committed to family. Despite difficult times, family always came first. There was little money, but there was fun and adventure. I was always proud to be one of the "Crowe kids."

My father sought for his students, his readers, the larger society to be "gooder"—a simple and clear summons for a troubled world. I think his writings have a message for us today.

LAST COLUMN

I *close with my father's last column for the Green Bay Diocesan newspaper, originally called* The Register, *later changed to* The Spirit. *His weekly column ran for 15 years. Most of the pieces included in this book came from that collection.*

* * *

Last Column for *The Spirit*
ca. December 1976
Handwritten copy found in files

This is my last column for *The Spirit*.

I've been writing this thing just about every week for almost 15 years. I've made a lot of friends—and some foes—in this part of the state because of it. Sometimes it has been reprinted by one journal or another in distant parts of the country. I've had mail in response to some of the columns, from far corners of the world.

Well, that's all over now and I would not be quite truthful if I did not say it makes me kind of sad.

As I understand the communication from the front office, they are changing the thrust of the paper (more features on religious themes and less of the secular stuff) I gather. And the decision was made, therefore, to close the door on the column.

I have enjoyed writing it. Maybe not quite so much in the past two years when I've been asked to deal pretty exclusively with sports. (That all started with a "controversial" piece I did a couple of years back in which, among other things, I came out for shorter sermons at Mass. That didn't go over too well with some people with influence and that's when a kind of limitation on subject matter began. I still think what I had to say that time deserved a better hearing!) but I like writing sports and so the directive was OK.

It's just that there are so many things.

A few years ago, somebody asked for the chance to get some of my columns together and put them out in some kind of book form. Nothing ever came of that, as far as I know, but at the time I did look back through some of the pieces over the years and I found some of those I liked best had nothing at all to do with sports.

There were several on my old dog, Aristotle, and especially one at the time he died. There was one on my "old lady"—my mother—and on looking back on that long ago late afternoon and seeing her standing on the porch with her shawl on her shoulders as my team and I drove away from her modest little house in St. Paul.

I reflected that my mother is long gone now, and the wrecker's ball had come, and the house is gone too, now—but there are some things that stay on after the wrecker has done its best. Or worst. Some things no one can really destroy.

Some about my dad, too—and some about our kids in those sweet, swiftly gone days of their growing up. One about the abandoned swings and the teeter totters at Henes Park in Menomonee in late November got mail from a lot of places.

Some were about teams I had, and especially about some of the boys whose lives touched mine for a little while. One I liked dealt with how it is when you sit in your office and another football season is almost over—and the kids come in from practice and shower and then say one more goodbye and go their separate ways on home.

And another day of being young is over. Another season. Another year. I guess that's the kind of thing I like to write the most.

There are a lot of people who walk through a teacher's life in thirty-five years. There are sad moments—and some very precious ones. Proud people. Desperate people. Boys crying out in the silence for help.

Sometimes we hear. Most of the time we miss it. In there, somewhere, it's a challenge to any teacher. And the story of his failures.

I go around the state a lot to give talks here and there. And people come up to meet me because "I always read your column—first thing."

Some, maybe we're just being kind. But many quoted to me from pieces I had long forgotten that I ever wrote. I really believe more people read the column than some of the front office ever realized. Maybe not. Maybe they were kidding me all that time.

But I don't believe that.

Anyhow, this is "so long" now. Goodbye. Like the song says, it's been good to know you. And to know you were there. May God grant to all of you good years and worthy dreams. Remember that you can climb as high as your mind can climb—and reach as far. And every good and kind thing you do or say—especially for those who need it most—is written down somewhere and will be there to the end.

Maybe I could do worse than close with that quotation from Will Durant: "A good man who is not great is infinitely more precious than a great man who is not good." That's true, you know.

Marty Crowe, c. 1982

BIOGRAPHICAL SKETCH

Next to Martin Crowe's senior class yearbook picture was written the verse,

"Of course, those arts in which the wise excel Nature's chief gift is writing well."

He won the Annual Lincoln Essay Contest three times in high school and wrote for his college newspaper. After college he organized a theater group in St. Paul that performed plays, some of which he wrote. In the late 1940s and early 1950s he wrote scripts for his radio programs in Eau Claire. Some are included in the book. A weekly column in the Green Bay diocesan paper ran for 15 years and he wrote a weekly column, "Commentary," in the Green Bay Press Gazette for one year. His human interest and sports columns were regularly published in several state newspapers. Some of his pieces appeared in national publications. Marty was also a popular public speaker.

Marty Crowe grew up in Stillwater, Minnesota. He attended the College of St. Thomas in St. Paul, Minnesota, majoring in English and Social Studies. He competed in oratory and debate and was a pitcher on the baseball team. He graduated in 1938.

Hired for his first teaching job in 1938 with the WPA in St. Paul, his next teaching positions were brief stays in a series of schools. In those early years Marty was not sure that teaching was for him. In 1944, he was hired as a teacher and coach at Hudson High School to replace a man who had been called up for military duty. He remained at Hudson for two years, beginning a career in teaching and coaching that would last nearly fifty years.

Marty's high school teams won four state championships, three in Wisconsin and one in Minnesota, and competed in a national invitational tournament in Washington, D.C. Marty was inducted into the Wisconsin Basketball Coaches Hall of Fame in 1982, and the Wisconsin Football Coaches Hall of Fame in 1996. In 1972, Marty was hired to coach the Manitowoc Chiefs, a semi-professional football team and that year was selected the Central States League "Coach of the Year."

Marty ran for Congress in 1940. He remained aware and engaged in national and world events throughout his life.

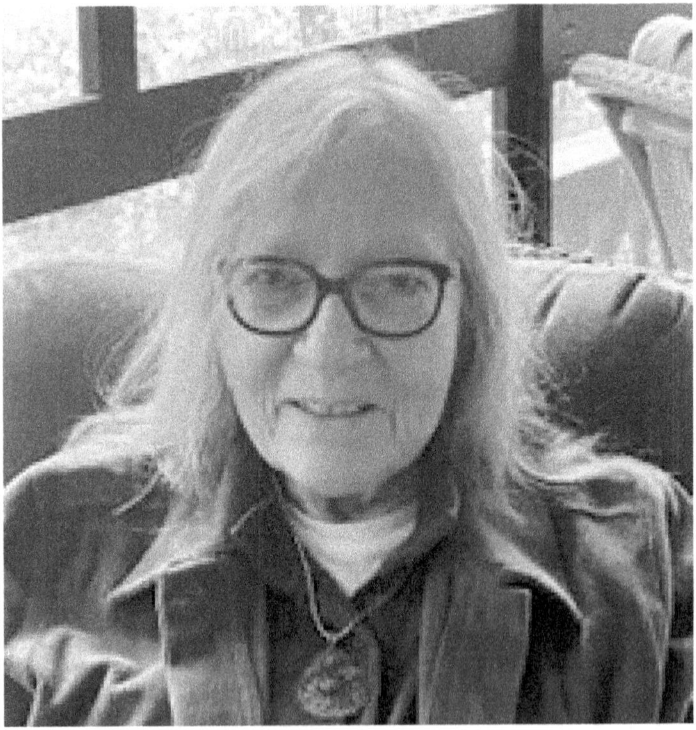

MAUREEN SLAUSON grew up in Eau Claire and Marinette Wisconsin, and Austin Minnesota, the second of six children in the Crowe family. She earned a B.A. in English and Psychology at the University of Wisconsin-Eau Claire and an M.A. in Guidance and Counseling at the University of Montana-Missoula. Maureen worked for 30 years as a School Counselor, 27 at the high school level. Her father was a mentor and major influence in her work with students and inspired her efforts to promote a climate of humanity in schools.